WARS OF THE MODERN ERA
General Editor: Justin Wintle

The *Wars of the Modern Era* series is designed to give the reader concise, clear and authoritative overviews of the major conflicts of the twentieth century, focusing equally on their military, political and social aspects.

ALREADY PUBLISHED:
Dick Wilson, *China's Revolutionary War*

FORTHCOMING:
Saul Landau, *The Guerilla Wars of Central America*
Dilip Hiro, *The Longest Civil War: Armed Conflict in Lebanon*

The Viet Nam Wars

Justin Wintle

Weidenfeld and Nicolson (Academic)
London

George Weidenfeld and Nicolson Ltd
91 Clapham High Street, London SW4 7TA

Phototypeset by Deltatype Ltd, Ellesmere Port
Printed in Great Britain by
Butler & Tanner Ltd, Frome & London

For Ed Berman

In their own persons, Lafayette and Talleyrand embodied the split personality of the French Revolution. For while it is commonplace to recognize that the Revolution gave birth to a new kind of political world, it is less often understood that that world was the product of two irreconcilable interests – the creation of a potent state and the creation of a community of free citizens. The fiction of the Revolution was to imagine that each might be served without damaging the other and its history amounts to the realization of that impossibility.

Simon Schama, *Citizens* (1989)

Contents

Maps

Editor's Foreword

'Ye shall love peace only as a means to new wars,' wrote Friedrich Nietzsche in 1885, 'and the short peace more than the long' (*Thus Spake Zarathustra*). Forty years later Adolf Hitler said much the same thing: 'Man has become great through perpetual struggle. In perpetual peace his greatness must decline' (*Mein Kampf*). Like it or not, war is likely to remain not only one way of resolving disputes (the continuation of politics by 'other means' in Clausewitz's famous phrase), but also a vehicle of self-aggrandisement, of self-expression even.

In the modern era the twin forces of political ideology and nationalism have added to, and somewhat replaced, more traditional motives for war: dynastic enlargement, economic expansion and religion.

The present series sets out to furnish tolerably concise overviews of what may be termed the major military conflicts that have shaped twentieth-century history. The intention is to provide both the general reader and students of various disciplines (history, politics, warfare itself) with accounts that balance narrative (what happened when) with analysis (why it happened). But there is a wider aim as well, which is to show how modern wars, however they may begin, sooner or later take on a geopolitical complexion.

For this reason – the meddling of superpowers underpinned by a single global economic trading system – every war deserves our attention, just as every war threatens us with its consequences: themes which, it is hoped, *Wars of the Modern Era* will in due course bear out.

Justin Wintle
1990

Preface

Viet Nam is a nation like any other nation: its history is riddled with wars. Many were the consequence of the country's geographic vulnerability, and were fought against powerful aggressors. On occasion Viet Nam itself turned aggressor, sometimes for plausible strategic reasons, as in the 1978 invasion of Cambodia, sometimes not, as in the fifteenth-century subjugation of the Kingdom of Champa. The wars described in this volume belong principally to the period after the Second World War. In effect they number three: an anti-colonial war, directed against the French and brought to a conclusion by the Viet Minh's victory at Dien Bien Phu in 1954; a war of national reunification, pursued in the main by the northern Vietnamese against their southern counterparts, culminating in the Ho Chi Minh Campaign and the fall of Saigon in 1975; and, intimately connected with this internal conflict, a war against American forces that lasted eight years, from 1965 until 1973. But because no war can be understood except in the greater continuum of time, in the first chapter I have offered a résumé of Viet Nam's whole history; and in the last chapter I have endeavoured to bring the story up to the present.

Customarily the wars of the modern period go by other names. Sometimes they are called the Indochinese Wars, sometimes, more simply, *the* Viet Nam War. I have elected to call them the Viet Nam Wars because for a majority of Vietnamese perhaps the overriding issue was the regaining of Viet Nam's independence and national integrity. Geopolitical and ideological complications, though increasingly manifest, were not the original cause of war. It also needs to be said that in writing this book I have been mindful that future volumes in this series will cover separately the wars in Cambodia and Laos. The fighting in those countries, therefore, although of the utmost consequence to the Cambodian and Laotian peoples, as well as impinging on the global political order, is largely ignored in this volume, except where it had a direct effect on the course of affairs in Viet Nam.

Because of the international complexion of nearly every military conflict that has taken place in South-East Asia during the last hundred-odd years, any attempt to limit enquiry to one country in particular represents a distortion. Conversely, in the same period, nationalism has undoubtedly been a mainspring of Asian politics. There is therefore some justification in continuing to frame our descriptions of those military conflicts in terms of this or that national identity, whether or not that identity – usually expressed in terms of one people, one country – is real or merely perceived.

That, and the need for a relatively brief overview account of the Viet Nam Wars, have supplied the motives for the present volume. An enormous, even a disproportionate, number of books, many of them overweeningly long, have been written on Viet Nam and its many aspects. That many further books will be written is beyond question. The consequences of America's defeat upon America's own political, military and cultural evolution are still being played out, while the gradual dissipation of an austere, doctrinaire Marxist-Leninist regime inside Viet Nam itself will lead to a re-evaluation by Vietnamese historians of their own history. For the present I have endeavoured to tell what by any measure is a remarkable story in a way that makes few or no concessions to ideological imperatives. This may upset some Vietnamese readers, just as it may upset some American readers; but it is perhaps the historian's duty to fall between two stools wherever possible.

Finally, it should be noted that, with the exceptions of Hanoi, Haiphong and Saigon, I have chosen to represent Vietnamese names as the Vietnamese themselves usually present them, as separated syllables. Thus, for instance, I have preferred Da Nang to Danang, and Dien Bien Phu to Dienbienphu. The same applies to Viet Nam itself, except in the period when the country was divided in two, giving North Vietnam and South Vietnam. Any irony in this arrangement is circumstantial.

J.W.

Outline chronology

200 BC   The northern part of present day Viet Nam is conquered by Chinese.

AD 939   Chinese rule is overthrown, although Vietnamese independence is not finally established until 1428. The Viet people continue expanding southwards eventually establishing themselves in the Mekong delta.

1545   Viet Nam is divided north and south by warring factions. Two dominant and rival clans emerge: the Trinh in the north, and the Nguyen in the south.

1772   A rebellion by the Tay Son brothers begins a process of national reunification.

1802   With French help, Nguyen Anh becomes Gia Long, the first of the Nguyen dynasty of emperors.

1859–83   Indochina is colonized by the French. Viet Nam is divided into three: Tonkin, Annam and Cochinchina (north, centre and south).

1930   The Communist Party of Indochina is founded by Ho Chi Minh, in exile in Hong Kong.

1940   Control of Indochina effectively passes to Japan, although French administration remains.

1945   In the vacuum created by the defeat of Japan in the Second World War, the Viet Minh (a 'broad' front of Vietnamese patriots and nationalists, but controlled by the Communist Party) seize power. Ho Chi Minh announces his country's independence in Hanoi, August – the August Revolution. The Emperor, Bao Dai, abdicates.

1946   French forces attack the Viet Minh in Haiphong,
        November. Beginning of the war of resistance against
        France.

1950   Ho Chi Minh's Democratic Republic of Viet Nam is
        recognized by China and the USSR.

1954   The French Expeditionary Force is decisively defeated
        at Dien Bien Phu, March–May. At the Geneva
        Conference, Viet Nam is divided North and South at
        the Seventeenth Parallel, pending nationwide elections.
        Ngo Dinh Diem, an American-backed Catholic, heads
        new Saigon government.

1955   Diem rejects Geneva Accords. He becomes President
        of a newly promulgated Republic of Vietnam.

1956   Diem begins his campaign against political dissidents.

1957   Beginnings of communist insurgency in the South:
        many former Viet Minh will become Viet Cong.

1959   The Central Committee in Hanoi formally decides to
        support insurgency in the South. Weapons and men
        begin infiltrating down what will become known as
        the Ho Chi Minh Trail. Diem steps up persecution of
        dissidents.

1960   The National Liberation Front is established in
        Saigon. Increased American aid to Diem.

1961   John F. Kennedy becomes President of the United
        States. Revival of 'domino theory': containment of
        communism again becomes the priority of US foreign
        policy.

1962   The number of US military advisers in South Vietnam
        rises to 12,000. Growth of 'strategic hamlet'
        programme.

1963   Battle of Ap Bac, 2 January: Viet Cong defeat South
        Vietnamese Army (ARVN) units, 1 November:
        President Diem is overthrown in US-backed coup. 2
        November: Diem and his brother Nhu are murdered.
        22 November: Kennedy is assassinated in Dallas.

1964   General Westmoreland is appointed to head Military
        Assistance Command, Vietnam (MACV) in Saigon.
        The *Maddox*, a US destroyer, is attacked by North
        Vietnamese patrol boats in the Gulf of Tonkin, 2
        August. Pre-planned American bombing of North
        Vietnam begins almost at once. Congress passes Gulf
        of Tonkin Resolution.

1965   US Marines land at Da Nang, 8 March: officially the
        first American combat troops to arrive. 200,000 more
        arrive by December. First draft-cards burned in
        America.

1966   Many US search-and-destroy missions against Viet
        Cong. Increasing use of chemical defoliants and
        herbicides on South Vietnamese landscape to deprive
        communists of cover. The number of US troops
        committed in Vietnam rises to 400,000, . . .

1967   . . . then 500,000. Large anti-war rallies in many
        American cities.

1968   The Tet Offensive begins, 31 January: a combined
        NVA (North Vietnam Army) and Viet Cong assault
        on US positions. Siege of Khe Sanh. My Lai massacre
        in March. 5 May: 'Post-Tet' communist offensive.
        American forces' presence peaks at 549,000. US
        government begins to lose the publicity war. Formal
        peace negotiations inaugurated in Paris. President
        Johnson withdraws from presidential elections and
        halts bombing of North Vietnam in October.

1969   President Nixon begins withdrawal of US ground-
        troops from Vietnam. At the same time he begins
        'secret' bombing of Cambodia. 2 September: death of
        Ho Chi Minh.

1970   Henry Kissinger and Le Duc Tho begin secret talks in
        Paris. 4 May: four students killed during anti-war
        demonstration at Kent State University, Ohio. 24
        June: US Senate repeals Gulf of Tonkin Resolution. By
        December, fewer than 300,000 US troops in Vietnam.

1971   Further US troop withdrawals: only 139,000 by year-
        end.

1972   The NVA strikes across the Seventeenth Parallel. Fall
        of Quang Tri. Bombing missions against the North
        intensified in an attempt to expedite peace
        negotiations in Paris. Haiphong Harbour mined.

1973   Ceasefire agreement is signed by Kissinger and Le Duc
        Tho in Paris, against the wishes of President Thieu.
        Peace Agreement signed by all parties, 27 January. US
        troop pull-out completed by end of March.

1974   9 August: Nixon resigns as President, following
        Watergate scandal.

1975   The 'Ho Chi Minh Campaign': the NVA and Viet
        Cong co-ordinate attacks on Saigon army positions.
        Fall of the southern cities, culminating in the fall of
        Saigon, 30 April. The war finishes as Viet Nam is
        'reunified'.

1976–7 Repeated Khmer Rouge incursions into Vietnamese
        territory.

1978   In December Viet Nam, now aligned with the USSR,
        launches invasion of Cambodia, Khmer Rouge ousted.

1979   In February China retaliates by attacking Vietnam.
        Chinese forces repulsed. Swell in the number of 'boat
        people': illegal emigrants leaving Viet Nam, hopefully
        to begin life again elsewhere.

1986   At its Sixth Congress, the Communist Party, under the
        leadership of Nguyen Van Linh, promulgates *doi moi*,
        a policy of economic renovation designed to save Viet
        Nam from bankruptcy. Limited liberalization as
        attempts are made to create a market economy.

1989   In September Viet Nam withdraws its army from
        Cambodia, despite continued activities of the Khmer
        Rouge. The United States, however, maintains its
        trade embargo against Viet Nam. At the end of the
        year, despite the collapse of communism in eastern
        Europe, Linh insists that the one-party system will
        remain in place in Viet Nam.

1990   Talks in Washington preparatory to normalization of
        relations between the United States and the Socialist
        Republic of Viet Nam.

VIET NAM: THE PHYSICAL GEOGRAPHY

CHINA

Clear River

Red River

Black River

Battle of Bach Dang River

Hanoi

Haiphong

Gulf of Tonkin

LAOS

Hué

Da Nang

THAILAND

Mekong River

Central

Highlands

Cape Varella

CAMBODIA

Phnom Penh

Saigon

Gulf of Siam

SOUTH CHINA SEA

Land over 500m

0   km   250

0   miles   150

VIET NAM UNDER THE FRENCH

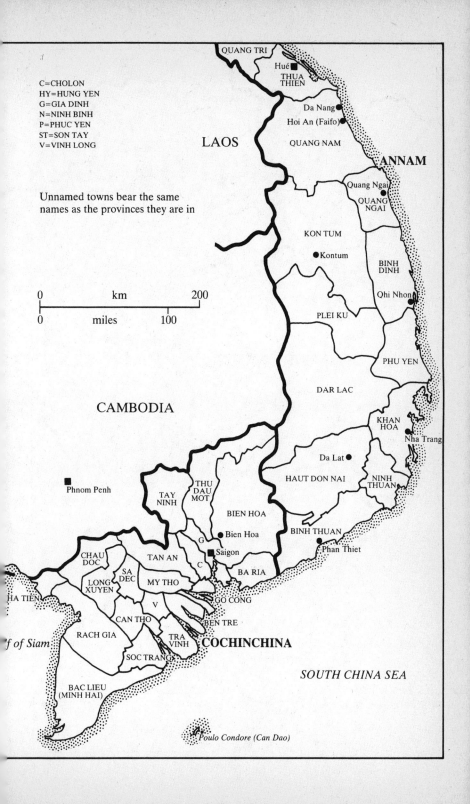

C=CHOLON
HY=HUNG YEN
G=GIA DINH
N=NINH BINH
P=PHUC YEN
ST=SON TAY
V=VINH LONG

Unnamed towns bear the same
names as the provinces they are in

LAOS

QUANG TRI

Hué
THUA
THIEN

Da Nang
Hoi An (Faifo)

QUANG NAM

ANNAM

Quang Ngai
QUANG
NGAI

KON TUM

Kontum

BINH
DINH

Qhi Nhon

0   km   200
0   miles   100

PLEI KU

PHU YEN

DAR LAC

CAMBODIA

KHAN
HOA

Nha Trang

Da Lat

Phnom Penh

TAY
NINH

THU
DAU
MOT

HAUT DON NAI

NINH
THUAN

BIEN HOA

BIEN HOA

Bien Hoa

BINH THUAN

G   Saigon
CHAU
DOC

TAN AN

C

BA RIA

Phan Thiet

SA
DEC

MY THO

LONG
XUYEN

GO CONG

HA TIEN

V

CAN THO

BEN TRE

f of Siam

RACH GIA

TRA
VINH

COCHINCHINA

SOC TRANG

SOUTH CHINA SEA

BAC LIEU
(MINH HAI)

Poulo Condore (Can Dao)

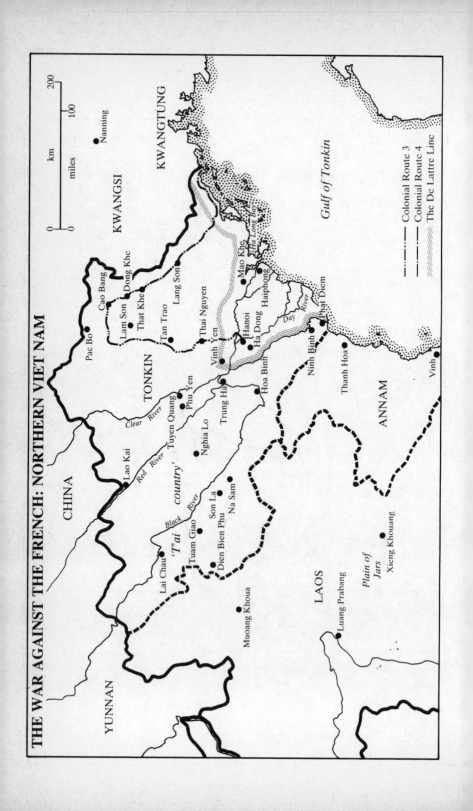

THE WAR AGAINST THE FRENCH: NORTHERN VIET NAM

CHINA

YUNNAN

KWANGSI

KWANGTUNG

Nanning

km
miles
0   100   200

Pac Bo

Cao Bang
Dong Khc
Lam Son
That Khe
Lang Son

Lao Kai

Red River

Clear River

Tuyen Quang
Phu Yen

TONKIN

Tan Trao
Thai Nguyen

Vinh Yen

Mao Khe
Ha Long Bay

Hanoi
Ha Dong   Haiphong

Day River

Gulf of Tonkin

Trung Ha

Nghia Lo

Black River

'T'ai country'

Lai Chau

Tuam Giao
Son La
Na Sam
Dien Bien Phu

Muoang Khoua

LAOS

Luang Prabang

Plain of Jars
Xieng Khouang

Hoa Binh

Phat Diem
Ninh Binh

Thanh Hoa

ANNAM

Vinh

- - - Colonial Route 3
- · - Colonial Route 4
········ The De Lattre Line

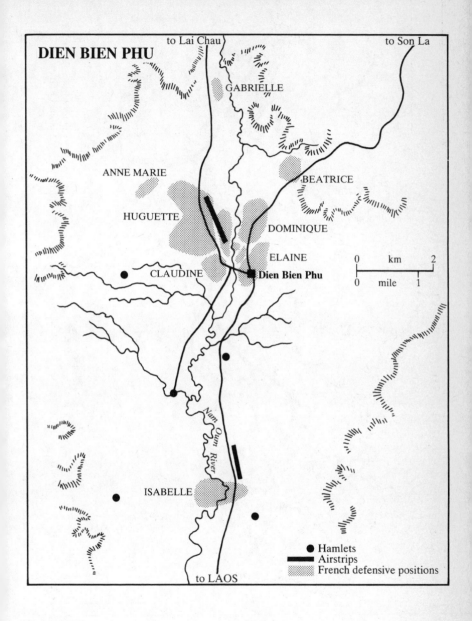

DIEN BIEN PHU

to Lai Chau

to Son La

GABRIELLE

ANNE MARIE

BEATRICE

HUGUETTE

DOMINIQUE

ELAINE

CLAUDINE

Dien Bien Phu

0   km   2

0   mile   1

Nam Oum River

ISABELLE

to LAOS

● Hamlets
▬ Airstrips
░ French defensive positions

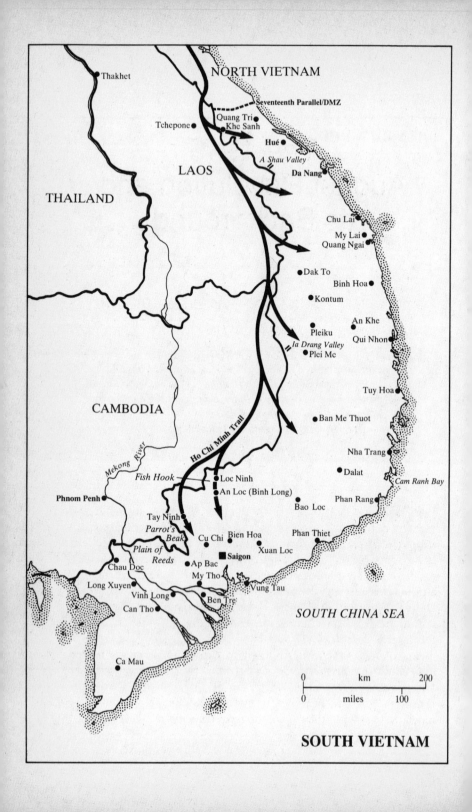

Thakhet

NORTH VIETNAM

Seventeenth Parallel/DMZ

Tchepone

Quang Tri
Khe Sanh

Hué

LAOS

A Shau Valley

Da Nang

THAILAND

Chu Lai

My Lai
Quang Ngai

Dak To

Binh Hoa

Kontum

An Khe

Pleiku

Qui Nhon

Ia Drang Valley
Plei Mc

Tuy Hoa

CAMBODIA

Ban Me Thuot

Nha Trang

Mekong River

Ho Chi Minh Trail

Dalat

Cam Ranh Bay

Fish Hook

Loc Ninh

An Loc (Binh Long)

Phan Rang

Phnom Penh

Bao Loc

Tay Ninh

Parrot's Beak

Cu Chi

Bien Hoa

Phan Thiet

Plain of Reeds

Xuan Loc

Saigon

Chau Doc

Ap Bac

My Tho

Long Xuyen

Vung Tau

Vinh Long

Ben Tre

Can Tho

SOUTH CHINA SEA

Ca Mau

0   km   200

0   miles   100

SOUTH VIETNAM

1

The 1945
August Revolution and
its Background

*They have gold in their mines and rivers, even in the excrement of
their ducks; there is hardly a country in Asia where labour is
cheaper than in Cochinchina.*
Abbé de Saint-Phalle, *circa* 1750

*Every time we returned to our headquarters and saw him, we felt
as if we returned to our own homes, a home where revolutionaries
lived together like brothers of a family, keeping in mind that they
must endure hardships, and that revolutionary work must be long.
He often said, 'In everything we must be prompted by the Party's
interests. The Party is like our own family.'*
Vo Nguyen Giap, 'President Ho Chi Minh, Father of the Vietnam
Revolutionary Army', in *Uncle Ho* (Hanoi, 1980)

In Europe's indecent assault on the Far East, so vital to sustaining the
exponential dynamic of the industrial revolution, France lagged well
behind its rivals. Spain, Portugal, Holland and Britain were all ahead
in the scramble for global resources. But when the French did catch
up, by colonizing Indochina, they did so with a curious brutality.
Curious, because no other nation – except perhaps the newly formed
United States in North America – had done so much to promulgate
the Rights of Man. Successive French governments of varying
ideological complexions, and later successive American governments of less varied hue, refused to extend those rights to the
indigenous inhabitants of South-East Asia. Yet the people of Viet
Nam would have those rights, or at least the right of self-
determination, and at any cost; and their eventual triumph had as
much to do with their own dogged tenacity as with political

miscalculation, wrong analysis and tactical ineptitude on the part of their militarily much stronger foes.

A part of that tenacity was vouchsafed by the strongly systematic character of Marxism-Leninism; another part emanated from the character of the Vietnamese people, honed by a long tradition of resistance to foreign invaders and authoritarian rule.

That history is set by contemporary Vietnamese scholars as lasting four thousand years. This figure, though, is largely imaginary, just as the notion of a 'pure' Vietnamese people is also largely conjectural. A distinctive feature of present-day Viet Nam is the presence of various ethnic minorities, which account for up to ten per cent of a population of sixty-five millions. These are known as the montagnards, because for a long period their living space was confined to mountainous areas. Broadly they can be divided into two distinct groups. One – including the T'ai, the Meo, the Man, the Nung, the Tho – are assumed to have come southwards into the region from what is now China. The other – including the Stieng, the Rhadé, the Sadang, all Austro-negroid in character – may have penetrated northwards from the Malay archipelago as part of a much wider migration which was necessitated by the expansion of peoples who formerly had their provenance in the Indian sub-continent. The picture is further complicated by the existence, in the south of the country, of another people – the Chams – who are of Indonesian stock.

The Viets belonged to the first group. To what extent the other tribes took to the hills out of natural preference, and to what extent they were forced into the hills by the rice-growing Viets, is not entirely known. It is conceivable that the Viets did not emerge from China until as late as the sixth century BC; and it took them the next two millennia to spread through the entire length and breadth of the country. But while they may be thought of as being the dominant, and ultimately 'successful', tribe, their expansion should not be regarded as one of simple displacement of other peoples. As that clan or group of clans calling themselves Viets, and ultimately 'Vietnamese', moved first into the Red River delta in the north of the country, then down through the arid central coastal strip, and finally into the vastly fertile delta of the Meking River, there was a gradual absorption of and reciprocal assimilation by rival populations, mainly through the institutions of parenthood and marriage. In its crudest expression this will have meant killing the menfolk and seizing the womenfolk. But to the geneticist, impervious to the imperatives of nationalism, the spoils of conquest belonged equally to the conquered.

'Viet Nam', like its older formulation 'Nam Viet', literally means 'land of the Viets'. What triumphed was the Vietnamese language, and with that tongue Vietnamese culture; and together these have commandeered such traces of prehistory as can be found.

Archaeological evidence points to a flourishing bronze-age culture during what is sometimes called the 'Hung' period, which perhaps lasted a thousand years from about 1200 BC. It seems clear that there was an aristocracy, a land-owning peasantry and a small body of slaves. Of more significance, well before the Hung dynasty – about which very little is known – was replaced by the definitely Vietnamese kingdom of Au Lac around the year 250 BC, is that the people inhabiting the Red River delta (in the north) developed a remarkable skill in wet-rice farming. In a climate made inhospitable by a scorching summer sun, typhoons and a cold penetrating damp in the winter, the first intra-village irrigation systems were laid down.

The Viets will have shown a leading hand in this, perhaps *the* leading hand. It is often said that the feeling of unity among the Vietnamese people stems originally from the need for mutual cooperation between settlements spaced apart upon the endless flatlands of the two great basins that comprise the most fertile parts of Viet Nam. If there is any truth in this, then there should also be some truth in the proposition that the same circumstances made the Vietnamese and their associate populations receptive to the practice of relatively strong centralized government.

The kingdom of Au Lac, established by Thuc Phan (An Duong Vuong), and with its capital at Co Loa, lasted less than half a century. In or around 207 BC, according to Chinese records, it was invaded by a Chinese army led by Trieu Da and sent by Emperor Ch'in Shi Huang Ti. For the next seventeen hundred years at least, Nam Viet, the land of the Viets, was regarded by the Chinese as their province. When not actually governed by the great empire to the north, the Vietnamese were obliged to pay a vassal's tribute.

Having conquered the Red River basin in a war that perhaps endured ten years, Trieu Da renounced his fealty to the Peking court. The events of the next hundred years are obscure. But in 111 BC the Han Emperor decided to resolve an unsatisfactory state of affairs by sending an expeditionary force to annex Nam Viet to the Chinese empire. Thereafter a mandarinate governor-system was installed.

This lasted until AD 939.

Viet Nam had become, for the first but not the last time in its history, a colony, ruled by an élite that was as foreign as its language. Probably no other event has so shaped the people and their country.

One important consequence of the lengthy Chinese occupation was the consolidation of the indigenous village-system through the imposition of a formal, legalistic feudalism. Another was the introduction of Confucianism, that pre-Christian ideology that reveres the family, the ruler, elders and the 'will of heaven' – values that help explain why, two thousand years later, another imported and authoritarian creed, Marxism-Leninism, had relatively little difficulty in penetrating the Vietnamese mind. Long after the Chinese had withdrawn, Viet Nam was ruled by a class of mandarins, presided over by a hereditary, but not always strong, emperor.

A third consequence was the more or less permanent disequilibrium created in Sino-Vietnamese relations, to the extent that, to this day, Peking's attitude towards its southern neighbour is that of the master toward his servant, while, for Viet Nam, China represents a frequently unamiable big brother.

As the Red River delta and its peripheries became a Chinese province called Chiao Chi, civil, military and religious authority were rolled up into one and invested in a single class of Confucian mandarins. The collapse of the Han dynasty in AD 220 ushered in a period when Viet Nam, as far south as Hué in central Annam, was virtually autonomous. But the country continued to be governed by ethnic Chinese, and it was not long before the imperial hegemony resumed. Increasingly, however, Chinese rule was challenged, even though contemporary nationalist propaganda probably exaggerates the exploits of a long list of ancient and medieval 'patriots', sometimes imbuing them with uncannily modern conceptions of the nation-state, and of 'guerrilla' warfare.

In an age when a people and a country were defined more by the land they worked than by the frontiers they kept, there was always 'insurrection' on the perimeters. In Viet Nam this tendency was encouraged by the terrain, two-thirds of it mountainous and jungle-ridden. But while the 'remote regions' provided rebels with natural hide-outs, they also prompted the need for strong-armed, even totalitarian, government.

The most glamorized, most mythologized of the early patriots were the Trung Sisters, who led a revolt in AD 39, after the elder sister's husband had been murdered, and during a period of internal upheavals in China itself. So successful were they in uniting and inspiring the native landlords, who as a class had been tolerated by the mandarins, that a genuinely independent Vietnamese kingdom was established for four years, between AD 40 and 43. This experiment ultimately rebounded on its perpetrators, however. The rebellion was smashed, the greater landlord class dismantled and the two Trungs left to drown themselves.

Voluntary inundation as the price of failure thereafter became something of a routine. Another woman who eventually immersed herself was Trieu Thi Thanh. Wearing ivory clogs and golden hairpins, she raised the standard of rebellion for six months in 248. Of more significance was a revolt in 542, organized by a Chinese mandarin, Ly Bon. Like the British in America, some Chinese, once they had pacified the indigenous population, saw that it would be to their advantage to sever their links with the empire they served. Feuding between the bigger landlords, or, as they are more appropriately called, local warlords, set in; but more often than not this activity was broadly contained and limited by an enduring respect for the Will of Heaven, and its human embodiment, the Emperor. In a constantly changing web of alliances and rivalries, in which the marrying off of sons and daughters played a conspicuous part, no one warlord was able to cut too large a figure.

Ly Bon's revolt succeeded for a while, then collapsed in the face of an imperial army dispatched from Peking. Nonetheless, the Chinese occupation gradually atrophied, falling prey to its own internal divisions. A junior élite of native Vietnamese aristocrats, permitted to enter the civil service examinations, slowly assumed more prominence. Eventually in 938 the people of Nam Viet, under the leadership of Ngo Quyen, threw off the Chinese yoke. Famously, a counter-revolutionary force sent by the T'ang Emperor was humiliated at the first battle of Bach Dang River in 939. The Vietnamese drove long stakes into the river-bed, concealed at high tide. The Chinese flotilla approached the shore, where the Vietnamese army appeared to be in two minds as to whether or not to fight. The tide turned and the Chinese vessels were helplessly impaled.

Viet Nam belonged once more, or perhaps for the first time, to the Vietnamese. For the ordinary peasants, however, forming the bulk of the population, there can have been little change. Chinese mandarins were simply replaced by homespun equivalents. And in another key respect there continued to exist a profound difference between the rulers and the ruled. Buddhism had first come to the Land of the Viets during the third century AD. The most fatalistic of all the great faiths seems to have been widely embraced by the lower classes, thus inaugurating a psychologically vicious circle which finds an echo in contemporary Viet Nam. Officially despised by communist dogma, Buddhism is nonetheless tolerated in the present-day village and proletarian household. Similarly, Viet Nam's medieval mandarins, raised according to the stricter tenets of Confucianism, saw in Buddhism a powerful tool for underpinning their rule. Then as now, a peasantry subsisting within an unmechanized agricultural economy was inherently more pliable when sustained by parables of forbearance and passivity.

The first hundred years of Viet Nam's new-found independence were turbulent in the extreme. After the death of Ngo Quyen in 947 rival factions schemed and fought for possession of the throne. Meanwhile the threat of renewed Chinese occupation hovered in the background. To the south as well there was pressure from the kingdom of Champa, which had, over several centuries, established itself in central Viet Nam as well as in the upper Mekong delta. In 1009, however, the resolutely Confucian Ly dynasty, which was to survive almost four hundred years, established itself as the ruling house of Viet Nam, and its capital within the boundaries of what is now greater Hanoi.

The relative stability of the Ly dynasty and their mandarin bureaucracies enabled the Viets to consolidate their independence and begin the long southwards expansion that continued into the late eighteenth century. The Ly also created a large and generally effective army. This was needed. In 1076 the Sung dynasty in Peking decided to reclaim Nam Viet, and an invasion force was duly dispatched across the border. This was repulsed, as were co-ordinated Cham attacks from the south. Two hundred years later a far more potent threat developed in the shape of Kublai Khan's Mongol armies. Three invasions were attempted, in 1257, 1284 and 1287. In the last of these wars, at the mouth of the Bach Dang River, the Vietnamese employed identical tactics to those which had defeated the Chinese in 939. Stakes were driven into the waters and a Mongol navy floundered. On land, enfeebling guerrilla operations, including scorched-earth actions, were also successfully directed against the great central Asian horde. Even though it was eventually defeated only in a set-piece land-battle in the Red River valley, these lesser tactics provided lessons that were keenly remembered and sometimes emulated by the communist military in the twentieth century.

Containable Cham incursions revived during the fourteenth century. At the beginning of the fifteenth, under the new and powerful Ming dynasty, Chinese interest in Nam Viet also re-awakened. Indeed for twenty years, from 1407, the country was again subjected to direct Chinese rule. This time, however, the occupation was never easy. Rebellions flared up in all directions. In the event it was a landowner's son, Le Loi, who united and organized Vietnamese resistance. For ten years he patiently built up an effective army in the inaccessible mountains around Lam Son while regularly harassing the enemy in hit-and-run raids, until at Tot Dong, to the west of Hanoi, in 1426 he decisively defeated his foe on open ground.

The Chinese were routed and Le Loi became Emperor, the first of a new dynasty (the Le) that was to survive almost as long as its Ly predecessor. It was now that what is called 'The Great March To The South' began in earnest. A growth in Viet Nam's population, coupled with periodic famine, dictated expansion. The kingdom of Champa, already contracting, was invaded in 1471 and thereafter ceased to exist. Its capital, Viyapura, was sacked and forty thousand of its inhabitants were put to the sword. The Vietnamese kingdom now spread as far south as Cape Varella, just to the north of modern Nha Trang. Over the next two hundred years what was to become southern Annam gradually fell into Vietnamese hands. By 1697 a garrison was established at Phan Thiet, on the very edge of the Mekong delta, which, within another sixty years, also passed into Vietnamese hands. Only the arid and sparsely peopled southern peninsula, the modern province of Minh Hai, remained un-subjugated.

In a sense, however, the Vietnamese had overreached themselves. The essentially bifurcated geography of Viet Nam – the two unequal rice panniers separated by a long pole – became a political factor well before the southern delta had been fully overrun. New lands meant new riches and greater autonomy for new chieftains, not all of whom wished to continue in obeisance to Hanoi. While culturally Viet Nam enjoyed its 'golden age' under the Emperor Le Thanh Tong (reigned 1460–98), as time went by the Le proved less and less of a match for their vassal lords. With the threat of war against at least one neighbouring power removed, local potentates had that much more scope to feud among themselves. By the mid-sixteenth century a tension between 'north' and 'south' was already manifest, and soon two rival mandarin clans emerged to reduce the Emperor to no more than a figurehead: the Trinh and the Nguyen, the latter based in Hué.

The Nguyen effectively oversaw the conquest of the south. It was not unnatural that, having organized that effort, they sought to monopolize its benefits. However, their forces were unable to defeat decisively the northern Trinh, and following a civil war that lasted the best part of forty-five years, a hundred-year truce between the shogunate families was concluded in 1673. Whether this did more to heal or deepen the divisions within Viet Nam is a moot point. During this same period armed European traders first began arriving in Indochina in numbers, and they were quick to identify and exploit the Trinh–Nguyen face-off. Limited military assistance was exchanged for mercantile concessions. Generally, the Dutch sided with the Trinh, and the Portuguese with the Nguyen. In the sense that the Dutch were northern Protestants, and the Portuguese southern Catholics, these dispositions exhibited an insidious and prognostic elegance. Both groups also undermined the long-term capacity and willingness of Viet Nam as a nation to defend itself against the technologically more advanced interloper. Although the colonization of Indochina was still two centuries away, and was eventually undertaken neither by the Dutch nor by the Portuguese, nor even by the British, but by the French, the principle of European influence and interference was established.

The first recorded European trader, a Portuguese named Antonio Da Faria, put in at Hoi An ('Faifo') in 1535. A few miles south of modern Da Nang (French Tourane), Hoi An was already a flourishing international port, much visited by Chinese and even Japanese vessels. In 1617 the first French missionaries arrived, followed in 1627 by Alexandre de Rhodes of Avignon, a 28-year-old Jesuit who headed immediately for Hanoi. There he quickly won the favour of Trinh Trang, the effective ruler. Until his expulsion in 1630, inspired, it is said, by Court concubines disaffected by the Catholic's strictures against polygamy, de Rhodes worked tirelessly to build a church in the capital. He preached up to six sermons a day, and personally baptised six thousand converts. Quickly mastering the local tongue, he evolved the romanized, phonetic spelling of the Vietnamese language (*quoc nghu*) that gradually replaced the hieroglyphic system (*mon*) adapted from the Chinese.

European commerce intensified during the course of the seventeenth century, but for a variety of reasons fell away during the
eighteenth. The climate and people were inhospitable compared to
other Far Eastern stations, and the pickings less immediately
compelling. Missionary work, carried out principally by the French,
continued however, so that little by little a sizeable Catholic
minority, sometimes called 'rice Christians', built up.

For a while it looked as though Viet Nam, along with Laos and
Cambodia (the other two components of Indochina), would rob
Siam (Thailand) of the distinction of being the only South-East Asian
nation to avoid colonization. In hindsight, however, the decisive
event was Robert Clive's crushing victory over Surajah Dowlah at
the battle of Plassey in June 1757. Britain seized Bengal, and with
Bengal not only effective mastery over the whole of India, but a
controlling position *vis-à-vis* the entire Far East.

Geopolitically, the losers at Plassey were the French, whose
presence in India, now doomed, had provided France with access to
the prized spice routes. Their eventual response was to establish
themselves in the three countries of Indochina. But this could not be
done immediately. The French were hampered from early action by
British and Dutch mastery of the southern seas, by domestic political
crisis (the French Revolution) and by the further containment of
French sea-power resulting from successive *grande alliance* naval
victories during the Napoleonic Wars. Yet France was never entirely
forgetful of its Asian interests. Long after Antwerp and London had
closed down their onshore trading facilities, Paris, and to a lesser
extent Lisbon, continued to finance Catholic missionaries in Viet
Nam; and although Vietnamese rulers periodically withdrew their
tolerance of these ideological proselytizers, they had a lasting
impact. Indeed, the Catholic Church achieved a higher convert rate
in Viet Nam than anywhere else in the Far East save the Philippines.

The missionaries, their churches and their congregations were of
strategic value to the French. They kept alive the principle of a
French presence in Viet Nam, and offered scope for covert political
interference. An opportunity for such interference on a large scale
came during the final decades of the century, with the climactic Tay
Son Rebellion. Law and order in Viet Nam had long been on the
wane. In the 1730s there had been a plethora of peasant insurrections, and throughout the century there were montagnard revolts.
But in 1771 conflagration became more widespread. Three brothers
(Nhac, Lu and Hue) from the village of Tay Son in the central

highlands between Qui Nhon and Kon Tum raised their standard against the Nguyen. Their force of peasant soldiers was backed by small and middling traders, and they flaunted a red flag – encouraging Marxist historians to identify the Tay Son movement as a prototypical *petit bourgeois* revolution characterized by egalitarian values.

The Nguyen were overthrown. Between 1771 and 1785 the rebellion spread throughout the south. Gia Dinh (modern Saigon) was sacked in 1775, and several thousand Chinese merchants were murdered. Then, in 1785–6, it spread to the north. The Trinh were ousted and Viet Nam was 'unified'. The tottering Le dynasty finally collapsed. The rich and powerful mandarins were dispossessed and their lands redistributed. A Chinese army of invasion was repelled, as was a Siamese army. The brother Hue became Emperor.

The Nguyen were down, but not out. A civil war that destroyed much of Viet Nam's infrastructure continued until 1803. After the death of Hue in 1792 the revolt lost momentum. Nguyen Anh, the leader of the Nguyen clan, counter-attacked. He had already retaken Saigon in 1788. Over the course of the next fifteen years he conquered his way to autonomy. In 1802 he became Emperor, assuming the name Gia Long – the first of the Nguyen dynasty, which was to survive until the final departure of the last Emperor of Viet Nam, Bao Dai, in 1955.

Gia Long's passage to power was not, however, accomplished without outside assistance. The man who made the Nguyen dynasty possible was a French bishop, Pierre de Béhaine. De Béhaine, a visionary among colonialists, was committed to the creation of a French Catholic empire in Indochina that would counter Dutch and British power in the Far East and bring France commercial glory. As early as 1784 he vouched Nguyen Anh his support. In 1787 the two men concluded a historically important treaty, ceding Tourane (Da Nang) and the island of Poulo Condore (Can Dao) to France. Subsequently, de Béhaine supplied Nguyen Anh with finance, arms and men. A ragged army of four thousand, many of them deserters, but all possessing European rifles, was put at the future Emperor's disposal. Of equal importance was a small navy, which defeated the Tay Son navy in what was perhaps the decisive engagement of the civil war, at Thi Nai in 1801, after the usurpers' army had been routed at Qhi Nhon in 1799.

By then Pierre de Béhaine was dead. Had he not died, in 1799, then the French cause in Indochina might well have been advanced by half a century. As it was the bishop left behind a handful of French advisers, who saw to it that Gia Long was properly enthroned, and a historic debt to the troubled European power.

No sooner was Gia Long ensconced on the imperial throne in Hué than he ordered his soldiers to exhume the bones of the last Tay Son brother and urinate upon them. This was done in front of the man's wife, and also his son, who was afterwards torn apart by four elephants.

The Nguyen were in no mood to acknowledge whatever progressive tendencies had graced the Tay Son regime. As far as possible Gia Long and his successor Minh Mang (1820–41) worked to rebuild a feudal order. Foreign trade was discouraged and a standing army established. The south, where pockets of resistance remained for several decades, was invested with garrisons. The mandarin bureaucracy was swiftly and fully restored, but within the framework of an absolutist monarchy. Loyal supporters were rewarded with the grants of large estates, made up of lands confiscated from former Tay Sonists and their sympathizers. Landlords, civil service examinations and the imperial seal once again became the stuff of Viet Nam. A grand palace in the Chinese Han style was constructed at Hué. The broad peasant mass of the population was ruthlessly exploited. A sixty-day corvée was introduced, as were conscription and a poll or body tax. Punishment was extended to the relatives of criminals.

It seemed that Confucian autocracy had returned for good. In Minh Mang's reign alone there were an estimated 230 petty uprisings, none of which achieved its objectives. But there were flaws to the Nguyen system. For a while nothing was done to discourage Catholicism, and the prohibitions on foreign trade meant that Vietnamese weaponry became progressively outdated. Both these factors were to benefit the French. Nor were the prospects of Viet Nam's survival as an independent nation enhanced when, a few years into his reign, Minh Mang reversed state policy toward missionaries. In 1825 an imperial edict forbade the entry of new missionaries into the country, and soon afterwards those already in Viet Nam came under government censure. Between 1833 and 1840 some ten missionaries were put to death. The immediate repercussion was a major rebellion in the Saigon area, led by Le Van Khoi and lasting two years (1833–5). The long-term consequence was that it gave the French what in French eyes was a legitimate excuse for military intervention in Viet Nam. Under attack, the Catholic interest had to be defended.

It is estimated that in 1840 there were up to a quarter of a million Catholic converts. The French missionaries, for the greater glory of God and their country, refused to be intimidated. Instead they regularly appealed to France for help. Nor were they short of local protectors, either within the native Catholic community or among self-serving mandarins. Even so the response from Paris was slow: the eventual colonization of Viet Nam was to be a piecemeal business.

The first clear earnest of French intentions did not come until 1847. In that year, on 15 April, and on the pretext of 'rescuing' a priest, Monsignor Dominique Lefèbvre, a French naval force operating out of its base in China bombarded Da Nang, killing some thousands of its inhabitants. Largely as a result of this, fresh anti-Christian edicts were issued in 1848 and 1851, following which two more missionaries were executed. But these measures, unsupported by any arms that could withstand the onslaught of even a small European force, made French intervention more rather than less likely. The final approval for colonization, however, was not granted until 1859, when the Commission on Cochinchina, set up by Napoleon III under Baron Brenier in 1857, delivered its report. The Commission's conclusion, augmented by the legal argument that the 1787 treaty between de Béhaine and Gia Long had been breached, was that Indochina offered substantial commercial opportunities, and that the region should indeed be annexed.

By then the Nguyen government had fallen into disrepair. Gia Long and Minh Mang's successors were weak individuals who had already lost their power before the French arrived to prise it from them. Arguably the social divisions created by the despotic Nguyen within Viet Nam made it unlikely that the country could stand firm against foreign aggression; but it is certainly the case that, at the critical moment, effective leadership was lacking.

Da Nang was seized by main force as early as 1–2 September 1858, even before Brenier's commission had formally delivered its verdict. Admiral Rigault de Genouilly, the commanding officer of the first French Expeditionary Force, made up of fourteen vessels and 2,500 men, thought first of striking north toward Hué, but in the event his troops, already suffering those fevers which in the decades to come would regularly decimate European troops, struck south. By

February the following year Saigon had been taken and a garrison installed.

The French now had the military foothold in Viet Nam necessary for conquest. In February 1860 a Vietnamese army twenty thousand strong was routed at Ky Hoa. This victory enabled the French, under Admiral Bonnard, to conclude an advantageous pact (the Saigon Treaty) with the cruel, effete and epileptic Emperor Tu Duc (1848–83). Confronted by a rebellion of northern Catholics led by Ta Van Phung to his rear, Tu Duc rapidly conceded French demands. Henceforth Saigon, the three Mekong delta provinces immediately surrounding the already burgeoning city, and the island of Poulo Condore (in time to become the most notorious prison camp in Asia) would be ruled directly by France. In addition, the interlopers were given extensive trading rights in Da Nang and other ports along the Vietnamese coast.

Little by little the foothold became a stranglehold. Admiral de la Grandière, appointed governor of the three 'eastern provinces' in the south, annexed three more 'western' provinces in the delta in 1863. At the same time, with a modicum of well-oiled rifles, neighbouring Cambodia was declared a protectorate. Thereafter the attention of successive governors, increasingly impervious to more cautious policies entertained in Paris, turned northwards. The whole of Indochina would be theirs. After a period of consolidation, in 1873 Governor Dupré sanctioned an expedition to the Red River delta, under the leadership of two archetypally swashbuckling colons, the merchant-explorer Jean Depuis and Francis Garnier, a naval officer.

Garnier, having at one point proclaimed himself the 'Great Mandarin' of Tonkin (as the northern third of Viet Nam was now called), was ambushed and killed in Hanoi in the same year. For a while the French contented themselves with occupying the rest of the south (Cochinchina) and making their presence felt in central Viet Nam (Annam). The beginning of the 1880s, however, marked a renewed and vigorous bid by the European powers (including Germany and Belgium) for overseas territories. It was now or never. In April 1882, on the orders of the first civilian governor of Cochinchina, Le Myre de Vilers, and led by Henri Rivière, a compact but highly disciplined force of six hundred men marched on and took Hanoi. Nam Dinh and Hong Gai were quickly added. And when Rivière in turn was assassinated in May the following year, even Paris reacted sharply. Parliament voted fresh funds for the Indochinese adventure, and these effectively sealed Viet Nam's fate.

In August Hué itself fell, obliging the captive Emperor, Tu Duc's newly crowned successor, hastily to agree terms. Tonkin and Annam became protectorates. Although fighting continued in several outlying provinces, Viet Nam, coincidentally ravaged by typhoons, famine and cholera, was now firmly under the French yoke.

In 1886 Vietnamese law was replaced by the French penal code. By then the Mexican piastre had already been introduced as the official currency. In 1887 the kingdom of Laos, to the north-west and west of Viet Nam, was coerced into abandoning its defensive treaties with Thailand (then called Siam) and accepted the status of French protectorate. This completed the 'conquest' of Indochina. Henceforward French Indochina was to be ruled by a governor-general presiding, by means of a central Indochinese Council, over the five regions, each with its own local governor: Cambodia and Laos; and Tonkin, Annam and Cochinchina – the three 'departments' of Viet Nam.

Yet while Cambodia and Laos were effectively and inexpensively run from Saigon, French suzerainty over Viet Nam at no point entirely lost its military character. This was mainly because Vietnamese resistance to foreign occupation was a constant from the beginning; but partly it had to do with the pervasively inconsistent style of the French colonial administration. Significantly, in the seventy-one years that France maintained a colonial presence, the governor-generalship changed hands no fewer than fifty-one times. While some of the men who held this post left their mark, the majority saw it for no more than it was: a temporary posting that represented but one rung on the ladder of imperial preferment. At the highest individual level the administrative commitment to Viet Nam was seldom more than lukewarm. The most powerful man in the region never had time to adjust to the history, traditions and needs of those he ruled without resort to any kind of consensus – unlike, it might be said, the Chinese mandarins of two thousand years before. Small wonder then that the details of the French occupation reveal a careless inhumanity that was only compounded by intermittent attempts to introduce a more liberal regime. Whenever the occupation ran into trouble, brute force was the normal, and preferred, remedy.

There were two added complications. Not all Frenchmen simply came to Viet Nam on a tour of duty. Those who came and stayed, who did acquire roots, were the traders, the entrepreneurs, the planters and their families. This after all was the *raison d'être* of the conquest. And because they stayed, and got to know the country and its people, albeit it from an essentially rapacious point of view, they were able with relative ease to manipulate those at government house, so that imperial policy was always apt to be undermined. This meant that liberal, progressive victories in France induced few echoes in Indochina.

Secondly, there was the matter of distance. Final authority over Indochina rested in Paris. Yet few who worked at the Indochinese bureau had ever set foot in South-East Asia. Decisions taken were often inappropriate, although there was always a strong likelihood that they would never be implemented. In the end, though, political interference from Europe, coupled with an inadequate understanding between the political and military wings of the French government, considerably reduced France's chances of retaining its Indochinese possessions after the Second World War. The culminating battle of Dien Bien Phu was fought against a backdrop of strategic disagreement between the commander of the Expeditionary Force, General Henri Navarre, and the French cabinet. Yet by then, in many circles, defeat had come to be looked upon as a blessing in disguise. Indochina, and in particular Viet Nam, had simply cost too many French lives.

But for sixty-five years that cost was discounted. The Mekong delta proved lucrative beyond the most sanguine expectations, and Viet Nam – 'the balcony of the Pacific' – became the jewel in France's colonial crown. Even after the Vietnamese–French war broke out, Saigon prospered, temporarily displacing Macao as the Orient's premier gold mart. The primary sources of wealth were rice, exported to China and Japan, rubber, increasingly in demand in the West, coal, tea and coffee. Service industries, including banking, also boomed, giving Saigon its international character.

This prosperity was enjoyed only by the few: by the French colons, of course, but also by members of two subsections of the Vietnamese community: a sizeable tranche of the mandarin class who preferred to work with rather than against their new colonial masters; and the compradors, usually but not exclusively Chinese. These latter were the senior local employees of the banks and the credit houses who spared the French the inconvenience of having to barter directly with the native producer. In return, they enjoyed whatever percentage they could squeeze for themselves, no questions asked. And they made millions.

The millions, on the other hand, made next to nothing. Despite the dramatic increases in paddi-production that followed the turn of the century, the lot of the peasant (or *nha qué*) diminished sharply under French rule. Many small holdings were swallowed up by larger landlords, who financed their acquisitions through 'city' deals and simple extortion. And as Saigon and other cities grew, so did urban drift, creating a new proletarian class of landless coolies soon forced to work on the plantations and down the mines in conditions that it is no exaggeration to call murderous.

In addition, the French introduced a series of sharply escalating taxes, on opium, salt and alcohol, that forced large sections of the population into chronic debt, enabling the colons and the compradors to acquire ever more land. The tax on alcohol is of particular interest, since alcohol consumption was made compulsory. Villages were obliged to purchase a certain quantity of alcohol each year, precisely in order to fill the colonial coffers.

The plight of the masses, however, so long as they remained politically unorganized, was an advantage to the French. It ensured the essential ingredient of any colonial-capitalist operation: an available workforce whose wages and upkeep were minimal. Brutality can succeed. Where, in retrospect, the French came unstuck was in their treatment of those members of the mandarin class who were not disposed to become operatives at the sharp end of the colonial wedge. In a sense this was a failure of will, a failure to take colonial logic to its conclusion. The Sûreté, probably the most efficient security force in the whole of Asia, strove tirelessly to track and arrest dissidents, but even its efforts were finally insufficient. Many thousands of Vietnamese died tending French rubber trees, or building the railways and canals designed to give Viet Nam a modern (and, ironically, very costly) infrastructure. But their deaths were not deliberate. They were simply tolerated, shrugged aside, in much the same way that for many hundreds of years the majority of mandarins had shrugged them aside. But some of those mandarins and their children underwent a slow, but ultimately critical, sea-change in their attitude towards the peasant and coolie classes. Just as the French could look upon those masses as an inexhaustible supply of cheap labour, so the architects of Viet Nam's eventual liberation saw in them a means to their nationalist ends.

In a sense the situation was tailor-made for Marxism-Leninism. In another sense, only Marxism-Leninism, with its strategy of mobilizing the underclass, could have succeeded against the fearful machinery of French oppression. But even Marxism-Leninism took

time to transform Viet Nam; and would have taken far lon,
not been for the opportunity created by Japan's defeat at the
America and its allies in the Pacific war.

Communist-oriented resistance did not surface in Viet Nai.. ... any
significant way until the late 1920s, and made progress only by
grafting itself on to an already entrenched nationalist politics. Before
that time there were a series of rebellions and insurrections that were
not dissimilar in character to earlier revolts against the Nguyen
dynasty. The first and longest lasting of these, called the Can Vuong,
began as early as 1883. To begin with it consisted of a largely anti-
Catholic, anti-Christian movement in Annam and Tonkin. The
Christians, it was felt, had decisively compromised Viet Nam's
independence by showing hospitality to the French. Soon, however,
it became anti-French and anti-Court. The French were astute
enough to see that Viet Nam would be more readily pacified if the
throne were tolerated at least in name, while the preservation of the
Court-system furnished a structure in which those mandarins willing
to serve the colonial administration could staff a bureaucracy that
formed a pyramid within a pyramid.

The acquiescence of the Nguyen emperors in these arrangements
meant that, in the long term, any potent resistance to colonial rule
was always likely to be anti-monarchical in tone. At the close of the
nineteeth century, the Can Vuong movement united those
mandarins unwilling to collaborate with their new *de facto* masters
and a number of spontaneous local rebellions that broke out as a
consequence of French occupation. In 1885 this resistance focused
on the figure of Tu Duc's nephew Ham Nghi, the boy-king swiftly
deposed by the French in favour of Dong Khanh, after he had
uselessly attempted to prevent the Europeans from entering Hué.

Ham Nghi fled to Tan So, in the mountainous hinterland of Quang
Tri province. There he was joined by other dissidents hopeful that
the French conquest would be short-lived. However, the real leader
of Can Vuong ('Loyalty to the King') was Phan Ding Phung, typically
the offspring of an established mandarin-scholar family from Ha
Tinh (the southern part of contemporary Nghe Tinh province).
When Ham Nghi was captured in 1888, Phan began building up
guerrilla bases in the highlands and jungles of Quang Binh, Nghe An
and Thanh Hoa provinces. Never strong enough to launch a
comprehensive attack, he nonetheless harried the French through his
use of guerrilla tactics, striking at enemy outposts and detachments
as and when he could.

Phan Ding Phung's death from dysentery in 1896 effectively marked the end of the Can Vuong movement. Although isolated episodes of resistance continued at the district and even provincial levels, the nationalist cause remained relatively muted for a decade at least, as all the while the French tightened their grip. Freedom of movement was restricted; a rigorous censorship was imposed; alcohol, salt and opium became state monopolies (the French even built an opium factory in Saigon); and separate administrations were created for the tribal montagnard peoples, thus potentially cutting Vietnamese rebels off from their traditional safe havens. In addition, the consolidation of the buffer class – the mandarin collaborators and their associates – obscured the plight of the newly landless peasantry, particularly in the south. Their immediate, perceived enemies were not so much the French, but their Vietnamese employers and Vietnamese landlords.

The man most responsible for these measures, and for the solidity of the colonial edifice in general, was Paul Doumer, Governor-General of Indochina from 1897 to 1902, and formerly Minister of Finance in Paris. (Later, he became President of the French Republic, before his assassination in 1932.) He it was who organized the state monopolies and set Viet Nam on the road to becoming a profitable business. Above all, and at considerable expense to the public purse, he created the necessary infrastructure – highways, railways, the postal service – much of which survives to this day.

No altruist, Doumer nonetheless recognized that if Indochina was to work then the aspirations of at least some indigenous Indochinese citizens had in part to be met. To an extent he encouraged native Vietnamese to play an active role in the running of the colony, giving them junior and even middling positions in the colonial bureaucracy. The higher positions, however, remained firmly in French hands, so that the concept of a 'Union d'Indochine' remained, even in the brighter periods of French rule, a piece of colonial propaganda.

A minority of Vietnamese did well for themselves. The majority suffered cruelly. Perhaps the most telling statistic concerns literacy rates. In pre-colonial Viet Nam between sixty and seventy per cent of the population could read and write. By 1920 this figure had dropped to around ten per cent. Since the function of the masses was to provide unskilled labour, there was no need to educate them. Along with the decline of schooling came a dramatic increase in poverty. Even though, under French dominion, Viet Nam rapidly became an export economy and the second largest exporter of rice in the 1930s (after Burma), domestic *per capita* consumption actually declined. In addition, consumer taxes were steadily raised. In order to build the roads and railways, the sixty-day corvée was revived. In effect, those who could not pay to be released from this obligation became, for two months a year, slaves.

Clearly, to combat the French system something as strong as the French system was required. Also needed was a strong leader, who would win, in the traditional Vietnamese way, great victories. But the quest for such a leader was in reality a vicious circle. Who could establish himself as such a man without first winning great victories? Eventually Ho Chi Minh was to resolve this dilemma by remaining *outside* Viet Nam, where he could be more selective about where and when to intervene, and where he could plan the future with legendary patience. For the immediate present, however, resistance was necessarily fragmented, even indistinguishable at times from traditional banditry on the fringes of society. Thus, for example, Hoang Hoa Tham, sometimes called De Tham, operated from a mountain base in Yen The. Up until 1913, when he was decapitated by hired assassins, he conducted lightning raids into the provinces of Thai Nguyen and Lang Son. But these failed to stir genuinely revolutionary ripples and had no long-term consequence. Most Vietnamese, unable to read, and with newspapers in any case closely controlled by the French, would never have heard of him.

Of more lasting importance was Phan Boi Chau, generally regarded as the leading Vietnamese nationalist of the early twentieth century. His career both reflects a maturation of the nationalist cause and exemplifies why simple nationalism was doomed to failure in Viet Nam. Born in Nghe An (the upper part of modern Nghe Tinh province) in 1867 of a 'poor scholar' family, and influenced in early adulthood by the Can Vuong movement, he established his reputation as a patriot with the publication in 1904 of his *Letters Written in Tears and Blood*. Significantly, an attempt in 1902 to contact Hoang Hoa Tham, by birth a peasant, had been spurned. Between 1905 and 1908 Phan lived in Japan, inspired like many other Asian nationalists by Admiral Tōgō Heihachirō's defeat of the Russian navy in the battle of Tsushima Strait, the first victory of Far Eastern over European arms. Wrongly it was assumed that Japan would lead Asia out of its European captivity.

Living poorly in Yokohama, Phan Boi Chau worked to build up a community of *emigré* Vietnamese patriots, while establishing links with the Nationalist Party (Kuomindang) of China. In 1907 he founded the Vietnamese Constitutional Association. At this time his principles were neo-monarchist. He had already selected Cuong De, a descendant of Gia Long, as the titular head of a future free Viet Nam government. In 1908, however, the Japanese adventure abruptly closed as the authorities, abiding by the terms of the Franco-Japanese Treaty of 1907, outlawed Phan's group, which thereafter dispersed into China, Hong Kong and Thailand. Phan Boi Chau himself lived first in Canton, then in Bangkok, then in Canton again. By the time of his arrest in 1914, following a Chinese 'counter-revolution', it would seem that he had given up constitutional monarchism in favour of democratic republicanism – in retrospect an important shift in orthodox nationalist politics.

Phan Boi Chau spent most of the First World War in prison. Released in 1917, he lived for the next eight years in Hangchow. In 1925 he was again arrested, this time in Shanghai, by French security forces. According to one version of events the French had been tipped off by Ho Chi Minh, in return for a bounty of 150,000 piastres ($50,000) which Ho then used to fund his fledgling communist organization. This has never been conclusively proved – or disproved. Phan Boi Chau was then deported back to Viet Nam, where he eked out his days under house arrest in Hué until his death in 1940, by which time his particular brand of republicanism had been largely superseded by Leninist revolutionaryism.

Inside Viet Nam, during the time Phan lived in voluntary exile, another patriot, Phan Chu Trinh, argued for the creation of a modern liberal democracy that would have room neither for an emperor nor for mandarins. Both men's ideas found a forum in the short-lived Dong Kinh Nghia Thuc, or 'Free School for the Just Cause', opened in Hanoi in 1907 and closed by the French after just seven months. Briefly, in that year, nationalist aspirations had been allowed free vent, conceivably to enable the Sûreté to identify potential subversives. In any event, a backlash followed. 1908 was a year of many arrests and imprisonments and some executions, inspired partly by anti-tax riots in May in Quang Nam, Quang Ngai, Binh Dinh, Nha Trang and Ha Tinh provinces. A month later De Tham, still operating out of Yen The, staged a 'poison plot' in Hanoi. The plan was to poison a detachment of French troops as they banqueted in their garrison. However, the poison failed, the French were alerted and reprisals were severe. Seventeen 'revolutionaries' were executed and many more were packed off to Poulo Condore.

These events established a pattern that was to last thirty years. Protests and revolts invariably failed and were invariably succeeded by a stiffening of colonial authority. Thus uprisings in Cholon (the Chinese quarter of Saigon) in 1913, Saigon itself in 1916 and Thai Nguyen in 1917 all came to grief. French feathers were never more than ruffled. So long as resistance to colonial rule was sporadic and uncoordinated, there was no real threat to the status quo. And even when, during the 1930s, the communists developed an intra-provincial organization, the French, backed up by their formidable security services, were always odds-on to retain control, if only because they had the fire-power and the opposition did not.

Nonetheless, the development of the communist resistance is of the essence of modern Vietnamese history because, somewhat against the odds, communism represented the shape of things to come.

The founding father of Vietnamese communism was Ho Chi Minh. He more than any other set the tone and the pace. Above all, he saw and insisted that the timing of a revolution inside his country must be attuned to wider, even world, events. An extraordinary, multi-talented individual, he was born Nguyen Sinh Cung in Kim Kiem village, Nghe An province, in 1890. Later he adopted a string of aliases, the most familiar being Nguyen Ai Quoc ('Nguyen the Patriot'), before becoming Ho Chi Minh ('He Who Enlightens') in 1941. His father, Nguyen Sinh Sac, was a scholar and a teacher who, having taken and passed the mandarin examination in Hué, turned his back on collaboration. Ho's elder brother, Nguyen Sinh Khiem, became a dissident and was an undoubted influence on young Ho. There was also a sister, Nguyen Thi Thanh. None of these children was ever to marry. Possibly this was a reflection on the character of Ho Chi Minh's mother, alleged to have deserted his father for drink, although official socialist history admits of no such stain on the record of what has become Viet Nam's Holy Family.

In his childhood Ho was taught by his father. Again according to modern state propaganda, the main lessons imparted were patriotism, nationalism, perseverance and abstinence. Later he attended the French-approved Quoc Hoc, an academy for budding mandarins in Hué. In 1908, however, he was expelled for having taken part in a student demonstration directed against 'poor teaching standards'. Nguyen Sinh Sac then sent his son to be taught the rudiments of school-mastering by Pham Ngoc Tho in Qui Nhon. (Later Pham's son, Pham Ngoc Thac, was to be Minister of Health in North Vietnam.) The French Governor of Annam, however, refused to allow Ho's name to be added to the register of approved teachers. He therefore travelled south to Cochinchina. For a few months he was given refuge by Trung Gia Mo, a former high-ranking mandarin turned nationalist, but a man rich enough to evade close attention from the Sûreté.

At the beginning of 1910 Trung Gia Mo arranged for Ho to be enrolled as a teacher at the small Duc Thanh school in Phan Thiet. There he stayed until September or October the same year, when, perhaps because the security forces were already on his heels, he moved on to Saigon. Not for the first time changing his name, he studied for a short while at a mechanical, or technical, college. Finally, on 5 June 1911, he signed up as an assistant cook on the packet boat *Latouche-Tréville* and set sail for Europe. He did not set foot in Viet Nam again for thirty years.

Ho Chi Minh's travels took him literally across the world. He visited France, Britain and other European countries; both the Americas; Africa; the USSR; and finally China. Paris and Moscow, however, provided the formative experiences. In the former he learned at first hand about the non-repressive, liberal side of French civilization. In the latter he acquired a thorough grounding in Marxism-Leninism.

Ho's ultimate ambition, to become the liberator of his country, or at least to assist in that process, soon became apparent. Having briefly worked as a wine waiter and under-cook (pastry) at the Carlton House hotel in London, he settled in Paris in 1917, earning his living as a signwriter and retoucher of photographs. His mind, however, was on other things. In 1919 he petitioned the Versailles Peace Conference, essentially to ask for a squarer deal for what today would be called Third World colonies. The following year he addressed the Congress of Socialists in Tours. In a short but impassioned speech he urged fellow delegates to apply the same standards to the peoples of Indochina as they did to the citizenry of France. His contribution was applauded, but he knew that few socialists would dare tangle with the economic imperatives of colonialism – as is suggested in the official transcript of the proceedings:

> *Ho*: The Socialist Party must certainly take action on behalf of my oppressed compatriots.

Longuet: I have already intervened on behalf of the natives.

Soon afterwards he joined the Communist Party of France, as a founder-member. Lenin's *Theses on National and Colonial Questions* became his bible. In 1923 he left France for Moscow, where he participated in the Fifth Congress of the Communist International (Comintern). Already he was a budding propagandist. In Paris, with Nguyen Tre Truyen, he had founded and edited *La Paria*, an agitprop broadsheet that manifested two of Ho Chi Minh's abiding characteristics: directness and sincerity. He had also written an extended, anarchical pamphlet on *The French Colonial Process*.

Swayed by the vigorous clarity of Lenin's writings and by the victories of the Russian Revolution, Ho at first clutched at Marxism-Leninism as a means to an end. If the people of Russia could overthrow the tsars, then the people of Viet Nam could overthrow the French and the puppet mandarinate. In time, though, he became committed to the ideology itself – although he was always to avoid the stilted terminology that besets the prose of many of his fellow Vietnamese ideologues, from Truong Chinh to Nguyen Van Linh, preferring instead a more lucid, more superficially liberal mode of expression. That, however, was a seasoned propagandist's window-dressing. Historians repeatedly ask the question: was Ho first and foremost a nationalist, or did he become first and foremost a Marxist socialist? The answer is, from the 1920s on, he was both equally. A desire for his country's independence drove him; the ideology guided him. There was no contradiction in this, just as, for example, there is no insoluble contradiction between Islam and Arab nationalism. In the first hectic months after his eventual return to Viet Nam in 1941, with national liberation firmly in his sights, Ho, living in a dank cave on the Chinese border, nonetheless found time to carve a bust of Karl Marx out of rock. It is unlikely that anyone who viewed Marxism-Leninism merely as a means to an end would have done this under those circumstances and in those conditions.

In 1924 he left the Soviet Union for China, in the company of Mikhail Borodin, a senior figure in the Comintern for whom Ho worked as an interpreter and secretary. Arriving in Canton, he at once set about organizing and training a corps of Vietnamese cadres, replicating Phan Boi Chau's Japanese experience of two decades before. Through Borodin's good offices, he was able to place some of these in the Whampoa military academy (run by and for the Kuomintang, or Chinese Nationalist Party), while others he dispatched to Moscow. It is estimated that between 1925 and 1927 Ho personally trained some two hundred fellow-nationals.

This, along with the creation of the Association of Vietnamese Revolutionary Youth (Viet Nam Thanh Nien Cach Menh Dong Chi Hoi, or Thanh Nien in short) in late 1925 or early 1926, more than anything else cemented Ho's pre-eminence in the revolutionary movement. From 1930 until his death in 1969 his leadership of the Marxist-Leninist faction was never challenged. Nor, with the single exception of a smouldering dispute between Vo Nguyen Giap and Truong Chinh in the mid-1950s, was there any serious wrangling among Ho's immediate subordinates, despite the many setbacks encountered. 'Uncle' Ho's ability to unite and inspire those around him, and to forge an effective team, was not the least of his talents.

The Thanh Nien meanwhile was a political masterstroke. Predating the formation of an indigenous Communist Party, and organized by Ho out of Canton, its very existence offered a critique of revolutionary conditions and revolutionary opportunities. Viet Nam was not ready for a revolution yet. A strong organization with undivided loyalties must come first. The old guard of nationalists must be sidestepped, jettisoned. Their liberal republican values were redundant. Something entirely new must be forged. Time, patience, discipline and secrecy must be of the essence. And also propaganda. Accompanying the new organization came a new broadsheet, also called the *Thanh Nien*, again supervised by Ho Chi Minh. More analytical than *La Paria*, it nonetheless embodied his no-nonsense, straight-talking approach.

The inspiration for the Thanh Nien came partly from Leninist revolutionary tactics imbibed by Ho in Moscow, and partly from the existence of the Revolutionary Party of Young Vietnam, dating back to the days of the First World War and known as the Tan Viet. Intermittently it carried out daring attacks on French installations, but it neither had nor sought a mass following. By the mid-1920s it had acquired some Marxist tendencies, and in 1927 it ruptured into two wings, one democratic republican, the other communist. The latter's more recent recruits included Vo Nguyen Giap and Tran Phu (later Secretary-General of the Indochinese Communist Party). When some of its members were sent to China to receive Kuomintang training, Ho Chi Minh became the beneficiary. A local official, not knowing what to do with them, referred them to the man who was now the representative of the Comintern for South-East Asia. Ho soon persuaded these volunteers to join his own association.

There were also, at this time, one or two autonomous Marxist groups inside Viet Nam, as well as a Trotskyist formation in Saigon. But of greater significance was the VNQDD (Viet Nam Quoc Dam Dong, or Vietnamese Nationalist Party), a republican body that adhered mainly to the ideas of Phan Boi Chau. This threatened to stand in Ho's way far more than any rival communist faction.

Founded in 1927 by Nguyen Thai Hoc, and modelled on the Kuomintang, the VNQDD appealed to the intelligentsia (mainly teachers), the *petit bourgeois* and some landowners. It did not appeal, nor did it seek to appeal, to the broad masses. As such, in Ho's view, it was distinctly counter-revolutionary. But if it was to have any chance of success, the Revolution would require the skills and resources of the VNQDD's typical membership. Further, since the French were adept at ruling Viet Nam by exploiting its internal divisions, there was always the possibility that they would before too long strike at the communists through the VNQDD.

To an extent this came about. The VNQDD sometimes informed on communists just as the communists sometimes informed on VNQDD activists – in much the same way that, a little later, rival communist factions in Saigon sometimes informed on each other. But left to its own devices, the VNQDD seemed quite capable of destroying itself. It favoured spectacular actions of a sort that had little lasting impact on the fabric of French rule, and it was easily infiltrated by agents reporting to the Sûreté. It lacked the communists' obsession with secrecy and it was organizationally weak. Above all, it failed to develop an equivalent to the Party cell, which inured the communists to all but the most draconian reprisals. Thus as early as 1929 the VNQDD lost four hundred of its members, all arrested after the assassination of René Bazin, the superviser of labour recruitment for the whole of Indochina. After this, some VNQDD supporters defected to the communists.

Not that, organizationally, it was all plain sailing for Ho Chi Minh. To begin with, he had Chiang Kai-shek's anti-communist coup of 1927 to contend with. Canton was no longer safe. Ho's group was obliged to remove first to Kwangsi, then to Hong Kong. Ho himself had to flee even further afield, to Moscow and Switzerland, before taking up residence in Thailand at the end of 1928, disguised as a Buddhist monk. In his absence things fell apart somewhat. A conference of the Thanh Nien was convened in China in May 1929. Delegates travelling from inside Viet Nam demonstrated impatience. There was a call from the floor to establish a

Vietnamese Party forthwith. Three delegates from Bac Bo (i.e. the north, or Tonkin) walked out and set up an Indochinese Communist League in Hanoi on their own initiative. A second, smaller break-away group set up an Annamese Communist Party. The rump, in order not to be wholly outmanoeuvred, formed themselves into the Indochinese Communist Party. Meanwhile the Indochinese Com-munist League, as best it could, attempted to take control of the Association's organization not only in Bac Bo, but also in Trung Bo (the middle, or Annam) and Nam Bo (the south, or Cochinchina).

Thus, in his absence, Ho Chi Minh's followers had divided into three distinct groups. It had not been Ho's or the Comintern's intention to form even one communist party at so early a stage. Rather the plan had been to allow the Thanh Nien, a communist organization, to spread to every part of Viet Nam and consolidate its power, as an ersatz Party. Now it was too late. In January 1930, at some personal risk, Ho Chi Minh travelled to Hong Kong and invited representatives of the three factions to join him. The critical meeting took place either at a safe house in Kowloon or at a football stadium during a match. Bowing to his leadership and swayed by his arguments, the three representatives agreed at once to bury their differences. Henceforward their parties would become one party, the Communist Party of Viet Nam, renamed the Communist Party of Indochina at its Central Committee's first plenum in October.

Technically, the effective Communist Party came into being on 3 February when a provisional Central Committee was appointed. An outline programme was promulgated on the 18th. As declarations of intent go, this was full-blooded. It called for the overthrow of the colonial regime, independence for Viet Nam, a government of workers, peasants and the military, the annulment of all public debts, the state ownership of all means of production, the redistribu-tion of all land among poorer peasants, universal education, an eight-hour working day, the abolition of many taxes and the reduction of others. Further clauses were addressed to the creation of a workers' militia, the development of agriculture and crafts, and the right of 'people to organize'.

In terms of the development of the nationalist movement in Viet Nam, the key injunctions concerned worker and peasant participa-tion. Cadres were instructed to build cells among both the urban proletariats and rural communities.

The assumption was that independence could not be won without the involvement of the masses. It was as starkly simple as that. It was also, given the well-armed nature of the French regime and the conditions inside Viet Nam, probably right. And yet prior to the advent of Marxism-Leninism, no nationalist seems to have thought of it: a reflection, perhaps, of the mandarin mind-set of the majority of patriots up until that time.

But that is not to say the masses were invariably inert. One of the factors favouring the spread of communism in the late 1920s and the 1930s was the growth of a labour movement, and of rudimentary trade unions. During the First World War a hundred thousand Vietnamese had served in France, both as soldiers and as auxiliaries. A number of Vietnamese were also regularly employed as cooks and kitchen staff on board vessels belonging to the French navy. Returning to their country, these men brought with them socialist ideas about the value of labour and about labour relations.

An interesting example is Ton Duc Thang, who was to succeed Ho Chi Minh as President of North Vietnam in 1969. Having trained at a technical college in Saigon, he joined the French navy as an engineer. In 1919, by way of expressing solidarity with the October Revolution, he hoisted the red flag on the mast of the ship on which he was serving as it sat in the Black Sea. Dismissed, he soon became a labour leader back in Saigon. The idea of a single union for all Vietnamese workers was partly his. In 1929 he was arrested, and he was kept on Poulo Condore until 1945. Imprisoned alongside communists, he quickly became one himself.

Strikes became a feature of Vietnamese life from the end of the war. Their declared objectives, however, generally related to wages, working conditions and hours. They therefore fell within the remit of industrial relations. An exception was a stoppage at the Ba Son naval arsenal in 1925, organized by Ton Duc Thang himself. Although the given reason for the strike was a demand for better pay, the real objective was to hamper the passage of French troops being sent to Shanghai to put down a much larger strike by Chinese workers. Not surprisingly, perhaps, the action was superficially successful. The French agreed to improve wages and the workers were even paid for the days they had refused to work.

Elsewhere industrial action met with more various results. Sometimes wages were increased, sometimes they were not. Whichever, militants were persecuted. Soon the unions and other illegal labour organizations were infiltrated, first by members of the Thanh Nien and then by Party cadres. Factories and plantations were natural hunting grounds for recruitment drives.

The Party also continued to benefit from the embarrassment of the over-ambitious VNQDD. Having suffered one disaster as a result of the Bazin affair, the VNQDD leader, Nguyen Thai Hoc, planned an event which he hoped would promote a general uprising. But the Yen Bay Mutiny, as it is known, backfired horribly. A scatter of actions was planned for 15 February 1930, but a lack of adequate coordination ensured that the uprising went off at half-cock. An arsenal at Yen Bay, on the edge of the Red River delta, was briefly seized on 10 February, five days ahead of schedule. The French, quickly learning what was afoot, retaliated swiftly and punishingly. On 20 February Nguyen Thai Hoc himself was arrested, to be executed with nineteen of his fellow VNQDD leaders. Many more were incarcerated, while others sought long-term refuge in Kuomintang China. Thereafter the VNQDD ceased to be a potent rival to the communists in nationalist politics.

The communists, however, were not beyond getting their own fingers burnt. The middle and end of 1930 witnessed the greatest explosion of colonial unrest to date, fuelled partly by a worldwide economic recession. The precise role played by the Party in what has become known as the Nghe Tinh Soviet Movement has never been adequately defined. There were over two hundred separate incidents up and down the country. Many of these seem to have been 'spontaneous' – villagers downing tools and marching on local mandarins and police stations by way of joining in the general tide of discontent. On the other hand, it is clear that Party cells used the unrest to further their own cause; that Party members were under instructions from senior cadres to assume controlling positions within the movement wherever possible; and that the considerable discomfort caused to the French was exacerbated by the Party's already efficient underground, intra-provincial organization.

Conditions in Vietnam in the spring and summer of 1930 were particularly bad. In addition to a slump in export commodity prices, there was famine in northern Annam. Unemployment in some districts affected up to a third of the workforce. And as land prices collapsed, foreclosures became endemic.

Beginning in March, there was an unprecedented wave of strikes, the biggest being at the Michelin rubber plantation at Phu Rieng near Bien Hoa, about twenty-five kilometres outside Saigon. In Saigon itself there were mass demonstrations that often turned to violence. Yet all this was just the background. The epicentre of the storm was not in Cochinchina, but in northern Annam. Similar protests in

Vinh, the capital of Nghe An province, led to a temporary political transformation, largely engineered by communist cadres.

On 1 May – May Day – a well co-ordinated demonstration of workers and students assembled in the city centre to demand better pay, better working conditions and shorter working hours. The French duly sent in the troops and the crowd dispersed. Four months later, however, an even larger crowd, twenty thousand according to official socialist statistics, massed at Hung Nguyen, a few miles outside Vinh. The plan was to march on Vinh, but the French, scared by the size of the affair, over-reacted. The air force was called up and the crowd was bombed. There were over two hundred deaths. Within days the whole of Nghe An and neighbouring Ha Tinh (the two provinces that today make up Nghe Tinh) were in revolt. And for once, briefly, revolt succeeded. In village after village the mandarins, police and other officials were driven out by peasant hordes using whatever crude weapons came to hand – ancient rifles, pitchforks, stakes. In their place, and with the Party assuming control of the rebellion, Russian-style collectives were set up. And for a few months, under the aegis of workers' councils, Nghe An and part of Ha Tinh were self-governing.

The French responded by declaring martial law in October. With measured brutality they mounted a military operation which one by one reclaimed the affected districts over the next six months. The eighteen soviets were put down. Many of the rebellion's leaders were arrested and shot. Many more were imprisoned and tortured.

Elsewhere the pattern was repeated. Short-lived soviets were also established in Thai Binh and Quang Ngai, only to be ruthlessly crushed. In other central provinces similar uprisings were attempted, orchestrated by communist cadres. Yet by the middle of 1931 the movement was over, for the simple reason that the revolutionaries could not match the fire-power of their colonial enemies.

This was an important lesson for the future. The next attempt at a general uprising, in 1945, was carried out with the backing of at least a rudimentary revolutionary army. But from the Party point of view, the Nghe Tinh Soviet Movement represented substantial gains as well as substantial losses. The gains were reflected by the communists' ability to insinuate themselves into and take charge of an insurrectionary situation. Rightly or wrongly, 'Nghe Tinh' became part of communist folklore. However briefly, it had been demonstrated that socialism was a viable alternative to colonialism. The losses consisted, in the main, of the numbers of activists arrested and imprisoned or executed by the French. The Party organization suffered a severe reduction of manpower. But the cell-structure ensured the Party's survival. Unlike their VNQDD counterparts, the communists were able to go underground in sufficient numbers to make continued resistance a possibility. The cells were rebuilt. Morale had been dented, but not shattered.

The French took the communists seriously. In April 1931 they rounded up the entire membership of the Central Committee, after it had held its second plenum in Saigon. Tran Phu, the first Secretary-General and a trusted colleague of Ho Chi Minh, was tortured to death. Many regional and provincial committees were also smashed. By the end of 1932 an estimated ten thousand subversives were in French gaols. Not all of these were cadres, but many were.

Ho Chi Minh himself also fared badly. In 1931 he was arrested in Hong Kong, and he was rearrested in Singapore the following year after escaping. At one point it was rumoured that he had died in a prison hospital. In 1933, at liberty again in Shanghai, he resigned himself to a further period of exile from Asia. He travelled to Moscow and attended Lenin University. Probably at no other stage of his career did the prospects for his country's independence seem more slender.

Nonetheless the communist cause bedded down and recovered. Particular attention was paid to the far north-east of the country, the mountainous region of the Viet Bac, backing on to the Chinese border. In Cao Bang province especially a strong organization was built, involving many of the indigenous montagnard peoples.

To the immediate post-Nghe Tinh period belongs the origin of the strategy that would one day deliver the long hoped-for victory over the French: the creation of an impenetrable mountain sanctuary that could be used both offensively and defensively. But the early to mid-1930s also marks the beginning of that process whereby the communist revolution became decisively rooted in the north.

For the present the Party was rebuilt and furtively expanded throughout Viet Nam. In the south, however, particularly in Saigon, the Party, always Leninist in character, had to contend with the rival faction of Trotskyites – the 'Indochinese Left Opposition' or 'October Group'. At this point, 1933, which wing of Marxism was in the ascendant was hard to judge. In a city that has always teemed with factions, perhaps neither was top nationalist dog. In a rare political concession the French had agreed that Vietnamese candidates could stand for the municipal elections, leading eventually to a minority representation on the Conseil Colonial, itself nothing more than a rubber-stamp for predetermined policies. The Constitutional Party, a group of non-militant republican nationalists, traditionally made all the running for the minority of seats available. The Communist Party of Indochina had avoided having anything to do with the council. In 1933 this policy was reversed. Temporarily, the Leninists and the Trotskyists combined forces to field agreed candidates. Of more significance, they also agreed to publish a common broadsheet, *La Lutte*.

The offices of *La Lutte* became the headquarters of the communist presence in Saigon. Since it was directly connected with the municipal elections, and since it was written in the European language, the French authorities decided at first to tolerate the paper. For a while, therefore, communism in the Cochinchinese capital took on a veneer of legitimacy. Nonetheless when two communists were elected, their candidature was immediately declared void by the Governor of Saigon's office, on a legal technicality.

Les Lutteurs, as they were called, continued their uneasy alliance until the late 1930s, well after they had been outlawed. Subsequently, those Trotskyists who would not mend their ways were unceremoniously liquidated by the Leninists – a reminder that, in the south at least, factional infighting could be as bloody as fighting between factions.

In the long term, a more substantial contribution to the progress of the Revolution was made on the island of Poulo Condore, or Con Dao. By gathering all the country's leading dissidents and insurrectionaries under one roof in a high-security prison, the French, as has often been remarked, created a subsidized college for the propagation of Marxism-Leninism. There was little else for inmates to do there except allow themselves to be proselytized by the likes of Pham Van Dong, Le Duan and Bui Cung Trung. Only those who were already Party members seemed to have the courage and endurance to make something of the incarceratory experience. Gradually a majority of prisoners, whose numbers ran to thousands, were welded into a brotherhood of believers.

The Party also built up bases outside Viet Nam, notably at Ban Mai in Thailand and at Lungchow and Canton in China. In June 1934, at the first Party Congress, held in Macao, a new provisional Central Committee was appointed. A year later, Ho Chi Minh attended the seventh World Congress of the Comintern in Moscow. Full membership of the Communist Party of Indochina was now ratified. More to the point, international communism redirected its hostility away from colonialism and towards fascism. It was also conceded that patriotism, or nationalism, should be allowed its place in the worldwide struggle for socialism. In the past Ho Chi Minh had been criticized in Moscow for placing too much stress on the winning of national independence; but now the defining characteristic of Ho's brand of communism had been approved by one of the highest bodies in the communist firmament.

In France the Popular Front, led by the socialist Léon Blum, whom Ho had met in Paris soon after the First World War, came to power in May 1936. Briefly, extravagant hopes were entertained for a new deal in Indochina. In the event, however, the Popular Front's actions, or lack of them, produced another surge of discontent. A parliamentary commission to investigate conditions in Indochina was promised, but it never materialized. No fresh set of socialist or even liberal instructions were handed down to the Governor-General and his staff. The only step forward taken was to allow the right of free association to be extended to the indigenous Indochinese.

Out of this grew the Congress Movement. Inspired by an article written by Nguyen An Ninh that appeared in *La Lutte* in July, the Party urged the creation of an Indochinese Popular Front that would bring under one umbrella all anti-colonial groupings. It also urged a congress, to be attended by representatives of such parties as well as by leaders of workers' councils and peasants' associations. In this can be detected, in embryonic form, the thinking that later forged the Viet Minh, the broad front that was to prove the 'envelope of the Revolution'.

During the summer months there was a frenzy of activity, principally in the south. In mid-August a preparatory meeting was held in Saigon, attended by three hundred delegates, most of them communist placemen. A nineteen-strong provisional committee was elected: five Constitutionalists and fourteen *Lutteurs*. Simultaneously, some six hundred local committees were set up, mainly at the village and district levels in Cochinchina and Annam. But then, seeing where all this would lead, the colonial administration abruptly overruled the Paris directive. From 15 September all public meetings were outlawed in Saigon and Cholon. The various committees were ordered to terminate their activities. The arrests began again.

The whole country, including Tonkin, was seized by a wave of crippling strikes. These lasted into the spring of 1937. Thereafter they petered out, largely because the French were astute enough to meet some of the striking workers' demands. Against a background of improved international trade, it involved no great sacrifice to accede to calls for higher wages and slightly shorter working hours. Once again, what had promised so much proved only a false dawn. The Sûreté had merely been given yet another opportunity to identify rotten elements within the fabric of the Indochinese 'Union'.

It was now that, in Saigon, the Communist Party of Indochina and the Trotskyists parted company, echoing Stalin's '3rd May Speech', by which Trotsky's followers were expelled from the Comintern. The Leninists' next move, following in the wake of the abortive Congress, was to set up the Indochinese Democratic Front, another earnest of the Viet Minh to come. This in turn was replaced by the National United Indochinese Anti-Imperialist Front in November 1939. Significantly, seventeen provincial 'self-defence' units were formed at the same time.

By then the country had already begun to be engulfed by events in the wider world. At the end of September, coinciding with the outbreak of war in Europe, the new Governor-General, Georges Catroux, formally declared the Communist Party of Indochina an illegal organization. Overnight two thousand of its members were arrested and placed in freshly built concentration camps. Catroux's motive for this was the growing threat from Japan. It was believed that the Japanese would seek to undermine colonial regimes in Asia and the Allied cause in general by encouraging internal dissidence.

The Japanese, however, had a different plan. Following the fall of France on 12 June 1940, they gave Catroux an ultimatum: surrender or face invasion. Japan wanted in the first instance to surround the Kuomintang, who were blocking its way in China, and in the second to amass, as quickly as possible, an empire in Asia that would furnish raw materials for its war machine, as well as bases throughout the Pacific region. Catroux capitulated. A Franco-Japanese treaty was concluded on 30 August. According to its terms the French would continue to run Indochina on behalf of Japan, on a caretaker basis. Japanese garrisons and supervisers would be inserted at all the key positions, and the fruits of Indochinese agriculture, industry and commerce would be made available to the new Asian superpower.

To underline their superiority the Japanese in any case stormed the French garrison at Lang Son in September. A detachment of the

French colonial army, disobeying Catroux, attempted to cross into China to link up with Chiang Kai-shek, but they were captured by a Japanese force coming the other way. Following this there was a communist-inspired insurrection in Lang Son province; but, acting on Japanese orders, French forces that had remained inside Viet Nam moved quickly to crush the revolt in the traditional manner.

The time to exploit the tensions inherent in the dual-control system that now prevailed in Viet Nam had not yet come. Nonetheless Japanese hegemony transformed the communist-nationalist cause. The immediate effects were adverse in the extreme. The French, anxious to appease their new masters, launched what was to become known as the 'white terror': the Sûreté and the police pursued dissidents and revolutionaries as never before. That, after all, was the only way to keep the Japanese off their backs. Simultaneously, Japan introduced its own security arrangements in the form of the rightly dreaded *Kempetei*. Two powerful southern religious sects, the Cao Dai and the Hoa Hao, were effectively co-opted into the Japanese scheme of things. But despite this concerted effort to purge Viet Nam of all nationalist elements, the Party leadership assumed a new confidence. Japan, Ho Chi Minh felt sure, would one day be defeated. And in that event, a situation would arise in which the strongest faction inside Viet Nam could seize power.

The communists now worked determinedly towards that moment. They had been given a new lease of life. While others merely wilted under the strain of a double occupation, the Party saw in this latest turn of events an escape from the endless game of cat and mouse they had played for over a decade with the colonial security services.

To test the waters, a second uprising was launched in Cochinchina in November. But once again the ensuing backlash inflicted more damage on the southern Party than the effort was worth, and only added to the 'northern' character of the Revolution when eventually it came.

Ho Chi Minh meanwhile prepared to return to Viet Nam after his thirty-year exile. At the end of 1938 he had slipped back into China from Moscow. This was a period of truce, even co-operation, between the Kuomintang and the Chinese Communists. He visited several provinces, arguing in favour of a 'popular front' strategy as a means to achieving revolutionary ends. In February 1940 he came to Kunming, where the Party-in-exile had its office. There, in May, he was joined by Vo Nguyen Giap and Pham Van Dong. His instructions to them were to return to Viet Nam to begin organizing effective guerrilla units immediately. And then, famously, on 8 February 1941 – a month after Thailand, supported by Japan, invaded western Cambodia – Ho Chi Minh himself crossed the border into Cao Bang, to live initially in a cave near the T'ai hamlet of Pac Bo, beside a stream that he renamed Lenin Stream and near a mountain that he renamed Karl Marx Mountain.

At Pac Bo a delegation from the Central Committee, led by Truong Chinh, was on hand to greet him. They were soon joined by Giap and Pham Van Dong. At once the comrades got down to work, to planning the future. Crash courses for new recruits were organized, and a fresh broadsheet, the *Viet Lap* or *Independent Viet Nam*, printed on a stone press, was launched.

In May the eighth plenum of the Central Committee, and the first to be presided over by Ho Chi Minh himself, convened. Truong Chinh – the revolutionary name adopted by Dang Xuan Khu and meaning 'Long March' – was confirmed in his position of General Secretary. It was now that the blueprint of the Revolution was drawn up. The most significant item was the sanctioning of a new popular front, the Viet Nam Doc Lap Dong Minh – the Vietnamese Independence League, always known as the Viet Minh. As with its predecessors, the idea behind this was to create an umbrella under which nationalists of every persuasion could fight for national liberation, while ensuring that the handle of the umbrella remained firmly in the Party's grasp. In this way, when the Japanese were defeated, the prize of independence would not be lost among squabbling factions.

But there were other critical policy decisions too. To maximize the chances of success, the Central Committee opted to concentrate its efforts on Viet Nam alone. The two other Indochinese nations, Laos and Cambodia, would be liberated in the fullness of time, but only once their larger partner had been made secure. Then, to strengthen both the Party and the nascent Viet Minh, cadres were to be instructed to work to create a broad gamut of organizations that, between them, could embrace every Vietnamese citizen: workers' associations, peasants' associations, youth associations, women's associations, soldiers' associations (for those enlisted as auxiliaries in the French colonial army), even associations for children and old people.

It was also emphasized that the creation of links between peasants and workers, the rural and urban wings of the Party, should be improved and consolidated. And finally, provision was made for the creation, at an as yet unspecified future date, of an army of regulars.

In December 1941, following Japan's pre-emptive strike on Pearl Harbor, Indochina was formally incorporated into Japan's Greater East Asia Co-Prosperity Sphere. Rice was requisitioned for the benefit of the Imperial Army, and many farmers were forced to grow jute. The Viet Minh, responding to Party directives, set about establishing 'national salvation associations' at the provincial level. Under the weight of the double yoke, that was as much as could be done for the immediate present.

Ho Chi Minh once again left Viet Nam in August. He returned to China, to seek out financial and political support against the day when the Japanese military bubble burst. Almost immediately, however, he was arrested by the Kuomintang, acting in league with the Free French. He was imprisoned first at Chinghsi, then moved to other gaols. During this period he wrote his *Prison Diary*, a series of poems dedicated to the theme of freedom, and obliquely to his country's independence. He was not released from captivity until September 1943, and even then he was not permitted to leave China. But among the vying warlords who made up the Kuomintang leadership he did succeed in befriending Chang Fa-k'uei. At Linchow, Ho's final place of detention, Chang Fa-k'uei agreed that several hundred Vietnamese should receive military training, and that some of these should be Viet Minh, or communist, cadres.

In October 1942, under Kuomintang tutelage, yet another umbrella organization, the Viet Nam Cach Minh Dong Minh Hoi (Viet Nam Revolutionary League, or Dong Minh Hoi) had been set up at Linchow. It was Chiang Kai-shek's intention that, as and when the Japanese empire crumbled, a government compliant to his wishes should be installed in Viet Nam. Not only would this restore the historical status quo between the two countries, but it would also deprive the Chinese Communist Party of potential support. The Dong Minh Hoi therefore, comprising the exiled remains of the VNQDD leadership and other non-communist nationalists, who in early 1941 had clubbed together to form the Dai Viet Quoc Dan Dang (Nationalist Party of Viet Nam, or Dai Viet), was fostered as part of the Kuomintang's long-term strategy. But because of the war situation already confronting him, because of pressure from his American allies, who at this time were well disposed towards Ho Chi

Minh in so far as they knew about him, and because of the strength of the Viet Minh in the Viet Bac region, Chiang Kai-shek had also to allow the Viet Minh to join the Dong Minh Hoi. His hope was that for the present the Viet Minh would assist him by harrying Japanese forces inside Viet Nam, but that later they could be isolated and discarded.

Thus a web of pragmatic and ultimately fickle alliances was spun. Ho Chi Minh, Truong Chinh and Phan Van Dong had few illusions about Chiang Kai-shek's deeper strategy; nonetheless, confronted by their own military and political frailty, they had no option but to cooperate with the Kuomintang whenever an opportunity was offered. As things fell out, and by a skilful manipulation of circumstances, Ho and his communist colleagues were the net beneficiaries. Not only did they now receive some much needed military assistance, but the Viet Minh's membership of the Dong Minh Hoi gave them a further lever on nationalist politics, enabling them to maintain the semi-fiction that, as far as the Viet Minh were concerned, Vietnamese independence was what mattered most.

Against this intricate background the war, and Ho Chi Minh's bid for power, now entered its climactic phase. Inside Viet Nam good progress had been made. Two Viet Minh guerrilla bases had already been created in the mountainous Viet Bac region. In addition, there was a third, independent but sympathetic armed group, calling itself the League for an Independent Viet Nam, led by Chu Van Tan. Large parts of Cao Bang province were effectively under Viet Minh—communist control, allowing the Viet Minh headquarters to be moved from Pac Bo to Lam Som, a few miles south of Cao Bang city along Colonial Route 3. The same applied in lesser measure to the other five provinces of the Viet Bac.

In late 1943 the French reacted vigorously. The China passes were blocked. Existing garrisons were strengthened and new watchposts installed. Villages deemed sympathetic to the Viet Minh were burned and levelled, and some thousands of villagers relocated to sites where they could be controlled by round-the-clock surveillance – a foretaste of the 'strategic hamlet' programme instigated by Saigon and American forces in the 1960s. And, as always, there were mass arrests and executions *pour encourager les autres*.

The new guerrillas, and the Viet Minh and Party cadres, were driven back into the forests and back up the mountains. There they survived, there they continued to train fresh recruits, and there, liaising with the Central Committee secreted in Hanoi, they prepared 'anti-imperialist' propaganda, now increasingly directed against the Japanese rather than against the Japanese and French.

Attempts were made to contact and develop a rapport with such Free French elements as there were in Viet Nam. But these were doomed to disappointment. Charles de Gaulle, though a fervent anti-fascist, had already committed himself to the restitution of French rule in Indochina once Germany and Japan had been defeated.

That defeat was edging ever closer. The tide of the Pacific war had turned against Japan on the Solomon island of Guadalcanal in January 1943. A few months later the British began their counter-offensive in Burma, which they had lost in 1942. Then in Europe the Axis was pushed back by Allied forces, first in Italy, then, in 1944, in Normandy.

In Viet Nam the regime remained as oppressive as ever. Indeed as Japan, unaware of American and British plans to drop nuclear bombs on its cities, prepared for a consolidated defence of its islands, the oppression intensified. Indochina, like the other parts of Japan's rapidly shrinking dominions, was ransacked for whatever goods and materials might benefit the imperial fatherland. With its long-term hegemonic ambitions in Asia clearly thwarted, there was no longer any need to pay even lip-service to the notion of co-prosperity.

The Viet Minh front, following the covert guidance of the Central Committee of the Communist Party of Indochina, and of the intra-provincial Committee of Cao Bang, Lang Son and Bac Can provinces, which convened in the early autumn of 1944, began its preparations for a general uprising. At the same time guerrilla operations were stepped up. In particular, attacks were carried out against local prisons to secure the release of captured cadres.

In the rebel camps and in the underground committee offices alike there was a mood of impatience, nurtured by long years of frustration. Yet the timing of the planned uprising was still all-important. If the Viet Minh showed its hand too soon, the Japanese and French between them might yet deliver a mortal blow. Conversely, any delay, any backwardness in preparations would either let the French back in, under cover of an anticipated Allied landing, or provide the Kuomintang with *carte blanche* to do whatever they pleased.

Ho Chi Minh returned to Viet Nam on 20 September. Conferring with his colleagues, he immediately made provision for the creation of an Armed Propaganda Brigade, a 'crack' unit which would carry out daring raids on enemy posts, partly to promote revolutionary morale, partly to seize much needed weapons from smaller enemy stockpiles. It was to include cadres who had received military training in China. At the end of November two platoons – the first regular troops organized by the communists, and thus the true antecedents of what, in less than thirty years, would become the fourth largest army in the world – came into being, commanded by Vo Nguyen Giap and Hoang Duc Thac; and at the end of December French outposts at Phai Khat and Na Ngan were successfully attacked.

Once again Ho slipped back into China. At Kunming he met General Claire Chennault, the commander of the 14th United States Air Force. He also had contact with the OSS (Office of Strategic Services), through one of its officers, Charles Fenn. In return for pledging the Viet Minh to render assistance to any American pilots shot down over Viet Nam by the Japanese, Ho extracted promises of limited material aid. As a result of this, some weapons and other supplies were airdropped onto a Viet Minh base in Lang Son. Of more importance, on this trip he learned about the Kuomintang's plans to invade Viet Nam in their own counter-attack against the Japanese.

Events were fast gathering momentum. On 9 March 1945 the Japanese abruptly revised their Indochinese policy. In what is usually described as a *coup de force*, Japan assumed full control over France's erstwhile colony. A section of the French army attempted to break out of Viet Nam across the Chinese border, but the great majority of French forces, some six thousand men, were now interned. At the end of the month de Gaulle reaffirmed his determination to restore French rule to Indochina. At the same time Japan promulgated Viet Nam's nominal independence. On 17 April a native 'government', composed of tame professionals – lawyers, doctors and teachers – and headed by the historian Trang Trong Kim, was inaugurated.

Meanwhile American bombing missions against Japanese targets intensified; and a terrible famine, largely induced by Japanese requisitions, swept across the Red River delta and upper Annam, claiming, over the summer months, an estimated two million lives. In mid-May, Ho Chi Minh once again returned to his country to take control of and shape the historic moment. With the Japanese edifice collapsing, the Central Committee met to decide on full coordination of all Party and Viet Minh activities. Guerrilla attacks, intensive training, propaganda, rice riots and rice seizures, strikes and local uprisings – the process of 'revolutionary effervescence' – would culminate in a meticulously planned nationwide insurrection.

Giap had already attacked Nghan Son in March. By the end of the month the whole of Cao Bang and Bac Can provinces had passed into Viet Minh control. Now the liberation of Thai Nguyen, Tuyen Quang and Lang Son was under way. Soon guerrilla units were operating in the northern part of the Red River delta itself. At the end of April a 'revolutionary military conference' was held at Bac Giang. There it had been decided to merge the two wings of the Armed Propaganda Brigade, together with Chu Van Tan's guerrilla organization, the Army for National Salvation, into a common Viet Nam Liberation Army. Then, at the beginning of May, a new headquarters, both military and political, was established at Tan Trao. On 4 June the six mountain provinces of Cao Bang, Bac Can, Lang Son, Ha Giang, Tuyen Quang and Thai Nguyen were declared a 'liberated zone'. Simultaneously, resistance bases were set up in other parts of Tonkin.

The Japanese launched a counter-attack, but without significant effect. Tan Trao and the mountain fastnesses held out. In the south, however, in Annam as well as Cochinchina, the situation was not as favourable to the communists. The Party was in place, with its secret cadre organizations, but the Viet Minh umbrella was slow to open. Only its youth organization, the Jeunesse d'Avant-Garde, led by Tran Van Giau, boasted any strength. Pitted against it were the 'counter-revolutionary' organizations of the Cao Dai and Hoa Hao sects, whose combined memberships now numbered between two and three million. The Cao Dai in particular was a force to be reckoned with. Long sponsored by the Japanese, and under its leader Tran Quang Vinh, it had developed a paramilitary wing. How this might deploy when the Japanese government finally collapsed was by no means clear. It might back a coalition of non-communist nationalists; it might collaborate with Allied forces seeking an early entry into Viet Nam; or it might even seek to seize power in Saigon for itself.

July was therefore spent, as far as possible, consolidating and extending Viet Minh organizations in all parts of the country. The signal for the long-awaited general uprising was not given until 13 August, seven days after the bombing of Hiroshima, five days after the Soviet Union declared war on Japan, four days after the bombing of Nagasaki and two days before Japan's surrender to the Allies.

The order came from the National Insurrection Committee, set up by the Party's second National Congress under the chairmanship of Truong Chinh. It was ratified by a Viet Minh People's National Congress on 16 and 17 August. The same body, claiming to represent the Dong Minh Hoi, also set up the Committee for National Liberation, headed by Ho Chi Minh himself – in effect, a provisional government.

Immediately the whole country was engulfed in a wave of local uprisings, in town and country alike. Government offices, prisons and police stations were besieged and in most cases taken without serious resistance being offered. Although the Japanese were now asked by the Allies to stay on in Indochina for peace-keeping purposes, pending the Allies' own landing, for them the war was over. Tran Trong Kim, the puppet Prime Minister, Bao Dai, the compromised Emperor, and the Civil Guard, placed at their disposal by the Japanese, were all that stood between the Viet Minh and power. As early as 16 August Vo Nguyen Giap set off from Tan Trao with a detachment of the Liberation Army to march on Hanoi. On 17 August Tuyen Quang was seized. The following day came the first of the provincial revolts, in Bac Ninh, Hai Duong, Ha Tinh and Quang Nam. Hordes of peasants converged from all directions on the capital towns, where their irresistable numbers were further swelled by the urban proletariats.

On the same day there was a mass meeting in Hanoi, in front of the French-style opera house. Originally this had been organized on behalf of Tran Trong Kim's provisional government; but suddenly Viet Minh cadres stormed the rostrum and turned the occasion into a Viet Minh rally. On the 19th, peasant phalanxes, accompanied by communist 'self-defence' units, moved in from the rural areas. At another rally the red flag was raised, a rifle salvo fired and a 'democratic republican' government proclaimed. The crowd, spear-headed by two thousand armed revolutionaries, then marched on the barracks of the Civil Guard. For a moment they were halted by the spectacle of Japanese troops and Japanese tanks; but the Japanese, overwhelmed by the sheer magnitude of the rebellion, capitulated without a shot exchanged. Hanoi had effectively fallen to the Viet Minh.

Elsewhere, notably in Ha Dong, Vinh Yen and Phuc Yen, the Japanese and forces loyal to the Tran Trong Kim government did put up token resistance. There was also trouble in Saigon where, stealing a march on the Viet Minh, a non-communist United National Front, heavily supported by the Cao Dai and Hoa Hao, briefly seized control; and it was not until the 25th that Tran Van Giau was able to rectify the situation in the Viet Minh's favour. But elsewhere the Viet Minh swept to power in city after city and in province after province. Hué was overrun on 23 August. A week later the Emperor, Bao Dai, stood on the balcony of the great southern gate of the imperial palace and read aloud his act of abdication. 'I would rather be the citizen of an independent nation,' he told the crowd assembled below him, 'than be the king of an enslaved country.'

By then the rest of Annam and Cochinchina had followed Tonkin's lead. The following day Ho Chi Minh, recovering from a near-fatal attack of malaria, and accompanied by a youthful Le Duc Tho, entered Hanoi. At once he set up a 'national united government', made up in the main of Party and Viet Minh leaders, but also including some outsider nationalists.

Finally, in the crowning act of the August Revolution, on 2 September, at a vast meeting held in Ba Dinh Square, Ho Chi Minh, the President of the new republic, was officially welcomed by the new government. In a frail voice he read out a declaration, which began with the words: 'All men are created equal, all men have a right to life, liberty and happiness.'

The contents of this speech were modelled on the demands Ho had sent to the Versailles Peace Conference in 1919. That Ho's tone was not more stridently Marxist reflected several factors. The strong echo of the American Declaration of Independence, while providing a testimony to the breadth of a political vision acquired during three decades' globetrotting, was also an act of high politics. It sought to indicate to the world at large, and to Washington in particular, that what the Viet Minh had achieved was first and foremost national independence; and it also sought to convince non-communist patriots at home – for example, members of the Dai Viet – that there was nothing to fear from a Viet Minh government.

As Ho well knew, Viet Nam was on the brink of reinvasion, by the British on behalf of the French, and by a Kuomintang army acting in concert with the Allies. Already a handful of Free French troops had been parachuted into the country, and Chiang Kai-shek's men were massing on the north-eastern border. In his hour of triumph he needed to keep all his available options open. With an ill-equipped and inadequately trained army that numbered no more than five thousand, the Viet Minh were still vulnerable to virtually any force that they might encounter; and it was unlikely that what had been

won without significant bloodshed could be held in the same
manner.

2

The War Against
the French

THE PRESIDENT *then said he also had in mind a trusteeship for
Indochina. He added that the British did not approve of this idea as
they wished to give it back to the French since they feared the
implications of a trusteeship as it might affect Burma.*

MARSHAL STALIN *remarked that the British had lost Burma once
through reliance on Indochina, and it was not his opinion that
Britain was a sure country to protect this area. He added that he
thought Indochina was a very important area.*

THE PRESIDENT *said that the Indochinese were people of small
stature, like the Javanese and Burmese, and were not warlike. He
added that France had done nothing to improve the natives since
she had the colony. He said that General de Gaulle had asked for
ships to transport French forces to Indochina.*

MARSHAL STALIN *inquired where de Gaulle was going to get the
troops.*

THE PRESIDENT *replied that de Gaulle said he was going to find the
troops when the President could find the ships, but the President
added that up to the present he had been unable to find the ships.*

Exchange between Franklin D. Roosevelt and Josef Stalin at the
Yalta Conference, 8 February 1945 (US State Department, 1955)

Far from securing Viet Nam's independence, the August Revolution
set the stage for three decades of war. The French, the British and the
Kuomintang Chinese were waiting in the wings to rob the Viet Minh
of their victory. Later the United States, the Soviet Union and Red
China would also become involved, to the extent that Viet Nam
became a potential flashpoint for a third global conflict. In 1945,
however, Viet Nam and the other parts of Indochina were still
regarded as relatively unimportant. Following the defeat of Hitler's
Third Reich, great-power interest continued to focus on Europe.

The West, having been outmanoeuvred by the Soviet army in the advance upon Berlin, now perceived a threat from its eastern ally. How far, and how fast, should communism be allowed to spread? Washington became quickly and firmly opposed to what American leaders saw as Soviet aggrandizement and an ideology that insistently negated American values. Harry S. Truman, assuming the presidency on 12 April 1945 after Franklin D. Roosevelt's death, and re-elected in 1948, made the containment of communism the cornerstone of his foreign policy. He sanctioned both the Marshall Plan, put forward in 1948 to bolster war-shattered western democracies with massive monetary aid, and the Berlin airlift of 1948–9, which saved the western half of the former German capital from falling into East German hands. He was also a willing sponsor in 1947 of the Central Intelligence Agency (or CIA, evolved out of the OSS), and an enthusiastic architect in 1949 of the North Atlantic Treaty Organization (or NATO).

An important corollary of these policies was a softening of American attitudes towards colonialism. Roosevelt had hoped that the end of the Second World War would spell the end of European colonial empires as well as the end of fascism. The United States, in its declared ideology, favoured self-government for all peoples. Yet the burgeoning cold war was to cloud and bedevil such clearcut polarizations and priorities; and in time Viet Nam was to become the hot safety valve of a prolonged struggle between two superpowers which increasingly had the capacity to destroy a world each sought to dominate.

A foretaste of that capacity had been unleashed on Hiroshima and Nagasaki. For the moment, however, the very idea of a 'war of containment', as the Vietnamese war in the 1960s was sometimes to be called, was in nobody's mind. Rather, Allied leaders were concerned to implement a framework that would provide a 'lasting peace' for all nations. Efforts to construct such a framework were made first at the Yalta Conference of February 1945, then at Potsdam in July. Yet the West was already suspicious of Stalin, and it was this suspicion that weakened American resolve with regard to colonialism. De Gaulle and Churchill both wished for the restitution of their countries' empires. As regards Indochina, nothing definite was decided, except that, when the Japanese surrendered, Allied forces would be dispatched quickly to maintain law and order. As regards Viet Nam, British forces would land in the south, while Chiang Kai-shek would send some of his Kuomintang divisions into the north. By this means a way would be prepared for the return of the French.

Ironically, the only power that could have prevented the August Revolution was the defeated power, Japan. The Japanese alone had sufficient men and arms in Viet Nam to have thwarted the Viet Minh. Yet at the critical moment, responding to Allied orders, they 'stood back and watched'. But more than that, in a limited number of cases they may even have assisted a process whereby some Japanese weapons fell into Viet Minh hands, just as in Indonesia they deliberately passed over their rifles to Sukarno's incipient nationalist army. The Japanese, humiliated in the Pacific, were weary of war; but they too were already looking to the future. An East Asia rid of European powers was preferable to a resumption of the pre-war order.

Even as the August Revolution unfolded, two hundred thousand Kuomintang troops, commanded by General Lu Han, advanced across the Chinese border in accordance with the terms of the Potsdam Agreement (24 July). Simultaneously, in the south, British and Indian units of the 20th India Division, under the command of Major-General Douglas Gracey, landed by air and by boat at Saigon. Gracey's orders, handed down by the Supreme Commander of Allied Forces in South-East Asia, Earl Mountbatten, were to disarm the Japanese, release French prisoners of war (but not rearm them) and maintain law and order in Cochinchina and Annam up to the Sixteenth Parallel. Specifically, he was instructed not to interfere in 'local politics'.

Saigon, when Gracey arrived, was in chaos. Government was nominally in the hands of the United Party, the broad nationalist grouping now controlled by the leader of the southern communists, Tran Van Giau; but other bodies, such as the Cao Dai and Hoa Hao, threatened to undo the Viet Minh's precarious hold. The streets were given over to riots and also to looting, as criminal gangs rampaged through the city each dusk. Gracey's reactions, however, ushered in an even greater turmoil. Far from disarming the Japanese, he used them as a ready-made police force. Ordering the immediate closure of every Vietnamese-language newspaper, he also rearmed the six thousand released French internees. The immediate consequence was that on 23 September French troops seized government and public buildings, ousting Giau. Force was also used to break up the following day's massed demonstrations. On the 25th Saigon's populace, organized by the Viet Minh working in harness with the biggest of the criminal gangs, the Binh Xuyen, retaliated. Four hundred and fifty French nationals were either killed or kidnapped in a short but devastating orgy of terror.

Gracey restored order by deploying his own and Japanese troops between the two sides. His aim, as it had been all along, in keeping with a tacit agreement between Churchill and de Gaulle, was to prepare the scene for fresh French forces. The first of these, three regiments (two infantry and one armoured) under the command of General Philippe Le Clerc, arrived in Saigon at the beginning of October. Thereafter Gracey progressively handed over the reins of power to his French counterpart. Le Clerc went immediately on the offensive. What amounted to martial law was imposed on Saigon and other Mekong delta cities, and everything was done to drive the Viet Minh back into the maquis.

The August Revolution fared only a little better in Tonkin. Although the Kuomintang made no immediate attempt to unseat Ho Chi Minh's government in Hanoi, Kuomintang soldiers nonetheless ruled the roost. In the villages of the Red River delta the newly inaugurated People's Committees were smashed. Chiang Kai-shek's soldiery, giving vent to the historic Chinese perception of Viet Nam as a vassal state, as an inferior Chinese province, regularly requisitioned everything valuable in sight: machinery, weapons, foodstuffs, women.

The Viet Minh Liberation Army, still numbering no more than five thousand semi-trained regulars, was powerless to intervene. Although Vo Nguyen Giap immediately set about expanding his forces as quickly as he could, Ho Chi Minh's only realistic hopes of survival were diplomacy and negotiation. Frantically and repeatedly he appealed to the United States, using the contacts he had built up with the OSS in the latter stages of the Japanese war. But Washington, unwilling to quarrel either with its European allies or with Chiang Kai-shek, and already aware of communist political advances in France and Italy, had no time for Indochina. As the weeks slipped by, Ho had reluctantly to concede that the only way forward was somehow to exploit the differences between the two occupying powers.

These differences were considerable. Both France and the Kuomintang had long-term designs on Tonkin. The French wanted to reclaim the whole of Indochina; the Chinese sought to create a biddable buffer-state that would render no assistance to Mao Tse-tung's communist army. In particular, Chiang Kai-shek sought to secure the Haiphong–Hanoi–Kunming rail-link, a vital route for supplies to the southern theatre of his coming campaigns.

Increasingly, the situation confronting the Viet Minh government boiled down to a straight choice. Eventually Ho chose the French. He is reputed to have declared: 'I would rather smell French dung for five years than eat Chinese dung for a thousand years.' Simply because China was so near and so vast, China would always find it easier to dominate Viet Nam. France, on the other hand, was on the far side of the world, and the divisions within France's domestic politics suggested to Ho that sooner or later Paris would have a government that would be sympathetic to his cause.

In November the new Governor-General, Admiral d'Argenlieu, a close supporter of de Gaulle, arrived in Saigon and the British pulled out. Le Clerc meanwhile began moving his battalions up the Annamese coast towards the Sixteenth Parallel. Since it was not yet apparent that the French already intended, in time, to repossess the whole of Viet Nam, the Viet Minh of necessity continued to treat with the Kuomintang. Very largely this meant appeasement. Bribes and other *ex gratia* payments to the Chinese commanders were arranged in order to forestall the further ravages of their troops. Pham Van Dong, in his role as Finance Minister, had even to organize a 'gold week', in which gold, jewellery and other precious 'gifts' were collected and handed over to Kuomintang officers. Lu Han himself was offered a set of solid gold opium pipes. Equally, there were political concessions. On 11 November the Communist Party of Indochina was supposedly dissolved, and it was agreed that, north of the Sixteenth Parallel, a general election would be held on 23 December to form a new government.

Although Ho Chi Minh had deliberately assigned some ministries to non-Viet Minh nationalists, including two Catholics, in an effort to vindicate his claims that his government represented the whole of the Vietnamese people, Lu Han had not been deceived. He knew that in reality the communists were in control. The purpose of the election was to give those nationalists excluded from Ho's team, in particular senior figures of the Dai Viet and former VNQDD leaders, a chance to assume power in their own right. But although the election was not in fact held until 6 January, the Viet Minh, trading on Ho Chi Minh's near-universal popularity, nonetheless won a great majority of seats to the new assembly; and through the Viet Minh the supposedly disbanded communists, who had no intention of relinquishing their ideology, retained their hold on the government.

But how long that government would last was uncertain. The longer the Kuomintang stayed in the north, the greater was the likelihood that their occupation would become permanent. Indeed, the only party who had both the inclination and the necessary muscle to remove the Chinese were the French. And since it now became clear that this is what the French planned to do in any case, Ho Chi Minh began negotiating with d'Argenlieu's envoy, Colonel Jean Sainteny, whom he had met previously in China.

On the face of it, there was reason for optimism. In January 1946 de Gaulle had resigned. His going was marked by a succession of relatively weak and predominantly left-wing governments whose commitment to colonial restitution appeared less than full-blooded. In reality, the French wanted all of Viet Nam, but they did not want to have to contest it with the Kuomintang. Therefore there was scope for discussion on both sides.

An agreement of sorts, for which Ho Chi Minh was subsequently criticized by some of his Viet Minh colleagues, was hammered out and, in the presence of the American consul to Hanoi, signed on 6 March 1946. Under its terms, which did nothing to address matters south of the Sixteenth Parallel, 'Viet Nam' was to be recognized as a 'free State having its own government, parliament, army and finances, and forming part of the Indochinese Federation and the French Union'. But France was to retain control of this free state's foreign policy, and was to be allowed to maintain a force of fifteen thousand men on Tonkinese soil for a period of up to six years.

Vo Nguyen Giap had some difficulty explaining this treaty to an assembled crowd in the capital the next day. 'We negotiated above all else,' he said, 'to protect and reinforce our political, military and economic position.' In real terms, however, the agreement was a humiliation for Ho Chi Minh, his government of national unity and the Viet Minh. True, the document did, by virtue of its very existence, acknowledge the legitimacy of a genuinely Vietnamese government, but both parties knew that there were no guarantees attached. Because the agreement was only bilateral, the French could, whenever it suited them, renege on it. Meanwhile, Ho Chi Minh had conceded the all-important point of a substantial French garrison in his territory.

Ho did, however, achieve one ambition: the withdrawal of the Kuomintang. Chiang Kai-shek agreed to remove his army in exchange for the demise of French concessions in Shanghai and other Chinese ports. It had also been agreed that a referendum would be held south of the Sixteenth Parallel to decide whether the south wanted to come under the same political roof as the north; and that a comprehensive settlement affecting the whole of Viet Nam would be negotiated in due course.

The Kuomintang now pulled out of Tonkin, although not before the spring opium crop had been gathered in and loaded on to the departing trucks. There was, however, no sign of any preparations for the promised referendum in the south. Rather the French strove hard to create for themselves a viable political base. And in the north they began moving troops into Haiphong, the great port to the east of Hanoi, and always the likely bridgehead for introducing a larger force than that sanctioned by the 6 March agreement.

The Viet Minh, reading these developments as proof of French duplicity, and recognizing that sooner or later it would have to resume armed struggle, continued to develop its military wing. It was in these early months of 1946 that the communist army took on its distinctive tripartite formation. At the lowest level were the village militias. To begin with these units were made up of five or six volunteers, who might be called upon at any time to assist in the operations of the next tier up, the regionals. The regionals, also volunteers, were organized at the provincial level and stood in an equivalent relationship to the top echelon, the regulars, as the militias did to themselves. In addition, they supported guerrilla units that subsisted on a semi-regular basis. The regulars meanwhile, soon to be formed into divisions, comprised a standing army, trained and maintained in two 'base areas', one in the Viet Bac, the other, newly created by Giap, to the south of the Red River delta in a segment made up of parts of Thanh Hoa, Nghe An and Ha Tinh provinces.

In time each part of this triple-decker army would play its role in defeating the French. Often they would become meshed in common operations. For the present, however, they were simply too ill-equipped and under-trained to represent a serious threat. Indeed, the French, unaware of the embryonic deep-structure of their enemy, for a while tolerated the Viet Minh's excesses. Although in May, when the Kuomintang finally withdrew, there was a race between the French and the Viet Minh to assert control over the cities and towns of the northern delta, attended by a plethora of minor skirmishes between units of the two sides, the Viet Minh also obligingly initiated a pogrom against those Vietnamese nationalists who had remained outside its political pale. Scores of mandarin-types were assassinated. According to one source-historian, Edgar O'Ballance, 'many prominent Indo-Chinese nationalists and their followers were liquidated' in a campaign of terror inaugurated by Vo Nguyen Giap in his new appointment as Minister of the Interior. Certainly, down the years, there is ample evidence that the Viet Minh and their successors were prone to dispose of their political opponents by unorthodox and violent means. Faced also by various insurgency campaigns in the south, the French at this stage naturally welcomed any reduction in the number of potential opponents.

More and more it looked like war. Even by the end of April, pouring troops into Hanoi and Haiphong, the French had exceeded their agreed quota. During the negotiations Sainteny had given Ho Chi Minh to believe that French forces in Tonkin would be deployed predominantly along the border with China, as a means of protecting the whole of Indochina against any Kuomintang incursions. Yet even now Ho, still cabling Washington, hoped that a comprehensive and satisfactory settlement could be achieved across a table.

In April bipartite talks resumed at the hill-city of Dalat, in the Central Highlands. There Vo Nguyen Giap came face to face with d'Argenlieu himself. Giap pressed the Governor-General to honour the 6 March agreement and hold a referendum in the south. D'Argenlieu refused point blank. Instead, it was decided that any further discussions must be held in Paris.

Thus was born the Fontainebleau Conference. Paradoxically Ho Chi Minh, himself making the journey to Europe in the company of Pham Van Dong, considered that French soil would furnish him with surer ground on which to make his case than Vietnamese soil. There, away from the autocratic d'Argenlieu, who frequently misrepresented his country's policies toward Indochina, he would be in a position to exploit leftist, anti-colonial tendencies within the French establishment. But it was not to be. The French in France were simply better at disguising their intentions. Although, when he arrived at Marseilles, Ho seduced reporters with his charm and erudition, in the capital he was treated shabbily by government officials. His talks with low-grade ministers dragged on through August and into September. All that he was offered were terms almost identical to those already agreed upon in March. Signing another useless scrap of paper on 19 September, known as the Modus Vivendi, Ho packed his bags and returned home.

The real outcome of Fontainebleau perhaps was the rebonding of the two dominant traits in Ho Chi Minh's political make-up: his nationalism and his Marxist-Leninist ideology. Before leaving for France he had announced the formation of a new government, the Hoi Lien Hiep Quoc Dan Viet Nam, called for short the Lien Viet, or

Popular Front. This was yet another manoeuvre to widen the catchment and appeal of the Revolution and conceal its communist character. In reality, however, although the Lien Viet promulgated laws that were distinctly liberal, it was controlled by the Viet Minh. Now, returning to Viet Nam, Ho and Pham Van Dong opted to apply that control.

On 28 October the National Assembly met and the 'government' resigned. In its replacement, Ho himself took on the foreign ministry, in addition to the presidency he already had; Pham Van Dong was appointed his deputy; and General Vo Nguyen Giap, as he now was, became Minister for National Defence. And while the term Lien Viet continued to be employed, there was a further purge of those nationalist elements that remained hostile to socialism. The assassinations resumed, in the south now as well as the north; and a vigorous propaganda campaign made it clear that, in the coming struggle, anyone not actively for the Viet Minh cause would be considered against it.

It had become very clear to Ho and his closest colleagues that armed conflict was now a certainty if the ideal of Vietnamese independence was to be kept alive. At the beginning of October the French had blandly announced that, as from the 15th, they would take over control of the customs service in Haiphong. This posed a double threat to the Viet Minh: firstly, the customs duties derived from the port formed a substantial part of Viet Minh revenues; and secondly, such small-arms supplies as the Viet Minh received from the outside world came in mainly through Haiphong. Even so, Ho Chi Minh was reluctant to make too great an issue of the French presumption, for the reason that he did not want to be seen by the world as the one who started the fight.

It was not until more than a month later that the storm erupted. During the intervening period the port had been subject to dual-control: Viet Minh regional cadres on the one hand, French soldiers on the other. But on 20 November the French seized, or endeavoured to seize, a small vessel carrying arms for the Viet Minh as it docked. At once a bevy of regionals descended on the French, temporarily taking them prisoner. Further French troops rushed to the scene and a general skirmish broke out. Within hours the city was in turmoil. The streets swarmed with Vietnamese, barricades went up and there were incidents everywhere. The Viet Minh brought out small mortars; the French brought out armoured cars. Street by street the Viet Minh were forced out of the city centre and into the suburbs.

The following day, 21 November, acting on orders passed from Hanoi, the local Viet Minh commander sought a ceasefire. He proposed that the two sides should return to the posts they had occupied before the affair started. But the commanding French officer, Colonel Dèbes, would have none of this. He agreed to the ceasefire, but insisted that all armed troops should stay as they now found themselves. Effectively this meant that the Viet Minh were denied access to the port area.

The Commander-in-Chief of the French forces, General Etienne Valluy, who had replaced Le Clerc in July, instructed Dèbes to exploit the situation in Haiphong in such a way as to wrest control of the whole city, thus finally securing the essential bridgehead for wider French operations in Tonkin. Accordingly, Dèbes demanded a complete withdrawal of Viet Minh from the area. His ultimatum, issued on the 23rd, allowed two hours for a reply. But even before this short interval had elapsed a French cruiser, the *Suffren*, prowling in the waters outside Haiphong, began bombarding those parts of the city where the Viet Minh regionals were thought to have taken refuge.

This onslaught, a throwback to the treatment of Da Nang in the nineteenth century, as well as a portent of the savageries that were to plague Viet Nam for the next thirty-five years, left several thousand Vietnamese dead, most of them civilians, and a great many more wounded. When the firing ceased, French troops moved forward to clear the town. The Viet Minh regionals, supported by some regulars, decided to hold their positions, and for five days the outer streets were given over to fire-fights. The French, better armed, progressed slowly but surely, and by 28 November the whole of Haiphong, including its airport, was theirs.

The crisis had come. In the weeks that followed Ho Chi Minh made a last attempt to negotiate a settlement, but even he now realized the immutability of French intentions. The decision that Ho and Giap had to take towards the end of December was whether to resist the French as they advanced through the delta town by town, or withdraw their forces to the safety of the jungle and the hills. Knowing that they lacked the *matériel* to confront the French Expeditionary Force (FEF), and sensing that the best hope still lay in patience and the dogged determination that comes of patience, they wisely chose the latter course. Regulars and most regionals alike were rapidly pulled out of all the urban centres and regrouped in the two 'base areas'. Those regionals who did not regroup stayed behind as an 'underground' force.

In Hanoi, as the regulars departed and the government prepared to evacuate, the regionals and militiamen took over essential security operations. On 19 December the commander of the French barracks demanded that all Viet Minh effectives in the capital disarm themselves. The French military police, he said, were to assume responsibility for law and order. Almost immediately that responsibility was put to the test. The following evening there was rioting throughout the city. The viciousness, the overstatement of French actions in Haiphong the previous month had only reinforced the Viet Minh's standing among the general populace. Every public building was attacked, and again the barricades went up. But the French were prepared. The next day, 21 December 1946, they counter-attacked, deploying mobile armour and mortars. Swiftly they surrounded the inner city, hoping to cast a *cordon sanitaire*. The remaining regionals and militiamen removed their uniforms and melted into the angry civilian population. Ho Chi Minh and his staff, by the skin of their teeth, escaped.

Thus began the First Indochinese War, or, as it was colloquially called, the Dirty War. It was to last seven and a half years. 'You may kill ten of my men for every one I kill of yours,' Ho Chi Minh is reported to have told a French negotiator, Paul Mus, in 1948, 'but even at those odds you will lose and I will win.' Ultimately the Viet Minh were invincible because they had the active support if not of the whole of the Vietnamese people, then of a substantial portion of them, particularly in the north where the decisive engagements took place. The French were never able to foster more than the dubious loyalty of some of the minorities: the relatively small Catholic community, sometimes the religious sects (the Hoa Hao and Cao Dai), the mainly Chinese southern compradors, the upper bourgeoisie, some criminal elements and some of the hill peoples, or montagnards, such as the T'ai and Tho in the north-west of the country. Outside the cities, in the south as well as the north, no part of the land was ever entirely theirs, while vast swathes of it belonged incontestably to the insurgents. On the roads built by their predecessors travel was habitually unsafe after dusk. And even as the war became increasingly internationalized, so that the fight against Ho

Chi Minh became overtly a fight against organized communism quite as much as it had been a fight against a seemingly ragged band of nationalists, the French failed to convince those Vietnamese who might have fought beside them that their ideology was worth dying for.

The Viet Minh, on the other hand, achieved precisely that. Dien Bien Phu, the climactic, decisive battle, was won by many means; but foremost among those means was the wave attack learnt from the Red Army of Mao Tse-tung: massive infantry assaults on strongly fortified positions under withering fire, great quantities of men rushing towards almost certain extinction.

Indoctrination, always a mixture of applied reason and stern discipline tinged with terror, was an important weapon in the Viet Minh arsenal. It allowed the communists to exploit to the maximum the one, and for a long time the only, advantage they had over the French: that the land 'belonged' to them, as Vietnamese, and not to the foreign interlopers. But it could also be used sparingly, especially in the south, where communist cadres quickly discovered that offering the peasants practical assistance was a more effective way of winning their hearts and minds than filling their ears with Marxist-Leninist cant.

Amongst cadres and soldiers, however, a different standard prevailed. There indoctrination and the Revolution went hand in hand. The army that Vo Nguyen Giap and Ho Chi Minh between them forged was political as much as it was military. Operational secrecy was maintained to a remarkable degree, yet there was never any secret as to the rationale of the Viet Minh cause. Alongside every officer came a political commissar. Just as at the very top of the Viet Minh's military edifice Ho Chi Minh and Vo Nguyen Giap may be said to have shared the command, the Marxism-Leninism of the one blending with the tactical principles of the other, so at the battalion, company and even platoon levels, army men and political officers sat side by side as they digested orders and planned their activities. The theory, which worked so well in practice, was that only a willing fighting force could be effective in the field, and that only a properly 'enlightened' force would prove willing. Much of the propaganda disseminated year in, year out by the commissars appears crude; but in the 1940s, within the equally crude context of the French occupation, it could be startlingly apposite.

Ultimately the war was what Giap has called it: a people's war. It was also, successively, a guerrilla war, a war of attrition, a positional war and a war of all-out assault. But these were only the labelled phases of a truly elaborate design in which the ordinary villager had as important a role to play as the soldier in his forest or mountain camp.

Vo Nguyen Giap, nicknamed 'the ice-capped volcano' by the French, was born in An Xa village, Nghe An province, in 1912. Like so many other Viet Minh leaders, he came from a family of teachers and scholars that had minor mandarin status. His early years were spent in different locations in northern Annam, mainly between Hué and Dong Hoi. In 1924 he entered the same *lycée* in Hué from which Ho Chi Minh had been banned in 1908. Student strikes in 1925 drew Giap into political activities, and the following year he too was expelled for participating in a 'Quit School' movement. In the same period he visited Phan Boi Chau under house arrest in Hué and joined the nationalist Tan Viet youth association. In 1930 he was briefly imprisoned following his involvement in revolutionary activities. Released for good behaviour, although now secretly a communist, Giap convinced the Sûreté that he had reformed his ways, and was allowed to take the *baccalauréat*. Subsequently, he enrolled at the University of Hanoi to study law and political economy. But although he took his *licence en droit* in 1937, his extra-curricular activities consumed more and more of his time. In 1938 he failed his law exams, and he had thereafter to earn his keep as a schoolmaster at a private school in the capital. He contributed regularly to communist broadsheets, and in other ways became an integral part of the Hanoi underground.

As early as 1939 Giap had established his pre-eminence in the Tonkin section of the Indochina Communist Party. Only Pham Van Dong and Truong Chinh exercised more influence. Following the Japanese takeover in 1940, Giap and Dong went into voluntary exile, travelling dangerously by train to Lao Kay and thence across the Chinese border to Kunming, where in June Giap had his first meeting with Ho Chi Minh. At once he became a member of Ho's inner circle. Thereafter Giap travelled through south-west China, visiting Keiyang, Kweilin and Nanning, picking up valuable political and military information. It was at this time that he first encountered the writings of Mao Tse-tung, although whether, as has been claimed, he met Mao personally on a separate journey to Kangta in the north-west in 1942 is open to question. What is beyond dispute, however, is that Giap began imbibing deeply such tracts as *The Strategic Problems of the anti-Japanese War* and *Guerrilla Warfare*, containing the essential principles of Mao's theory of revolutionary tactics. And it was Giap's enthusiasm for this new military learning that caused Ho to prime him as the future commander of the Viet Minh's forces.

No other soldier of comparable stature came to his calling so late in life. Until he was almost thirty Giap had no first-hand experience of military affairs whatsoever. But neither had anyone else among the communist leadership, and someone had to take the brief. In 1940 therefore, no more than a novice himself, Giap undertook to raise and train the first guerrilla units. From December 1944, with Kuomintang and American assistance, he further undertook to forge a platoon at least of regulars. By the August Revolution he was in command of some five thousand troops, and in the year leading up to the final outbreak of hostilities with the French Giap raised this number sixfold.

The Haiphong incident and the Hanoi Uprising of December 1946 left Giap with two urgent tasks: in the first instance, to keep the reality of war alive when his men were, in the main, poorly armed and unlikely, in the foreseeable future, to be much better armed; and, in the long term, to contrive an army that could defeat the French military machine.

The answer to the first was to resume guerrilla warfare, to constantly harass and undermine the French with ambushes and acts of sabotage. The answer to the second was to enlarge his regular army to scale. By 1948 Giap's regulars numbered sixty thousand, organized in five officered divisions: the 304th, the 308th, the 312th, the 316th and the 320th, each trained and maintained in one of the two 'base areas'. Yet even an army as substantial as this was, without effective fire-power, inconsequential; and it was not until Mao's Red Army swept to power in China in 1949 that the Viet Minh's main force, now in receipt of supplies to its rear, could begin to be effective.

In 1946–7 Mao's victory was still a distant prospect few cared to prophesy. For the next three years Giap could only wait and hope. While his divisions were nursed towards maturity in the mountain fortress of the Viet Bac, and to a lesser extent in the Nghe An–Ha Tinh–Thanh Hoa base area, it was too hazardous to risk using them. 1947 understandably became, in the slogan of official communist history, the 'year of strategic defence'.

Much of the groundwork undertaken before the August Revolution had to be redone. The whole of Indochina was now divided into fourteen regions, each with its own committee, military commander and political commissar. Cadres were infiltrated into every village, in the first instance to prepare militias, and in the second to spread Viet Minh propaganda. At the same time the Viet Minh developed a new agency, a secret police, to deal with recalcitrants. Giap's newly formed divisions needed rice just as much as they needed weapons, and where rice was not voluntarily forthcoming it sometimes had to be extorted by one means or another. And yet the same Viet Minh agents performed another invaluable role. They created an intelligence network that, in the campaigns to come, gave Giap a steady edge over his enemy. The Viet Minh nearly always knew what the FEF was about to do, for the simple reason that the French could not function without Vietnamese auxiliaries; whereas the French were increasingly left guessing at what the Viet Minh's next move would be. But more than this, any movement by even the smallest French units would be observed and reported. When the conflict entered into the stage of positional warfare this, for Giap, was a critical advantage.

The French meanwhile, despite disagreements between militarists and politicians, made apparent headway. Just as Le Clerc had deployed his battalions swiftly in the south, so the new French commander, Valluy, rapidly dispatched his detachments to the cities and towns of the Red River delta. Further, realizing that Viet Minh forces were concentrated in the Viet Bac, he now, somewhat against the wishes of Governor-General Bollaert, began planning for a dry-season offensive. At the same time Bollaert initiated what was to prove a lengthy courtship of the erstwhile Emperor, Bao Dai, presently embarked on a life of ease in Hong Kong. If Bao Dai could be persuaded to return under French auspices, then the French occupation would acquire a patina of legitimacy.

In March 1947, to encourage Bao Dai, Cochinchina was declared a 'free state' within the French Union. A provisional government, headed by Nguyen Van Xuan, was formed, although the Governor-General's office continued to control all the significant functions of government: finance, foreign relations, security and everything military. For their part, the Viet Minh continued to blow up bridges, disrupt communications, assault police stations and arrange assassinations in all parts of the country.

By now Valluy had fifty thousand men under his command, including several battalions of Algerians, Moroccans, Tunisians, Senegalese and mainly German Legionnaires. While in Paris arguments raged between left and right as to what form colonial rule in Indochina should take, Bollaert, having sent Paul Mus to reopen secret negotiations with Ho Chi Minh, ordered a unilateral ceasefire for 15 August. He would, he said, talk to anyone to resolve the 'situation'. But as soon as he heard of this, Valluy flew to France to beg Prime Minister Ramadier and his cabinet to recall the Governor-General. Not for the first time the civil and military wings of colonial authority in Viet Nam were at cross purposes.

In the event the ceasefire was cancelled, although Bollaert was allowed to remain in Saigon since it was felt he was making significant progress in his negotiations with Bao Dai. Indeed, at the end of the year Bollaert almost brought it off. On 7 December he met the erstwhile Emperor on board a French battle-cruiser in Ha Long Bay and persuaded him to sign a protocol that, in effect, restored Bao Dai to the throne under French trusteeship. But before the year was out Bao Dai panicked and fled to Europe; and it was not until the early spring of 1949 that he would be coaxed, with meaningless concessions, into honouring his pledge.

For now Valluy was free to launch an offensive the simple aims of which were to smash Giap's main force in the Viet Bac and capture the Viet Minh leadership. With Chiang Kai-shek and the Kuomintang still strong in Yunnan, Valluy felt confident that his enemy would have no easy escape. Such optimism, however, was soon dispelled. Operation Lea quickly ran into trouble, bringing home to the French the true nature of the struggle on their hands. Of necessity, because of the size of his armour and the fighting habits of his soldiery, Valluy was obliged to move his forces, in what he hoped would be a pincer movement, northwards along the only two passable roads through the Viet Bac region: Colonial Route 3, which connected Hanoi to Cao Bang via Thai Nguyen, an industrial town on the rim of the Red River delta forty-odd miles from Hanoi; and Colonial Route 4, carved through the mountains between Lang Son and the same destination.

Valluy committed some fifteen thousand of his men to this adventure. He would have committed more, except that this would seriously have risked undermanning the many garrisons in the rest of the country, all needed as points of resistance against continuing guerrilla incursions. He had at his disposal in all sixteen battalions: three mobile armour, six infantry, two paratroop, four artillery and one of engineers. None of these was either trained or particularly suited to the kind of jungle-trekking that would have been the only realistic hope of flushing out the Viet Minh. Pitted against this force was an army of up to sixty thousand regulars. Although these were ill-equipped, they were attuned to a wild and difficult terrain that stretched several thousand square miles.

In its first few hours Operation Lea, commencing on 7 October 1947, went well for the French. A paratroop battalion dropped with such precision into the heart of Viet Minh territory that Vo Nguyen Giap and Ho Chi Minh had to take cover in a ditch to avoid capture. But the problem was that the enemy would not fight. They simply melted into the dense surrounding landscape. Then it appeared that the paratroopers were surrounded. Shortly they came under fire and a desperate week-long battle began. Meanwhile the two convoys of the intended pincer movement were only just beginning to trundle their way up Routes 3 and 4. Giap, advised of this by his intelligence, at once set about blowing holes at regular intervals along both roads. Nonetheless Valluy's engineers, supported by artillery and from the air, managed to advance his columns, albeit at unequal speeds. On 16 October a motorized regiment of Moroccan infantrymen broke through from Route 3 to relieve the stranded paratroop battalion. By then, however, Giap had managed to evacuate the area, moving his main force northwards over the mountains and thus evading danger.

Operation Lea was abandoned. In its stead, at the end of November, the more modest Operation Ceinture was mounted. Restricted to the southern tip of the Viet Bac, this once again failed to locate and engage any sizeable Viet Minh units, although the capture of some supply dumps meant that Valluy could claim limited success. On 22 December Valluy again withdrew, allowing two Viet Minh regiments to slip quietly back into those areas they had previously evacuated.

The point had been made. Outside of the Red River delta, which formed but a small wedge pointed from the sea towards the geographic centre of Tonkin, the Viet Minh were untouchable by conventional forces. The era of heliborne search-and-destroy missions was two decades away. Isolated garrisons apart, only two sectors were reliably brought under French control. One was to the sparsely populated north-west, a largely mountainous area on either side of the upper reaches of the Red and Clear Rivers. Here the French had persuaded the local T'ai, H'mong and Tho tribes to fight with them; and, being montagnards, the tribalists knew how to work the terrain to their advantage. The other was Route 4 itself, between Lang Son and Cao Bang. Securing the Chinese border was considered imperative, but it was only through a chain of heavily fortified garrisons, principally at That Khe and Dong Khe, as well as at Cao Bang itself, that the fiction of this security could be maintained. Convoys servicing the posts along the way were frequently ambushed, and over the months French casualties climbed steadily. And when Giap's regulars eventually launched their counter-offensive in 1950, it was precisely here that France suffered its first great and humiliating colonial defeat.

Similarly, the other 'safe' region was to prove a nightmare. The French may have persuaded the montagnards for a while that the Viet Minh were untrustworthy friends, but the Viet Minh propaganda specialists in time convinced them that the French were a far greater evil fit only to be expunged from the land; and the final battle, Dien Bien Phu, was fought in the middle of T'ai territory.

Valluy's campaigns revealed a stalemate. 1948 passed without major engagement. The French had not the skill to pursue effectively the Viet Minh regiments in the mountains, and the Viet Minh had not the strength to launch frontal attacks against the French in any of their strongholds. Yet it was the Viet Minh who kept up the pressure, through constant, unpredictable guerrilla activities. Such advances as the French were able to make were on the political front.

Despite Bao Dai's febrile vacillations, the French were confident that sooner or later he would return to head a native government pliant to their wishes. A more immediate advantage was obtained *vis-à-vis* the Cao Dai, who were weaned away from a fleeting alliance with the Viet Minh. They now joined the Catholics in an anti-communist concert that the French endeavoured to tune to the point of stridency. But with regard to the balance of forces in Saigon, the most significant move to consolidate control of the city was achieved when the puppet government successfully wooed the Binh Xuyen.

The Binh Xuyen, under its seedy strong-arm leader Le Van Vien, was in effect the biggest of the Saigon mobs. It had its own armed force and had perfected the art of 'protection'. Now the Binh Xuyen became Saigon's police force: a classic example of poacher turned gamekeeper, except that the extortion continued. Vien's ambition had always been to control the city's larger casinos, including the Grande Monde in Cholon. Now he achieved that ambition. By institutionalizing corruption (which included farming Saigon's many brothels) the French, through 'Prime Minister' Nguyen Van

Xuan, sought to run the city's affairs in the same way that the city affairs ran themselves. The gain resided in the fact that the Binh Xuyen furnished an effective counter against the Viet Minh, even though, for a while, Le Van Vien paid over a share of his ill-gotten profits to communist cadres.

In due course, following the Elysée agreement of March 1949, Bao Dai returned to Viet Nam. Once again forgoing his royal title, he became 'head of state', placed by the French in nominal command of the Vietnamese government. But although he presided over a native cabinet, that cabinet had little real power except in the appointment of its own officials and those of the native bureaucracy. Eschewing Saigon, Bao Dai set up instead at a hunting lodge in the pleasant hill resort of Dalat. There he and the French could ignore each other to their hearts' content. But Bao Dai did have just sufficient power to come to terms with Le Van Vien. The Viet Minh's share of their profits was rerouted by Binh Xuyen officials into the former Emperor's various bank accounts.

The French Expeditionary Force had meanwhile swollen to 150,000 men. In May 1949 the French Chief of General Staff, General Revers, visited Viet Nam to assess the situation for himself. Although the Viet Minh were as yet in no position to topple the French, their incursions were enough to remind the French continuously that there was a war on. In Paris it was also appreciated that Mao Tse-tung's imminent victory in China threatened a transformation of the uneasy status quo in Indochina.

In his less than optimistic report which at the time went largely ignored, Revers made some telling recommendations. He urged that the defences of the Red River delta be strengthened against any attack by the Viet Minh's main force; that the Chinese border garrisons be dismantled before they were destroyed; that after a thorough 'pacification' of the northern delta, a counter-offensive be launched against the Viet Minh's Viet Bac divisions; and that the 'native' army, serving alongside the FEF, be substantially enlarged.

The Viet Minh meanwhile, finding that the fourteen regions of their previous devising inhibited rather than improved the flow of commands down their three-tier army, had divided Viet Nam into six definitive military 'zones': north-west Tonkin, north-east Tonkin, the Red River delta, northern Annam, southern Annam and Cochinchina. In addition, military and political commands were integrated. Much of 1948 had been spent in an endeavour to strengthen the resistance in the south, which as ever lagged behind the north. Pham Van Dong and Pham Ngoc were sent to Annam and Cochinchina to encourage the expansion of the village militias and provincial irregulars. But while progress in these respects was made, and some small regular units were formed, the creation of a hoped-for third base area was indefinitely postponed.

The guerrilla war, however, intensified. French convoys were regularly attacked in all parts of the country by shock troops who melted into the surrounding countryside at the first sign of counter-attack. Bridges continued to be dynamited and roads mined. To this period of the war also belongs the initial excavation of underground tunnels in the maquis that furnished the Viet Minh, and later the Viet Cong, with safe hiding places whenever the enemy attempted to clear guerrilla-infested provinces in central Viet Nam and the Mekong delta. A system of watchtowers, on the other hand, constructed by the French along roads and rivers alike, proved a valuable source of small arms to the communists. Attacked by night, their mainly Vietnamese defenders chose more often to flee than to fight.

The reality of the situation was that in two and a half years neither side had made significant progress. While the French could claim with some justification to control the cities and towns of the two deltas, the Viet Minh were seemingly committed to a campaign of perpetual harassment while striving to win over the hearts and minds of an at times suspicious and obdurate peasantry.

In July 1949, to further this latter end, the Viet Minh announced that the *nha qué* would be allowed to own the land they worked. Temporarily, plans for the collectivization of all arable land inside Viet Nam were shelved. But while this increased the appeal of the Viet Minh considerably in the sourthern part of the country, as well as in Annam, the event that was ultimately to turn the tide in Ho Chi Minh's favour took place outside his country. In April, having already entered Peking, the Chinese Red Army crossed the Yangtse River. Within a few weeks Nanking, Hangchow and Shanghai belonged to Mao Tse-tung. In August Changsha fell. On the mainland, at least, Chiang Kai-shek was finished. In October the People's Republic was formally proclaimed.

The effects of the Kuomintang's defeat were far-reaching in the extreme. On the one hand, it led to the creation of a separate, trimmed-down Chinese state on the island of Formosa (Taiwan) that in time would join the 'Pacific Century' club, whose other members included Japan, South Korea, Hong Kong and Singapore. On the other hand, it fostered a new communist bloc in Asia that has outlasted its East European counterpart. Ho Chi Minh was no longer isolated internationally. He could now look to Viet Nam's traditional enemy for both material and political support.

In early January 1950, finally abandoning the idea of a negotiated settlement with France, Ho announced that his was the only legitimate government of Viet Nam. Immediately, his confidence was rewarded. Peking effectively recognized the Viet Minh on 18 January; Moscow on the 30th. Poland, Romania, Hungary and North Korea quickly followed suit. In February General Giap, abiding by Mao Tse-tung's strategic terminology, proudly declared that the struggle against the French was ready to advance to its next phase: that is, the 'war of position'. Already, from November 1949, all males aged between eighteen and forty-five living in 'liberated' areas had been made liable to military service. The elimination of all enemy outposts now became the liberation army's immediate objective. At the same time China's 2nd Field Army extended its training facilities to Viet Minh regulars. Vietnamese gunners could build up their skills on the artillery ranges at Tsin Tsi and Long Chow. Conversely, Chinese 'technicians' began crossing the border into the Viet Bac.

The French responded quickly. In a continuing effort to sustain the myth that Viet Nam was in some way an independent nation, Paris came up with a new formula. Viet Nam, Laos and Cambodia were henceforward to be called the 'Associate States' of the French Union of Indochina. Tonkin, Annam and Cochinchina were to become figments of the past. Bao Dai's position as head of state was confirmed, although in fact real power was still denied him by a series of secret resolutions. A new government, under the prime ministership of Tran Van Huu, was installed.

The upshot of these manoeuvres was that, overtly, there was no longer any legal hindrance to 'Viet Nam' seeking aid from the United States. Accordingly, at the behest of his Secretary of State Dean Acheson, President Truman allowed an immediate $10 million worth of aid to be earmarked for Saigon, where in 1950 the Pentagon installed a Military Advisory and Assistance Group (MAAG). Thereafter aid to Viet Nam, most of it destined for the FEF but some $10 million finding their way into Bao Dai's personal coffers, flowed from Washington like water, rising to $1 billion in 1954 and a total of $2.5 billion for the five years leading up to Dien Bien Phu; so that by the end of the war seventy-eight per cent of the French effort was being funded by the United States.

Reassured by the promise of American support, Paris now increased its Indochinese forces to 175,000 men. At the same time a decision was made to reinforce the garrisons guarding the Chinese border, particularly along Colonial Route 4, in order to prevent Chinese aid reaching Giap.

Everything portended a dramatic face-lift to the conflict. Even so, the guerrilla war was far from over. On the contrary, it was vigorously renewed and continued unbroken until the cessation of hostilities in July 1954. Indeed, it formed an integral part of the overall plan whereby Giap's regular divisions could be gainfully deployed. The French army of occupation being subjected to pinprick attacks in every quarter of the country, the French command had of necessity to disperse its strength to cover not just its rear, but its entire provenance. Repeatedly, attempts to pursue the Viet Minh's massed forces were stymied by broken supply and communication lines.

As early as the spring of 1950 Giap felt sufficiently emboldened to launch his first, semi-successful large-scale offensive. While in the Mekong delta Nguyen Binh was instructed to 'isolate' Saigon by using both village militiamen and regional irregulars, in the north Giap concentrated his activities on the China border posts. In February the small French garrison at Lao Kai, sometimes called 'the gateway to China', was overrun with the help of 80mm mortars. Then in May, Route 4 was targeted.

Convoys supplying That Khe, Dong Khe and Cao Bang had long been subject to sniper fire and ambush. One reason for this is that Route 4 provided the Viet Minh with perfect cover. The high, narrow road snakes through craggy, densely foliated limestone mountains from one small valley to the next. Boulders abound, as do overhangs. Paths leading from the interior and cutting into the road are entirely obscured. For the colonial footsoldier it was an evil forced march at the best of times. And now that the Viet Minh had Chinese mortars, mines and bazookas, even driving Route 4 in an armoured vehicle was an intimidating prospect.

But despite Revers' recommendations, the French continued to operate Route 4 and the garrisons it served. By this means alone they could convince themselves that the Viet Minh were in some manner surrounded, or at the least confined, in their mountain 'fastness'. It was also essential to monitor and deter the flow of arms and perhaps men from Red China. If the border was abandoned, it was felt, then the Viet Minh might indeed become a match for the FEF.

On 25 May Giap launched four infantry battalions against the French fortification at Dong Khe, in a valley midway between Cao Bang and That Khe. Again mortars and other small field pieces were used, as was, for the first time in the war, the 'human wave' tactic. Although the garrison was eight hundred strong, it fell. Two days later, however, it was recaptured. The French had mobilized and dropped a battalion of paratroops. The Viet Minh were prevented from mounting a second counter-attack by the sudden onset of summer rains.

For the moment Route 4 was 'safe'. But only until the rains stopped. In the dry autumn season Giap made a second campaign. Dong Khe was attacked on 16 September. For two days German Legionnaires resisted, but finally, after heavy fighting, they were overrun. General Carpentier, the Commander-in-Chief of the FEF, now reluctantly conceded that Route 4 would have to be abandoned. But the real defeat came in the manner of the withdrawal. First it was decided to evacuate Cao Bang. On 3 October a convoy of 1,500 troops, accompanied by civilians and their baggage, set off from the head of Route 4 for Lang Son. At the same time 3,500 men from That Khe – mainly Moroccans – set off northwards to reinforce the Cao Bang convoy. The two columns failed to meet. Those coming from Cao Bang were ambushed. Forced to abandon both the road and their vehicles, they fled to the hills. Then the second column, advancing from That Khe, received the same treatment.

French casualties were already high, but worse was to come. Off the road, the two FEF groups finally managed to conjoin, whereupon they were attacked *en masse* for a third time with terrible consequences. In a desperate rearguard action, the French lost an estimated four thousand men. There was no retreat, only escape. Those who survived a ferocious Viet Minh assault on what at best was a semi-entrenched position between two hills fled, in many cases to be hunted down individually in an unfamiliar jungle. Finally, a fresh battalion of paratroops, dropped into the area to offer some defence against Giap's marauders, was also mauled, suffering an eighty per cent casualty rate.

The French had been humiliated. Not only had the whole of Route 4 from Lang Son to Cao Bang been lost, but Lang Son itself had hastily to be abandoned, allowing a substantial arsenal to fall into Viet Minh hands. Six thousand troops had been either killed or taken prisoner, and the FEF found itself the poorer by 13 field guns, 125 mortars, 950 machine guns and 1,200 sub-machine guns. Several hundred trucks had also been either destroyed or abandoned.

For the Viet Minh, on the other hand, 'Route 4' was precisely the kind of 'brilliant' victory that its propaganda required. The whole of north-east Tonkin was now a liberated zone. Chinese weapons and Chinese supplies could flow into the Viet Bac without fear of impediment. But just as important, the army of national liberation had shown it could outfight the French in a large-scale manoeuvre.

Yet it was also in part an illusory and therefore dangerous victory. The terrain had been outstandingly favourable to the Viet Minh, as indeed had been the weather: a more or less permanent cloud-cover, at points coming right down upon the upper reaches of Route 4, had prevented Carpentier from deploying his air force in bombing and strafing missions. How well Giap's divisions would perform on flat, open and possibly sunlit terrain was another matter.

In Paris the alarm bells rang. In December 1950, as Giap pushed forward units to the edge of the Red River delta, both General Carpentier and High Commissioner Léon Pignon were recalled. They were replaced by Jean de Lattre de Tassigny, who assumed political as well as military command. The expectation was that de Lattre, a Second World War hero renowned for his grit as well as his generalship, would put backbone into the French effort.

Arriving in Saigon on 17 December, de Lattre's first action was to call a halt to the exodus of French families returning to France. He then implemented several of the recommendations in General Revers' forgotten report. In particular he ordered the expansion of the Vietnamese National Army (later to become the Army of the Republic of Viet Nam, or ARVN), to the extent that by the middle of 1951 there had come into existence four indigenous divisions; and he organized the defence of the perimeter of the Red River delta by means of the eponymous De Lattre Line: an unbroken chain of mini-fortresses, each one within sight of its two neighbours.

Publicly, he exuded great confidence, although in private he conceded that his country's cause was probably doomed to failure, and for much the same reason that Ho Chi Minh and Von Nguyen Giap were optimistic about their own cause: the broad mass of the people were behind the Viet Minh in a way relatively few Vietnamese were behind the French. Of all the commanders sent to Viet Nam by Paris, de Lattre was undoubtedly the most astute; and had he lasted, the war might well have dragged on longer.

For the moment, the northern delta held out against any encroachments by Viet Minh troops, although it soon became apparent that Giap was mustering his forces for another spring offensive. His army was now augmented by two new units: a heavy division (the 351st), armed with Chinese-manufactured field pieces, mortars and anti-aircraft guns; and a battalion of engineers. In addition, some twenty-five thousand 'regionals' had been upgraded into regulars, so that the communist army now numbered sixty full-strength battalions. These were now equipped with radio sets, again courtesy of Peking – something that had previously been in short supply.

The second spring offensive began well before the winter ended. As early as 22 December French air reconnaissance spotted Viet Minh detachments near Tien Yen, north of Ha Long Bay. Paratroops were dropped, as was napalm (petroleum gelled with aluminium soaps), and the force was dispersed. Thereafter Giap was to insist that, unless circumstances absolutely dictated otherwise, the movement of his troops was to take place by night, and that by day his men should be camouflaged against aerial survey. As it happened though, no great damage had been done. Giap had already decided to attack the Red River delta perimeter from the west. Like so many Viet Minh manoeuvres, Tien Yen was a feint, designed to prevent the French concentrating their forces in any one sector and to keep them scattered instead.

The French response to this tactic was to create 'mobile groups', forerunners of US 'combat teams'. These were integrated units, around three thousand strong, comprising infantry, armour, artillery, engineers and signals, which could be deployed rapidly wherever they might suddenly be needed. Unlike their American heliborne successors, however, they were, despite the availability of paratroops, mainly wheelborne, and therefore their mobility was restricted to serviceable roads.

At the beginning of 1951 Giap duly launched an attack in the area around the large town of Vinh Yen, about forty miles north-west of Hanoi and just north of the Red River itself. If he succeeded, he would advance two divisions on the capital while his remaining forces launched diversionary attacks elsewhere.

However, Giap was too ambitious. He had yet to learn that if not discretion, then caution is the better part of valour. On 13 January an outpost at Bao Chuc was easily overrun. De Lattre, flying immediately to Vinh Yen but under-estimating the enemy's strength, next day dispatched the 14th Mobile Group to the scene of action, only to have it severely mauled. The remnants came back to Vinh Yen, and during the course of the night several more outposts were stormed by the Viet Minh. At once de Lattre organized an airlift relief operation, and on 15 January Giap's forces were pushed back into the surrounding foothills. On the 16th, with the aid of a second mobile group, the foothills themselves were attacked. Giap imprudently responded by throwing both his available divisions, the 308th and the 312th, into a counter-attack. The wave tactic was employed, but it was thwarted by the guns and the bombs of the French air force. Once again napalm was used, to devastating effect.

The fighting continued through to the afternoon of the 17th as the Viet Minh, as though refusing to acknowledge the damage that was being inflicted on them, continued to send men forward. But it was to no avail, and by early evening the communists had shown their tail. Six thousand of them had been killed, the equivalent of one-half of one division. As many more had been wounded and a further six hundred prisoners were taken.

In his defence Giap claimed that at least he had come close at Vinh Yen. De Lattre had been forced to employ all his available reserves. In the face of a relatively new and deadly weapon (napalm) many commanders would have ordered an immediate retreat. But Giap, always prepared to sacrifice men for his objectives, instead dug deep into the morale of his troops. Yet because of de Lattre's undisputed mastery of the air, it is difficult to see how even a victory would have advanced the Viet Minh cause, for Giap would still have had the problem of advancing across relatively open ground towards Hanoi.

Of the two commanders, though, it was de Lattre who was perhaps the more appreciative of his own weaknesses after Vinh Yen. He perceived that the delta remained vulnerable to attack and immediately set about expediting the construction of the De Lattre Line: twelve hundred reinforced concrete blockhouses that stretched all the way from Ha Long Bay to Vinh Yen itself, and then back south-eastwards as far as Phat Diem.

By the end of the year the project was complete. A formidable undertaking, it was however finally a quixotic one. For while the line looked outwards towards the Viet Minh-infested mountains and forests that surrounded the delta, there was little point to it if the area it enclosed was not secure. Once installed, it was also a further drain on available manpower.

These shortcomings de Lattre realized. His intentions were that the blockhouses should in time be manned entirely by local soldiers, and that the mobile groups should be developed in such a way that they became mixed French–Vietnamese commando units. He also saw the need for a pacification programme within the delta itself. Yet the obstacles were formidable. His officers were decidedly disinclined to mix their own men with 'natives', and the level of Viet Minh infiltration and allegiance in the delta villages and towns was close to saturation.

Giap, by contrast, remained bullish, opting to strike again while the irons were hot. At the end of March he moved his 316th Division toward the north-eastern section of the delta perimeter. On the night of the 23rd he attacked a garrison at the small inland village of Mao Khe, between Haiphong and Ha Long. Again, however, he was unsuccessful. For two days the garrison resisted, giving French gunboats, travelling up the Da Bac River, time to position themselves against the enemy. Paratroops and the air force were also deployed. On the 27th Giap launched a mass assault on French positions outside Mao Khe; but although these yielded, Mao Khe itself held firm.

Twice now the delta perimeter had withstood the Viet Minh's new-found fire-power. Another two months passed and Giap tried a third time, on a broad front along the Day River to the south. By dint of an impressive logistics operation he manoeuvred three of his divisions – the 304th, the 308th and the 320th – into position. His plan was to thrust the 320th past Phat Diem (a Catholic centre) towards Thai Binh, while creating 'diversions' further up the river at Ninh Binh and Phu Ly. His tactics were flexible, however, in the sense that if either or both of the secondary attacks prospered then they could be converted into the main thrust.

Since the summer monsoons had already arrived, the Day River campaign took the French unawares. For this reason Giap scored some initial successes. On 29 May the 304th and 308th Divisions crossed the river and attacked their targets, destroying several outposts as well as the armed vessels that the French had in the area. Simultaneously, guerrilla incidents were staged all around the circumference of the Red River delta itself. Then in the late afternoon, using sampans, the 320th surged over the Day River in two separate places, one directly opposite Phat Diem and one to the south-east. The intention was to link up with a regiment that had been infiltrated behind French lines a few days before. But because of the rains, the Viet Minh quickly became bogged down, trapped by the accuracy of de Lattre's riflemen. Several mobile groups were swiftly moved into defensive positions, and once again the French air force proved too much for the insurrectionaries. But the greatest damage was inflicted by an armada of river boats that cut the Viet Minh's supply and communication lines.

The fighting continued until 10 June. It then took Giap another eight days to withdraw his forces back across the Day River. He had held very little of his army in reserve. He had also, in seeking to overstretch the French, overstretched himself. The net result was that in five months the Viet Minh had suffered three major defeats. Up to a third of the regulars had been lost in battle, along with much of the *matériel* supplied by the Chinese, whose patrimony was now diverted to the war in Korea.

The mood within the Party (since February 1951 relaunched as the Viet Nam Dang Lao Dong, or Viet Nam Workers' Party) was bleak. But rather than blame the failure on Vo Nguyen Giap, Ho Chi Minh looked at the broader picture. In particular he was aware that in the south of the country not enough had been done to undermine French control and French confidence. The Party's Saigon deputy, Nguyen Binh, was now recalled to the northern headquarters. He died, however, in shadowy circumstances *en route*. Giap and his colleagues then sat down to rethink and reformulate their strategy.

Almost for the sake of appearances, and to keep up battlefront pressure on the French, when the dry season arrived at the end of September 1951 the Viet Minh made a scaled-down attack against Nghia Lo, a French garrison on the eastern edge of the predominantly T'ai north-western highlands. But after ten days the action was called off as de Lattre smartly reinforced the outpost with three paratroop battalions. For the moment it was back to guerrilla warfare, as Party propagandists worked to repair the damage done to the Viet Minh's credibility, and to extend revolutionary loyalty, especially in the south.

Recriminations within the leadership gave way to a prolonged bout of auto-criticism – always one of the strong features of Vietnamese communism. Out of this came a hard-nosed analysis of how to conduct guerrilla (or people's) war, in both its political and military aspects. In particular, still relying on Mao Tse-tung as his guiding inspiration, but modifying the Chinese leader's doctrines to suit conditions inside Viet Nam, General Giap defined the seven principles that should govern the behaviour of small units: they should keep the initiative, they should be cunning and deceptive in their operations, they should maintain an aggressive spirit, they should be resolute, they should at all times maintain secrecy, they should act promptly and they should aim at perfection. He laid down guidelines for 'co-operation with the people', stressing that all cadres must be prepared to assist the peasantry in its agricultural work, and he spelled out step-by-step procedures for acts of sabotage and small assaults.

But guerrilla warfare by itself would never win the war. Giap and his fellow generals also busied themselves rebuilding their shattered regulars, paying particular attention to the creation of an efficient and independent supply service. Again it was envisaged that the whole people should have the opportunity to participate in this essential aspect of warfare. Henceforward those villagers who did not join either the militias or the upper echelons of the Viet Minh war machine could expect to be conscripted, for up to a hundred days a year, as porters.

The deeper resilience of the people's army was soon put to the test. The French themselves now decided to mount an offensive. At daybreak on 14 November three paratroop battalions were dropped in and around the town of Hoa Binh. Situated almost due south-west of Hanoi on the banks of the Black River, and some twenty miles outside the delta perimeter, Hoa Binh was a Viet Minh stronghold, an important staging-post in the line linking the two base areas. If it could be taken, the French would effectively drive a wedge between Giap's divisions, as well as extend the area protected by the De Lattre Line.

The town was quickly occupied. The Viet Minh garrison melted away into the surrounding low-lying hills. Six mobile groups were rapidly brought up to reinforce what looked for a while like an easy French picking. The Black River became the new frontier of the occupying force, and fresh concrete blockhouses were soon being constructed. Giap, however, was biding his time, having learned the folly of throwing his forces forward too hastily. As he gathered elements of three of his divisions (the 304th, 308th and 312th) for a counter-attack, two other divisions (the 316th and 320th) created small diversions elsewhere along the De Lattre Line. In the area around Hoa Binh he restricted his actions to sniper fire and sabotage for the best part of a month. Then, from 9 December onwards, he escalated his attacks to hit-and-run raids on the outposts created by the French. His objective was not to reclaim lost territory, but to make life as difficult as possible for the enemy, while keeping his own casualties to a minimum.

French morale was accordingly dented. As the New Year arrived, soldiers of the Expeditionary Force discovered that they were the ones who were uncomfortably dug in. In the second week of January 1952 Giap again turned the screw. Having taken measures to cut Route 6, connecting Hoa Binh to Hanoi via Xom Pheo, Xuan Mai and Ha Dong, and also to block both the Black and Day Rivers against French boats, he brought forward his main force and encircled the occupied township. The French suddenly found that they had some ten battalions tied down. Convoys sent down Route 6 to bring reinforcements and effect a rescue were ambushed; and it now became apparent that the Viet Minh not only had anti-aircraft guns, but knew how to use them.

For a while there was a kind of stalemate. Giap realized from his previous experience that any attempt to retake Hoa Binh ran the risk not only of failure, but also of another crippling loss of men. The French, on the other hand, realized that they could not remain in Hoa Binh for ever. To extricate themselves they decided simply to widen the road all the way back to Xuan Mai close to the Day River, and then make what they hoped would be an orderly retreat.

As soon as he saw what the French were doing, Giap ordered his troops to modify their fire. The enemy, it seemed, were constructing their own trap. In due course, beginning on 22 February, the French began their evacuation. The Viet Minh let the enemy column advance just so far, then opened up from camouflaged positions. Although this did not amount to a full-scale assault, and although the main body of the French force managed to return behind the De Lattre Line, it was nonetheless claimed as a victory. For two days the fighting was exceptionally intense, and the French sustained considerable casualties as well as the loss of much equipment.

The Viet Minh could justifiably feel pleased with themselves. The enemy had had its nose badly bloodied. The 'hell of Hoa Binh' became a catch-phrase among the colonials. Above all, Giap's army had behaved with admirable restraint. No unnecessary risks had been taken, and morale in the army had been restored. Arguably, it could have pursued the enemy column into the delta, but this would almost certainly have meant facing another reversal. In particular the supply service had shown what it was capable of: over 150,000 porters had been engaged in ferrying rice, weapons and ammunition behind the lines. And, as an added bonus, de Lattre had been seen off. On 20 November the French supremo had been taken ill, and he was flown back to France, where shortly he died. His military replacement, General Raoul Salan, was a capable soldier; but he lacked de Lattre's singular vision and his understanding of the true nature of affairs in Indochina.

Positional warfare was once more a possibility. While the FEF spent the summer months endeavouring to flush out guerrillas inside the delta area, the Viet Minh regulars concentrated on improving their battlefield skills. Arms supplies from China, having fallen off, now picked up again, coming in through three safe 'doors': Lang Son, Cao Bang and Lao Kai in the far north. These included some 75mm recoilless field guns and an assortment of American weapons captured in Korea. In addition, the Soviet Union emerged as a new donor of military aid. Much needed heavy-duty Molotova trucks had already been presented to Ho Chi Minh by Moscow. Now all around the edge of the delta sizeable arms and ammunition stores were built in secret places, against the day when the Viet Minh resumed the offensive.

For his part General Salan was also in receipt of American arms, although these came direct from the manufacturers in the United States. In Korea the major battles had been won and lost. The United States' 8th Army, having successfully regained South Korea from the communists, had failed to secure North Korea. China's Red Army, advancing in waves, had pushed the United Nations' forces back to the Thirty-eighth Parallel. Although hostilities would continue for another eighteen months, the essential logjam had been achieved. In Washington, however, President Eisenhower's government, aware that America's Korean campaign had been only partially successful, was becoming increasingly wary of further communist encroachments. While attitudes towards France's continued colonialism remained negative, combating the 'Red Menace' was perceived as the priority. Accordingly, aid to Viet Nam was raised.

Thus was the conflict progressively internationalized. It no longer merely concerned the Vietnamese and the French. Rather it was locking into the mainstream of global affairs whose frame of reference was, for forty-five years after the Second World War, the mutual opposition between authoritarian communist and supposedly liberal-capitalist political systems. The fact that anti-colonial America was prepared to back colonial France was simply one of many political paradoxes that arose out of the interaction between geopolitical imperatives and the histories of individual regions. Elsewhere in the world the United States was to support many illiberal dictatorships, while the Soviet Union, in theory equally anti-imperial, evolved its own constellation of 'satellite' states.

But there was also a spatial dimension to the expansion of the war in Viet Nam. The Viet Minh had already launched one probing attack against Nghia Lo, in the autumn of 1951. Now Giap deliberately made the opening up of the north west and of Laos as a second theatre the cornerstone of his strategy. And it was his success in this undertaking that led to the great and conclusive battle of Dien Bien Phu.

In a sense the French brought this upon themselves by simple virtue of having endeavoured to combine the three separate king-doms of Viet Nam, Laos and Cambodia into a single administrative entity. Just as in Viet Nam Marxism-Leninism was perceived as the most likely means of throwing off the colonial yoke, so too in Laos the communist programme became the likeliest way of re-establishing national integrity.

During the Japanese war, when Laos was subject to the same Vichy-style dual control as Viet Nam, two nationalist movements had emerged. One, led by Prince Boum Oum of Champassak, was merely anti-Japanese and Court-oriented. The other, the Lao Issara, or Free Laos Party, led by Prince Petsarath and opposed to both Japanese and French rule, was broadly democratic-republican. In 1945, however, when Laos again became a French protectorate, the Lao Issara was excluded from playing any active political role.

Out of these circumstances was born the Pathet Lao ('Laos Country'), a communist group that sought the complete removal of French interests and the abolition of the monarchy. Although in 1946 Paris recognized the autonomy of the then King, Sisavang Vong, and in 1949 elections were held that effectively granted political recognition to the Lao Issara, a minority of former Lao Issara followers chose a different course. The Pathet Lao, set up in 1950 under Prince Souphanouvong, aligned itself with the policies of the Viet Minh in neighbouring Viet Nam.

To a degree, in these early days, the existence of the Pathet Lao, with its royal leader, was a manifestation of convoluted Court intrigues traditional to the country. In addition, Laos itself was ethnically far more fragmented than Viet Nam, to the extent that only a minority of its much smaller population were in fact Laotians.

Nonetheless, the Pathet Lao had shown themselves adept at adopting the guerrilla tactics taught by the Viet Minh, and by 1952 large areas of the countryside, particularly in those areas adjoining Viet Nam, were effectively under their control. There was therefore every reason for the Viet Minh to believe that their war could be introduced into territory where responsibility for military security still rested on French shoulders.

In the autumn of 1952 Giap for the first time made clear this strategic departure. With three of his divisions – the 308th, the 312th and 316th – concentrated in the hills to the west of the delta well beyond the De Lattre Line, between the upper reaches of Red and Clear Rivers, he began targeting isolated French garrisons in a bid to cross the Laotian border. On 15 October a post at Gia Hoi was surrounded and cut off by the 312th. Two days later Nghia Lo was subjected to mass assault by regiments of the 308th. Another garrison at Tu Le, had also to be evacuated. Although Gia Hoi was successfully relieved and evacuated by paratroops, Nghia Lo and its adjoining ridge were taken by force. Despite, or because of, its remoteness from Hanoi, and even though French casualties were insignificant compared with the losses sustained on Route 4 or during the battle of Hoa Binh, this was an important victory. Suddenly the entire north-west of Tonkin, hitherto considered 'safe', was vulnerable to the communists.

General Salan, with half an inkling, but no more, of what was motivating the Viet Minh, responded by reinforcing his key garrisons in the north-western sector: at Lai Chau, Son La and Na Sam. Viet Minh attacks continued, but on a reduced scale. Thus on 30 November a French outpost at Dien Bien Phu, until now of little strategic importance, was easily overrun. The dry season's main contest, however, was the result of a French initiative. With Giap's forces apparently spread out, and distanced from their base area in the north-east, Salan decided that this was as good a time as any to mount a punitive expedition. If he could cut off Giap's rear then he might force him into something like a pitched battle, or at the least oblige him to withdraw from the region altogether.

Operation Lorraine began on 29 October. A combined force of thirty thousand assembled at Viet Tri on the Clear River and at Trung Ha, at the watershed of the Red and Black Rivers. Included were four mobile groups, paratroops and several armoured battalions. Sticking to the roads, the two columns converged at Phu Tho and then trundled their way up Colonial Route 2 towards Chan Muong. Where the road forked at Phu Doan a Viet Minh supply base was taken without significant resistance, on 9 November. The main body of Salan's army then turned left. Following the Clear River, it advanced as far as Phu Yen, some sixty-odd miles from base. A detachment was also sent to Tuyen Quang, along the right fork.

After two weeks neither column had made contact with the enemy. But then the Viet Minh, who had patiently allowed Operation Lorraine to unfurl, began attacking the supply convoys along Route 2. On 14 November, realizing that Giap had deliberately allowed his units to stretch their lines, and that a second Hoa Binh was in the offing, Salan ordered an immediate retreat. At once the Viet Minh increased their activities. On the 17th a large part of Salan's forces came under heavy fire at Chan Muong. Thereafter the fight developed into a running battle all the way back to Viet Tri on the edge of the De Lattre Line. Only French air-cover prevented a fiasco. Salan had lost over a thousand men, but he might have lost a good many more.

On this occasion Giap did not balk at pressing home his advantage. He successfully counter-attacked two outposts, at Ba Lay and Moc Chan. He then ordered the 308th Division to assault the larger garrison at Na Sam. But here he was thwarted. The local commander moved his men out of the town and into entrenched positions around an adjoining airstrip. The Viet Minh underestimated both the size of the French force and their willingness to resist. Massive wave attacks were launched on 23 November, and again on the 30th. But these achieved nothing except the loss of some five thousand men.

Yet despite this setback, the honours of the campaigning season undoubtedly belonged to the Viet Minh. They had established themselves in the north-west, which until now had seen little military activity during the war. This was essential if Laos was to be opened up. The Viet Minh not only required safe bases in the region, but they also needed to persuade the resident montagnards to support their cause – objectives that only time and a permanent presence could gain.

The autumn of 1952 also witnessed the strengthening of the Viet Minh elsewhere in Viet Nam. Two regiments of regulars had been formed in the central provinces, and throughout the south generally there had been a steady increase in the incidence of guerrilla actions. In particular, there had been heavy fighting around An Khe, on the edge of the Central Highlands inland from Qui Nhon. Little by little, General Giap was wresting the advantage.

The French had made some efforts to improve their own position. The FEF was maintained at around 175,000 men, while a secondary army of 100,000 Vietnamese, as yet untested in battle, had been recruited. Supplies from the United States now included landing craft and river patrol boats as well as C47 transport planes. Yet for Raoul Salan, as for his successor General Henri Navarre, without an adequate intelligence system the central problem lay in trying to second-guess Viet Minh initiatives. It looked as though the enemy planned to diversify to Laos; but then again this might always prove a feint. Giap might just as easily march the other way and try again to smash his way through to Hanoi. Because of this uncertainty, and because of Giap's ability to move his divisions undetected through mountainous terrain, French defences had to be maintained at all points – quite apart from the constant hazard presented by guerrilla actions. Moreover, in pure fighting terms, as recent main force encounters had demonstrated, the Viet Minh soldier was rapidly achieving parity with his European or North African counterpart.

1953 began quietly, with neither side willing to show its hand. Giap, however, kept his main force in the north-west, and at the beginning of April began moving three of his divisions into Laos. The 316th advanced on Sam Neua, the 308th up the Nam Seng valley and the 312th from Dien Bien Phu towards Luang Prabang, the 'royal' capital (as opposed to the administrative capital at Vientiane).

Salan had failed to anticipate his Viet Minh counterpart. On 14 April he ordered the evacuation of Sam Neua. Catching up with the rearguard of the departing column, the Viet Minh inflicted heavy casualties. The French now concentrated their forces at Xieng Khouang in the Plain of Jars, in order to block the way to Luang Prabang. But while some of Giap's forces were held up by the French garrison at Moung Khoua, the main bodies of the 308th and 312th Divisons met up, and then separated again, to advance not only on Luang Prabang, but also on Vientiane. Again, Salan retreated his forces, abandoning Xieng Khouang; and by the end of the month the two most important cities in Laos were semi-encircled by Viet Minh battalions.

Giap had comprehensively outmanoeuvred his enemy, but in so doing he had overstretched his own lines. Even with the help of the Laotian communists he was in no position to launch a full-scale assault on either of the Laotian capitals, even had he wanted to. But in reality he had already gained his objective. The whole of northern Laos, an area of twenty thousand square miles, had come under communist control. Encouragingly, Laotian irregulars had swept swiftly through the countryside isolating French outposts, which could only be kept alive through air-drop supplies. The infrastructure had been created for future campaigns, including rice stores, ammunition dumps and intelligence networks. On 7 May Giap began withdrawing two of his divisions, the 312th and 316th, back to northern Viet Nam.

On 8 May General Navarre took over as commander-in-chief of the FEF from Salan. Anxious to discover the true state of affairs in Indochina, he was quickly disheartened by what he learned. Despite the De Lattre Line, over sixty per cent of villages inside the Red River delta were adjudged to be Viet Minh controlled. In central Viet Nam the situation was even worse. The French only exercised round-the-clock authority in the larger towns and cities. Even in the south, former Cochinchina, despite the apparent loyalty of the Cao Dai and the Hoa Hao, as well as the assured loyalty of the Catholic population, the situation was precarious. And it was now apparent that Laos too was no longer secure. The morale of Navarre's army was deteriorating, and the government in Paris was coming under increasing pressure, both at home and from abroad, to end the war.

In effect, Navarre had one hand tied behind his back. Above all he wanted to increase the size, range and effectiveness of the mobile forces – just as fifteen years later, after the Tet Offensive, General William Westmoreland would seek to enhance US forces in the southern republic. He clamoured for reinforcements, but the ten battalions he received after a short trip back to France in September were a fraction of what he believed was required. The United States, which had already provided $500 million toward the cost of the conflict, was willing to increase its percentage share of the overheads, but only on condition that part of the money was used to build up the indigenous National Army. John Foster Dulles, Eisenhower's Secretary of State, also began insisting on a timetable for the eventual withdrawal of the FEF from Indochina altogether.

In order to allay international anxieties, in July Paris had proclaimed the 'independence' of the three member states. A rumour had been put about that France was ready to concede power in Viet Nam to the Viet Minh. But this cosmetic declaration did nothing to bolster Bao Dai's position. Rather it exposed the continuing difficulties he experienced in holding together even a puppet government.

In these circumstances, Navarre tried as best he could to keep a palpably leaky vessel afloat. In July he scored a small success with Operation Hirondelle, when three paratroop battalions landed outside Lang Son and destroyed a sizeable Viet Minh supply base. His attempt to clear the coastal area between Quang Tri and Hué, however, met with less clearcut results. In the late summer and early autumn he devoted his energies to stiffening the defences of the two deltas. To appease his American allies he also promoted the training of two Vietnamese light infantry battalions, at Yen and Nha Trang. Sensibly, but too late in the day, he fostered mixed French–Vietnamese commando groups designed to operate inside areas held by the Viet Minh. These, it was hoped, would work with the minority peoples, using the same tactics that the enemy had made its own. But no great campaign against the Viet Minh was planned for the coming dry season.

All of this played somewhat into the Viet Minh's hands. While regiments of the 308th had been left behind in Laos to build up guerrilla bases, thus ensuring that the new theatre was kept open and alive, Giap was able to take advantage of the relative quiescence of the French, preparing his now battle-hardened army for what, according to Mao Tse-tung's rubric, was to be the third and final phase of the struggle: mobile warfare. He would march his battalions in all directions until the French were comprehensively outmanoeuvred, then close for the kill. With the fighting in Korea over, supplies from China increased, coming in through improved border road networks. Chinese military advisers, including much needed engineers, were also more forthcoming, to the extent that Giap's final campaigns of the French war are thought by some to have been the product of joint Vietnamese–Chinese tactical planning.

From October 1953 the Viet Minh began turning up the heat. All over the north detachments of Giap's regulars made lightning appearances, the object of which was to confuse the French command as to the real whereabouts of the communists' main forces. Thus regiments of the 320th made sorties against the De Lattre Line along the Day River; but when some of these sections were trapped under heavy fire, Giap declined to send in reinforcements. As Navarre soon realized, the greatest concentration of Viet Minh troops remained in the north-west, ready, if deemed appropriate, to launch another full-scale campaign in Laos.

It was at this point that Navarre decided to establish a strong garrison at Dien Bien Phu. His aim was to create a buffer between the Viet Bac and Laos, thus limiting Giap's options. From this position he hoped, in time, to mount expeditions against the Viet Minh's northern base area in the heart of the Viet Bac. Garrisons in remote places outside the two deltas had long been referred to as 'hedgehogs': in theory hard to overrun and bristling with menace against any enemy in their vicinity. Dien Bien Phu was to be a super-hedgehog; and if the Viet Minh unwisely chose to attack it, then so much the better: for it was a maxim of the FEF that once the Viet Minh could be drawn out into the open, then they could only suffer defeat.

Dien Bien Phu – meaning, in Vietnamese, the 'arena of the gods' – was sited at the top end of a twelve mile long, eight mile wide valley at an important crossroads: to the west, northern Laos; to the east, Son La and routes to the Red River delta; and to the north, a circuitous mountain road to Lao Kay via Lai Chau. On 20 November three paratroop battalions were dropped south of the town, and the small fortifications were quickly taken. The existing landing strip was repaired and extended, and a second one was added to the south. Soon heavy transport planes began flying in the materials needed to create an elaborate entrenched encampment.

The Viet Minh saw immediately the threat that Dien Bien Phu posed to their general strategy. But they also saw the French manoeuvre as an opportunity to deliver a crushing blow to the enemy's neck. If Dien Bien Phu could be taken, then not only would the Laotian front be kept open, but perhaps the folly of France's continued military presence in Viet Nam would be made manifest to the government in Paris. Ho Chi Minh, as keenly aware as ever of international opinion, knew well that the patience of the United States with its European ally was likely, in the event of a major defeat, finally to exhaust itself.

As the war entered its eighth year, then, there was a feeling on both sides that any substantial engagement was likely to prove decisive. And because of the new super-garrison's strategic position, such an engagement was destined to take place at Dien Bien Phu. Unless Dien Bien Phu was taken out, General Giap risked exposing his rear whenever he campaigned away from his strongest base area.

Navarre was confident that Dien Bien Phu could not and would
not be taken. At the top end of the valley he concentrated a vast
amount of weaponry. The flat ground around his encampment could
be protected, if necessary, from the air; his fortifications were
reinforced against the wave attack; and although the Viet Minh
might mass in the surrounding low-level hills, they would offer no
real threat. Indeed, his hope was that if they did attack, they would
impale themselves on the spines of his outsized hedgehog. His newly
expanded mobile forces could then pursue them into the hills and,
with their growing aptitude for guerrilla tactics, perhaps inflict
considerable harm.

Giap recognized each of these difficulties, but with his Vietnamese
and Chinese comrades he began plotting how the obstacles, both
natural and man-made, might best be overcome. However, he
proceeded with caution. The chance presented to him was simply too
good to be thrown away in a frenzy of rash aggression. His tactical
catchphrase had become: 'strike only when sure of victory'.

In the second week of December he began moving two of his
divisions towards Tuam Giao, forty kilometres by road to the
northeast of Dien Bien Phu. Navarre responded by evacuating Lai
Chau, the only other strong French garrison in the region, regroup-
ing the troops at Dien Bien Phu even though this was at the expense
of cutting off support for friendly T'ai guerrilla groups working in
the mountains. Giap quickly occupied Lai Chau for himself. Then, in
a surprise variation, the Viet Minh next moved units from the Nghe
An-Ha Tinh base area into and across the upper Laotian panhandle.
Thakhet, on the Thai border, was occupied and Laos effectively cut
in two.

After these repositionings there was a lull in activity that lasted
well into the new year. But in the second half of January 1954 Giap
unexpectedly launched a heavy attack on the Laotian garrison-town
of Seno. Navarre ordered Seno to be relieved, but the relief force was
ambushed and overwhelmed by Viet Minh effectives operating in
conjunction with Laotian guerrillas.

In a further show of strength the Viet Minh began advancing
detachments of southern regulars towards and into Cambodia. At
the same time, in an attempt to convince the American MAAG that
something positive was being done, Navarre launched his own
initiative, Operation Atlante. Starting out from Nha Trang with a
mixture of FEF and Vietnamese troops, this aimed to sweep the
surrounding coastal areas, which had become guerrilla infested, and

hopefully draw off Giap's second base area forces (essentially the 320th Division) from their wider Indochinese campaign. Giap refused the bait, however, and Atlante ran itself into the ground. By the end of March it had advanced a paltry hundred miles up the coast, constantly challenged by guerrilla units and by detachments of Viet Minh provincial irregulars. In particular, the Vietnamese nationals fared badly under fire, sustaining unusually heavy casualties. Their failure enhanced American criticisms that the French were mismanaging local resources; it also meant that Navarre was unable to count upon what should have amounted to a valuable strategic reserve force in the critical weeks ahead.

Giap meanwhile continued to push detachments into Laos. He now had four distinct groups working there. At the end of January Muong Khoua fell to the Viet Minh. By early February communist soldiers, including regiments of the 316th Division, were once again ranged against Luang Prabang. Of necessity Navarre flew in five battalions of his mobile reserve. On 23 February the 316th abruptly withdrew, taking the opium crop with it. Intelligence reports now confirmed that Giap was indeed converging his forces on Dien Bien Phu.

By the beginning of March the French, commanded by Colonel Christian Marie Ferdinand de la Croix de Castries, a gallant cavalry officer, had all but completed their preparations. The valley had become, at least in its upper half, a military machine. The second airstrip was already operational. Minefields had been embedded around the camp perimeters.

In all there were five concentrations of FEF soldiery. The main complex surrounding the command bunkers, to the north of Dien Bien Phu village itself, was divided into four subsections, dubbed – in clockwise order, and reputedly in honour of de Castries' mistresses –Dominique, Eliane, Claudine and Huguette. Then there were the heavily fortified outposts: Beatrice to the north-east, Gabrielle to the north, Anne Marie to the north-west and, four miles to the south and protecting the second airstrip, Isabelle. The total garrison now consisted of a massive twelve battalions. The artillery included 75mm, 105mm and 155mm guns, as well as heavy mortars. In addition, there were ten light tanks and the assurance of heavy air-cover: apart from whatever could be called up from other French airbases, there were six fighter-bombers permanently assigned to the Dien Bien Phu station. And morale was high. There was indeed a general air of impregnability.

The surrounding hills lay low, but they were steeply banked and amply blanketed with thick foliage. Here, in one of the great feats of modern warfare, Giap's team secretly created batteries of heavy field pieces, dug in among the rocks and invisible from either the air or the valley itself. The miracle was that the 105mm guns had found their way to the valley in the first place. The entire French artillery had been airlifted. The entire Viet Minh artillery was brought in over rough roads, footpaths and mountain passes. Before reaching their destination they had to be dismantled, and then they were re-assembled on site.

Enabling this operation was another, equal in importance and betokening the true scale and commitment of the Viet Minh's 'people's war'. By the end of February Giap had effectively surrounded Dien Bien Phu with a force of some forty thousand soldiers. These included three entire divisions – the 308th, the 312th and the 351st heavy – as well as three regiments from the 304th and 316th. Even to feed such an army, in such inhospitable terrain, required enormous planning and an enormous labour force. It has been estimated that upwards of a quarter of a million 'porters', in addition to an on-site task force of twenty thousand used to clear paths and roads through the jungle, were involved in ferrying rice, ammunition and other supplies, sometimes over distances totalling several hundred kilometres and usually on foot or on bicycle. All over northern Viet Nam men and women began leaving their villages with bundles of provisions, seeping through French defences and watchposts by night. For every kilogram of rice that reached the front, some twenty were consumed *en route*. While Russian and Chinese trucks carried heavier items by road as far as they could be carried, the bulk of Giap's war materials, certainly in the final stages, had to be taken by hand.

The French were only partly aware of what was happening. From the middle of January there had been skirmishes with guerrilla units on the edges of the valley. Navarre, however, had ordered his commanders at Dien Bien Phu not to pursue the enemy into the hills, at least for the time being. Above all, no one on the French side was aware that the Viet Minh had eighty-odd 105mm cannon or an even greater number of newly manufactured Chinese 37mm anti-aircraft guns. That they had some 75mm guns was well known; but even these, it was assumed, would never find their way through the mountains.

French perceptions of Giap's strength changed dramatically when, on 10 March, the Viet Minh began shelling the main runway, slanted through the central complex. Giap's plan was comprehensive. The airstrips were essential to the survival of the French because they had no other means of supply. If they could be taken out, then the valley garrisons would be under a true siege. In these circumstances he could begin systematically reducing the entire encampment, first by taking the outposts, then by attacking the centre. By day, operations would be conducted under cover of an artillery and anti-aircraft barrage from the hills; by night, under cover of darkness.

As the French reeled from the shock of this first blow, from surprise at the weight and accuracy of the enemy's shells, the Viet Minh on the following day, 11 March, mounted a preliminary assault on Gabrielle. The French endeavoured to destroy the hill batteries with their own heavy artillery, but short of a direct hit Giap's guns were too well concealed, hidden in caves or by rocks, trees and sometimes swirling mists. Beginning on the 12th, therefore, the air force began dropping napalm on what were assumed to be Viet Minh positions. But although this caused some loss of life, Giap's carefully spaced artillery was safe.

On 13 March, in the late afternoon, Giap assayed his first grand attack, principally against Beatrice to the north-east of the main complex, although Gabrielle and Anne Marie also came under fire. As the artillery barrage renewed, platoons of 'death volunteers' moved forward to cut holes in the wire that surrounded the Viet Minh's targets. Beatrice itself meanwhile received the full attention of Giap's 105mms. Then the infantry advanced. In a prolonged and close fire-fight, the Viet Minh inched their way through French defences. By midnight Beatrice had fallen.

The following night it was Gabrielle's turn. During the day fresh supplies were successfully landed on the main runway and a further battalion of paratroops was dropped. But the northernmost outpost was already doomed. By dawn of 15 March, half its defences had been destroyed, and later that day Gabrielle too was abandoned.

Famously, a French artillery officer, Colonel Charles Piroth, was unable to come to terms with his unit's inability to damage Giap's hidden guns. Having informed colleagues that he felt 'utterly dishonoured', he removed the pin of a grenade with his teeth and committed suicide.

By now both airstrips were inoperable, having been shell-battered into a rubble in just five days. Henceforward French supplies had to be parachuted; and as the area under French control shrunk, these fell increasingly into Viet Minh hands. And worse was to come. On 18 March, following the desertion of a battalion composed of supposedly loyal T'ai tribesmen, Anne Marie had also to be evacuated. The French garrison at Dien Bien Phu, after less than a week's fighting, had been robbed of its protective hood.

But the Viet Minh, often advancing recklessly under withering fire, had also suffered losses. Some two and a half thousand men had already been killed, and it was by no means certain that simple massed attacks alone would overcome the enemy's central encampment. In a lull in the fighting, Giap now ordered his men to begin digging trenches and tunnels from the edge of the valley inwards, towards the perimeters of Dominique, Eliane, Claudine and Huguette.

Soon a budding network of entrenchments was being mined to within half a mile of the outer French wires – a feature of the Dien Bien Phu landscape that later inspired post-battle visitors to compare what they saw with the Somme. The work had to be done at night to avoid aerial attention. For the stranded French it was an eerie sensation. They could hear the spades at a decreasing distance; but there were few other sounds.

By 22 March the road between the central complex and Isabelle to the south had been cut. The main force of the French was now closely encircled. The tanks, hit by artillery and bazooka fire, lay useless on their sides. Nor was it possible to evacuate the wounded. When a Dakota marked with the Red Cross had attempted a landing on the 18th, it had been shot at by the enemy. Only a handful of severe cases had been spirited away in helicopters by night. And even that had proved unsafe. Now, with diminishing foodstores, there began to be serious anxieties as to whether Dien Bien Phu could in fact be held.

The French air force continued its saturation bombing of the surrounding hills, but to no apparent effect. The Viet Minh opened fire at will. The Chinese anti-aircraft guns were regularly repositioned, so that each day French pilots faced a new set of targets and a new set of threats. During the course of the whole battle, upwards of sixty aircraft were downed. In addition, the communists were experiencing none of the shortages that the French had anticipated. Behind the lines, Vietnamese and Chinese engineers had advanced the solid road connecting Lao Kay and Lai Chau to within ten miles of the front. A fleet of five hundred Molotova trucks kept on bringing in food and artillery shells.

De Castries ordered sorties to be made against the enemy.

Although these caused some obstruction to the Viet Minh, their main purpose was to raise a dangerously flagging morale. It was not until 30 March that the battle proper resumed. Having brought his trenches within three hundred yards of the French lines, for six days Giap now hurled everything he had against his foe. His heavy guns concentrated their fire on Dominique, and his infantry moved forward in waves. At night de Castries counter-attacked, punching the communists back from many of the points they had gained by day. On 31 March there was a massive sortie from Isabelle, to the south. But little by little Dominique was overrun, and Eliane came under fire. On 1 April Huguette too was attacked, leaving only Claudine relatively unscathed.

Now the Viet Minh had dug a trench across the main runway itself. On the night of 2 April Isabelle was attacked, and on the 3rd and 4th there was 'all-out' fighting in every sector. By evening large parts of the central complex had been overrun, despite the sudden appearance of yet another battalion of paratroops from the sky. Yet now the battle abated. Viet Minh casualties had been stupendous, as many as ten thousand perhaps, and officers were encountering resistance among the ranks to further carnage. Temporarily, Giap had reached the point of diminishing returns.

This latest lull lasted ten days, during which time Navarre parachuted in further reserves, including his best paratroop battalion. It was thought that if the Viet Minh suffered as badly in their next attack as they had during the last, then Giap must consider abandoning the siege altogether. But Giap too was calling up his reserves, so that when activities recommenced there were approximately fifty thousand Viet Minh against sixteen thousand FEF. Perhaps of greater consequence than this superiority of numbers was the fact that Giap had managed to manoeuvre a further two hundred 105mm guns into the outskirts of the valley.

For two weeks, from 15 April until 1 May, during which time the summer rains arrived, Giap adopted a tactic of extreme caution. He no longer rushed his troops forward, but settled instead for a 'period of encroachment'. Despite the deteriorating weather conditions, he expanded his trench operations. Indeed, an almost unbroken spell of low cloud-cover enabled this operation, since French bombers and fighters were rendered largely ineffectual. There was much sniping and some laying down of artillery fire, but in the main it was a relentless tightening of the noose. The French meanwhile braced themselves for what they knew must be the decisive encounter.

There is evidence that, despite appalling living conditions, the French trapped inside Dien Bien Phu at this time were more optimistic than their compatriots who beheld events from the outside. Navarre in particular grasped the gravity of the situation, but his appeals for US air support, for heavy bombers to be sent from their bases in the Philippines and for aircraft carriers to be brought into the Gulf of Tonkin fell on deaf ears. While America continued to furnish material aid, which included over a thousand ground staff to service the heavy transports provided by the Defense Department, Eisenhower balked at direct military involvement. Among those in Congress who opposed US air-strikes were two younger Democrats, Lyndon Johnson and John F. Kennedy. A plan to deploy three small tactical nuclear weapons against Viet Minh bases, codenamed Operation Vulture, was rapidly shelved after its patron, John Foster Dulles, had flown to London in a vain attempt to enlist Prime Minister Winston Churchill's support. The President was aware of how closely both China and the Soviet Union supported Ho Chi Minh – during March, Moscow had earmarked $500 million for the Viet Minh cause – and feared 'another Korea'. Rather there was a strong feeling among many White House officials that the French should be allowed to fail at Dien Bien Phu, so that a more direct relationship with an independent, i.e. non-communist, government based in Saigon could be developed.

The issue of US intervention soon became academic, however. On 1 May Giap resolved the question of whether he would risk a second all-out attack. In the evening, all around the French position, which now measured no more than a mile across at any point, the final assault began. The Viet Minh had crept so near that, after an initial barrage, little artillery cover could safely be given them. Further sections of Eliane and Huguette were stormed. Concurrently, to the south, the new outer defences of Isabelle were smashed, although Isabelle's central defences continued a staunch resistance.

The next day witnessed further efforts by the Viet Minh to reduce the area occupied by the French. It also saw the arrival of yet more paratroops. But the fighting was inconclusive, the battle favouring first one side, then the other.

On 3 May there was a respite, but this was only the last lull before the final storm. On the 4th, the attack was resumed with a ferocity hitherto unimagined. After a concentrated artillery barrage, the Viet Minh began relentlessly mortaring such French positions as remained.

The FEF at Dien Bien Phu was doomed, and yet de Castries insisted it fight on, even though maggots had begun burrowing into the wounds of those hospitalized in underground shelters. It was not until the late afternoon of 7 May, when amid rain, smoke and blood, and with French ammunition supplies virtually exhausted, units of Giap's 308th Division penetrated to the very heart of the broken complex and stuck the Viet Minh flag atop the command bunker, that the issue was conceded. Isabelle held out until the morning of the 8th. Its garrison attempted a break-out, but seeing themselves entirely surrounded, offered the white flag.

In total, the French had lost some seven thousand of their best soldiers, set against eight thousand survivors. Of these latter, half died of hunger and exhaustion as they were force-marched by the Viet Minh towards Hanoi. Although the corresponding figures for the Viet Minh side have never been published, it is estimated that some eighteen thousand revolutionaries died at Dien Bien Phu, with perhaps twice as many wounded.

Nonetheless, the outcome of the battle represented a clearcut and decisive victory by any standards. Militarily, the last word belonged to the Viet Minh. Commemorating the event ten years afterwards, General Giap was to write:

> The enemy's morale was most shaken. Large contingents of newly replenished puppet troops were disbanded. What was more serious for the enemy was that by liquidating the Dien Bien Phu entrenched camp, our troops defeated his highest and most powerful form of defence, and put before him the prospect that the other defence systems, much weaker than Dien Bien Phu, would be threatened with annihilation.

Ho Chi Minh was later wont to quip that Giap had beaten the French without losing a single plane or tank – for the simple reason that he had never had any. This, however, belies the broader significance of the Viet Minh's 'war of resistance'. In the nineteenth century France had colonized Viet Nam in order to sustain itself as an industrial nation. Yet it was the industrial revolution that, in the long term, undermined and rendered impractical the colonial project. Without the mass-produced, engineered weapons which were either supplied by the Chinese or snatchd from the enemy, no victory would have been possible. The process that put rifles into the hands of the early colonizers evolved into the process that also put a rifle into the hand of every revolutionary.

At Dien Bien Phu Chinese-made howitzers and Chinese-made

mortars sealed the fate of what remained of French pretensions to rule Viet Nam by force. Yet this was scarcely the complete picture. While some critics have accused Navarre of madness ever to think Dien Bien Phu could work, the theory behind it was not unsound. If the whole of Indochina was not to run amok, then a strong presence in the north-west of Viet Nam was required. Where Navarre failed was in imagination, and in his deficient intelligence services. He did not imagine that the Viet Minh could do what was required of them, and he was not informed that they had the means to do it. Above all he did not see that, accustomed as they were to mountainous terrain, the Viet Minh's natural instinct would be to turn the valley into a cauldron.

But the material, logistical, numerical and locational advantages enjoyed by the Viet Minh at Dien Bien Phu do not alone account for Giap's victory, or its impact. As far as the military conflict went, Dien Bien Phu was but the crowning glory. What made it possible was the wider context of nationwide insurrection and nationwide participation. Again it has to be emphasized that the Viet Minh's achievement lay not so much in individual feats of arms, but in its leadership's ability to involve a significant proportion of the population in a prolonged and arduous struggle. In the two world wars, the same or even greater percentages of European, American and Japanese populations had been mobilized in the 'war effort'; but the difference in Viet Nam was that Ho Chi Minh and his colleagues did not have the formal apparatus of a *de facto* state to depend upon. Rather the Viet Minh had to rely on a shadow state, which was only made real by the rigours of Marxism-Leninism.

In the long term, those rigours were to turn sour, or at the least ambiguous. During the two months it took to reduce Dien Bien Phu, however, they assured the Viet Minh of success. All over Viet Nam, but particularly in the Red River delta and in the central provinces, there was an endless, co-ordinated welter of guerrilla activities that kept French forces perpetually stretched to breaking point. And in the Central Highlands, in the province of Kon Tum, those battalions of the 320th Division not tied up in Laos, and reinforced by irregulars, laid siege to the city of Pleiku: a major operation only overshadowed by the greater siege in Lai Chau province.

In the middle of May 1954 General Ely arrived with fresh instructions from Paris. On 3 June Navarre was relieved of his duties. Ely, as well as becoming commander-in-chief, was also appointed Commissioner-General for Indochina, with Salan as his deputy.

Their mission was to save whatever could be saved of the FEF, and to buttress the non-communist government in Saigon.

The Red River delta was now largely abandoned. Even though, in the shape of the Geneva Conference, peace talks aimed at reaching a comprehensive settlement for the whole of Indochina were already under way in Europe, the Viet Minh pressed home their military advantage. It was Ho Chi Minh's intention to secure as much territory as possible, in order to strengthen Pham Van Dong's hand at the negotiating table. By the beginning of July the French presence in north Viet Nam was restricted to the two centres of Hanoi and Haiphong, and the road that connected them. Province after province had been evacuated, with columns of the FEF harassed all the way as they retired. Further south, Ely's troops, similarly embattled, had been withdrawn below the Eighteenth Parallel.

It was now Ely's plan to withdraw his northern forces to the FEF's original bridgehead at Haiphong. But Operation Auvergne became a running retreat made all the more hazardous by the presence on the arterial highway of thousands of Catholic refugees, fleeing an anticipated 'communist terror'.

It was not until 21 July that an armistice, to take effect from the 23rd, was finally agreed in Geneva. In the interim some thousands more French and African soldiers had lost their lives. But now at last it was decided that the French would evacuate their last remaining units from Hanoi within eighty days, and all their forces from Haiphong within three hundred days.

On 5 October, nine years and a month after Ho Chi Minh's original proclamation of an independent Vietnamese state in Ba Dinh Square, Hanoi was formally handed over to his government. Regiments of Giap's 308th Division paraded in triumph through the streets of the capital. But in reality, because of the machinations of the superpowers in Geneva, the scene was already being set for another, even bloodier, war.

3

Viet Nam Divided

We have been exploring ways and means to permit our aid to Viet-Nam to be more effective and to make a greater contribution to the welfare and stability of the Government of Viet-Nam. I am, accordingly, instructing the American Ambassador to Viet-Nam to examine with you in your capacity as Chief of Government, how an intelligent program of American aid given directly to your Government can serve to assist Viet-Nam in its present hour of trial, provided that your Government is prepared to give assurances as to the standards of performance it would be able to maintain in the event such aid were supplied.

The purpose of this offer is to assist the Government of Viet-Nam in developing and maintaining a strong, viable state, capable of resisting attempted subversion or aggression through military means. The Government of the United States expects that this aid will be met by performance on the part of the Government of Viet-Nam in undertaking needed reforms.

Message from President Dwight Eisenhower to
Premier Ngo Dinh Diem, 23 October 1954

The outcome of the Geneva Conference, expressed as the Geneva Accords, was dictated by three factors: the Viet Minh's victory over the French Expeditionary Force; the United States' determination to contain communism; and the People's Republic of China's desire for Viet Nam to remain divided against itself, and thus be a weak, pliable buffer-state rather than a potentially strong neighbour.

The conference was convened, after preliminary talks in Berlin, in Geneva in the spring and early summer of 1954 to address and resolve two broad issues: Korea and Indochina. It was attended by delegates representing world powers and the local governments concerned. Through a series of unscheduled bilateral discussions, however, it was generally dominated by the 'big four': the United States, the Soviet Union, Britain and France, with China making a bid for equivalent status. Britain and the USSR were 'co-chairmen'.

Plenary sessions aimed at settling Korea's future lasted from 26 April until 15 June, but they were not conclusive. As a result Korea remained divided North and South along the Thirty-Eighth Parallel, following the earlier ceasefire agreement between communist and United Nations forces. Although this had no direct bearing on the Indochinese section of the agenda, and on the future of Viet Nam, it nonetheless reinforced a principle already established by the post-war partition of Germany: that a nation-state could be arbitrarily divided in such a way as to reflect and even enshrine the geopolitical rivalry between the liberal-capitalist West and the communist East.

Talks on Indochina commenced on 8 May. Giap's victory at Dien Bien Phu, achieved the very day before, could not, it seemed, have been better timed. Without it, the Viet Minh delegation, headed by Pham Van Dong, would probably have withdrawn. With it, the Viet Minh had every reason to be confident. They now controlled between sixty and seventy per cent of the entire country: all of the northern half of Viet Nam and most of the rural areas of the southern half, as well as some cities and towns. It was plausible, therefore, that the Viet Minh should claim complete victory and the right to govern throughout the land. But it was not to be. When the conference closed, on 21 July, Viet Nam too was effectively partitioned, along the Seventeenth Parallel.

The lobbying was intense, as were certain manoeuvres away from Geneva. Of these the most significant was the appointment of Ngo Dinh Diem as Prime Minister of the 'Saigon' government on 7 July, with the erstwhile Emperor Bao Dai, already titular head of state, taking on the presidency. Since Diem was in reality an American appointee and the United States, though present at Geneva, was not to be legally bound by whatever settlement the conference might reach, unless Washington so wished, this increased the prospects of continued hostilities, even though President Eisenhower was on record as saying that America would not intervene militarily in Indochina if the talks failed.

Ironically, it was the Chinese who, through the labyrinthine closed-door sessions that went on at Geneva, assured the United States a future platform in Viet Nam. Chou En-lai, the leader of numerically the largest delegation, worked to exclude the Americans from Indochina altogether. With this in mind he approached the French delegation. It was known that, despite the vast amount of aid given to France by the United States, the two western powers were at odds, each wanting the other out of Saigon. He would, he said, support a continued French presence in southern Viet Nam. In essence, Chou was proposing that Viet Nam be split in two.

The Viet Minh resisted this solution for as long as possible. The Chinese, however, were insistent. Hanoi, Chou En-lai said flatly, could expect no more help from China unless it fell in with Peking's wishes. Then the Soviet delegation muscled in appearing to support the Chinese position. Little by little Pham Van Dong was browbeaten into submission. Despite the Viet Minh's great victory, he knew that his party's resources had been strained to the limit, and that a settlement which gave him half of what he wanted would be better than no settlement at all.

Finally, on the afternoon of 20 July, Vyacheslev Molotov convened a meeting at the villa rented by the Soviet delegation. Neither Bao Dai's representative nor the American spokesman, Bedell Smith, were present. France, China, Britain and the USSR urged Pham Van Dong to agree to a partition at the Eighteenth Parallel. Pham Van Dong, having already conceded that he would be prepared to accept partition at the Thirteenth, responded under pressure by agreeing to a partition at the Sixteenth. France stuck to the Eighteenth. Abruptly Molotov intervened. He saw no reason, he said, why the two sides should not compromise and accept the Seventeenth.

And so it came about. Henceforward Viet Nam would consist of two separate states, North and South, even though the two documents that finally came out of the Geneva Conference fatally muddied the issue. The first of these was a ceasefire agreement, signed by France and the Viet Minh. Its essential provisions, apart from an almost immediate cessation of hostilities, were for a demilitarized zone (DMZ) stretching both sides of the new partition line; a mutual withdrawal of both sides' troops from each other's territories; and the setting up of an International Commission to monitor the agreement, composed of representatives from Canada, Poland and India. The second was the Final Declaration of the Geneva Conference, a series of accords signed by no one, but assented to by all parties except the United States. Critically, this prohibited the introduction of foreign troops into Cambodia and Laos as well as the two Viet Nams; and it provided for a general election to be held in both parts of Viet Nam in July 1956, in order that the country might be reunited.

Over two decades later, after relations with Peking had turned sour, Hanoi was to maintain that the Viet Minh were betrayed by the

Chinese at Geneva. In this charge there is undoubtedly a measure of truth. The question though remains: why, when they appeared to have a clear military advantage on the battlefield, did the Viet Minh accept a compromise?

The answer, never clarified by communist sources, is necessarily complex. Pham Van Dong was clearly susceptible to big-power pressure. The memory of the Modus Vivendi worked out with the French in 1946 still haunted the Viet Minh mind. What the Geneva agreements offered was something that the Viet Minh had not been offered before at a genuinely international forum: sovereignty, albeit a sovereignty limited to the northern half of their country.

Despite the final outcome of the Geneva Conference the Viet Minh could hold their heads high, the more so as they felt that the promised July 1956 election would vouchsafe them their ultimate goal, a single Viet Nam under communist rule. The Chinese had also failed in their original conference objective. The French were to remain in the South, but only for a limited period. Under pressure from the United States, France had undertaken to withdraw all its forces from Indochina within two years.

In reality, the Geneva agreements, far from achieving either a military or a political solution for Viet Nam, simply postponed further conflict. Their weakness was that, the frail, toothless International Commission apart, they furnished no guarantees. Even legally they were riddled with shortcomings. The terms of the ceasefire agreement were meaningful only so long as the French maintained a presence in Viet Nam. And as for the Final Declaration, could an unsigned paper be said to carry any weight at all?

Inevitably, over the coming decade, the situation inside Viet Nam deteriorated. The two states, far from unifying became implacably opposed to each other; and because, in their opposition, each side sought and obtained superpower sponsorship, the civil war when it came was unprecedentedly vicious.

From the beginning, the United States' intervention in Vietnamese affairs was predicated on a hostility toward communism. This was the mainspring of American foreign policy throughout the period of involvement, which lasted, directly or indirectly, from 1949 until 1975. To what extent intervention and hostility were justified has been the subject of a wide-reaching, interminable and finally insoluble debate. In essence, two contrasting political systems, both deriving from populist revolutionary theories promulgated in the latter half of the eighteenth century, vied for global dominance. Each region of the world was perceived as part of a chessboard where not to win was to lose. From the American perspective, strong communist gains in the immediate post-war period necessitated vigilance and action. Eastern Europe and mainland China had both succumbed to a rule whose authoritarian style was antithetical to professed American values. And down the years there were to be many other episodes which suggested communist hegemonism: the Berlin Blockade, Korea, Hungary 1956, subversion of neutralist governments in the Middle East, the Cuban missile crisis, Czechoslovakia 1968 – to name but a few. Certainly, in Washington's eyes there was no shortage of provocation, just as in Moscow's view the United States consistently worked to undermine the achievements of Lenin's revolution. Both sides made exalted claims for their political philosophies, and both sides allowed themselves to become trapped inside a feud that spawned suspicion, recrimination, posturing and intervention, covert as well as overt, in all quarters of the globe.

As regards South-East Asia, and in particular South Vietnam, American foreign policy achieved its classic formulation in the 'domino' theory as enunciated by Eisenhower and Secretary of State John Foster Dulles from 1952 onwards. After Mao Tse-tung's communist victory of 1949 the whole region encompassed by the western Pacific seaboard was felt to be under threat. It was vital for American trading interests – without which there could be no America – that Japan, South Korea, Formosa (Taiwan), the Philippines, Indonesia, Malaya, Thailand and if possible the countries of Indochina remain 'free', or at the very least 'neutral' as regards the communist/liberal-capitalist face-off. The theory stated that once one of these countries fell, then the others would quickly follow. This would not only significantly deprive the West of dependent markets and raw material; it would even destroy the world trading system on which the Western bloc relied, thus enfeebling American and European economies to the point of political vulnerability.

Whether or not the domino theory overstated its case is again the subject of contention. One argument put forward is that communism in Indochina was an internal matter, a way of resolving political and social imbalances created by an adverse colonial experience; that the surrounding countries, notably Thailand and

Malaysia (as it came to be called), were never in fact in line for a political–military takeover by a communist Viet Nam in league with a communist Cambodia and a communist Laos. Conversely, the existence of disruptive communist insurgency movements in Malaya in the 1950s, and in Thailand in the late 1960s and 1970s, as well as the increasing accommodation towards communism manifested by President Sukarno in Indonesia, indicated that American fears were in some measure appropriate.

Ironically, from the western liberal-capitalist standpoint, when the Viet Nam War finally ended in 1975 the general situation in South-East Asia (excluding Indochina) was markedly more stable than when the war started. The United States may indeed have 'lost' Viet Nam, but its broader strategic aims were probably accomplished by its having fought the war. In Malaysia and Indonesia communism had vanished as an effective political force, while in Thailand it was distinctly containable. The all-important Straits of Lombok, at the eastern end of Bali, and of Malacca, between mainland Malaysia and Sumatra, remained open to western shipping.

One of the key developments that enabled this outcome was the Sino-Soviet rift that developed through the 1960s and into the early 1970s. Although by the end of 1975 communist regimes held sway in all three of the Indochinese states, their victories were short-lived. Within three years they were fighting each other, supported variously by Peking and Moscow. The East–West geopolitical template was largely replaced by an East–East template.

In 1949, however, the culmination of Mao Tse-tung's revolution was perceived in the West as being firm evidence of a monolithic communist threat to the new world-order for which Allied forces had fought and died against Germany and Japan. It was this event above all others that persuaded President Truman, goaded by Secretary of State Dean Acheson, to consider granting aid to France in its war against the Viet Minh. Early in 1950 Congress approved a bill giving the President some $75 million to use as he saw fit in Asia. In March, Acheson secured $15 million of this fund to be deployed in Indochina. At the same time, the United States formally recognized Bao Dai's Saigon government.

By July 1954, with the Geneva Conference in full swing, the US contribution to the French war effort had escalated to some $3 billion. Such an investment, although apparently squandered by the French, was not about to be written off. Having effectively countered the Chinese Red Army in South Korea, Washington was resolved to shore up any other leaks that might spring in the Asian sector.

Secretary of State John Foster Dulles was the main architect of the United States' anti-communist crusade during the period in which he headed his department (1953–9). Although he criticized the French military campaign, he considerably increased American subsidies, and during the Geneva Conference he leant heavily on Paris not to give way to any of the Viet Minh's demands. Yet he and his equally combative Assistant Secretary for Far Eastern Affairs, Dean Rusk, recognized that after Dien Bien Phu France wanted ultimately to wash its hands of Indochina. With this in mind they underwrote a programme designed to maintain South Vietnam's membership of the non-communist world, and thus to provide the rest of South-East Asia with a breathing space in which to put its house in order.

The dubious vehicle of American hopes in Viet Nam was the freshly appointed Prime Minister, Ngo Dinh Diem. Born in 1901 in Annam, Diem was a self-proclaimed nationalist who served briefly as Minister of Justice under the French in 1933 before resigning. Momentarily he flirted with the Viet Minh, but in the end he went his own way. Like Ho Chi Minh, he travelled extensively abroad. He studied in America and then lived for a while in a Benedictine monastery in Belgium. Although free of vice in his personal affairs, he was an autocratic man who distrusted others and sought only to enhance the status of his immediate, much less virtuous family. As well as being an ardent Catholic he nurtured a private philosophy that he called 'personalism': a species of mandarinism cast in near-mystical terms. His greatest weaknesses were a thoroughgoing unconcern for the Buddhist majority who composed his subjects and an inability to distinguish between politics and diplomacy.

Washington backed Diem because, it was said, there was no other choice. Yet an important aspect of Diem's appointment as un-crowned emperor of the Saigon regime was the appeal he exercised for Colonel Edward Lansdale.

Lansdale was a key component in the plan to rescue Viet Nam. An air-force pilot, he had served as an OSS officer in the Far East during the Second World War, having previously worked in advertising. During the late 1940s and early 1950s he played a leading role in Ramon Magsaysay's successful campaign against communist insurgency in the Philippines. Viet Nam was logically his next port of call. In June 1954, now employed by the CIA, Lansdale arrived in Saigon and established the Saigon Military Mission, in effect a centre for covert operations. In Diem he saw another Magsaysay; and like Diem, he had scant regard for the Geneva Accords.

The Accords had provided that, following the ceasefire at the end of July 1954, and somewhat in contradiction of the promised elections, all Vietnamese should be free to choose on which side of the Seventeeth Parallel they wished to live. The immediate upshot of this was an exodus from North Vietnam of some eight hundred thousand Catholics. Naturally favoured by Diem – 'God has gone South' was how he described matters – these were resettled in and around the Mekong delta in secure villages and townships, sometimes at the expense of local Buddhist residents. Conversely, there was a far smaller flow of some (but not all) Viet Minh activists and supporters to the North. Lansdale, working through his CIA subordinate Colonel Lucien Conein, used this migration to infiltrate several groups of well-trained native operatives into the Red River delta.

Neither side, it seemed, was taking any chances. The Viet Minh had also infiltrated the Catholic convoys passing through the DMZ with its own spies and effectives; and some military cadres had been instructed secretly to stay behind in the South. Yet for the communists these were only precautionary measures. Because Diem had already expressed his opposition to the Geneva agreement, they were justified in believing that the scheduled election would not be held; and therefore there was always the possibility that what had begun as a political struggle could, sooner or later, become an armed conflict.

Unwittingly Diem, sometimes following Lansdale's advice, but more often pursuing his own obscure reasonings, set about creating circumstances which only encouraged a resurgence of communist insurrection. His regime, in many respects as harsh as anything the French had inflicted on Viet Nam, was medieval in its details. Members of Diem's immediate family quickly advanced to the fore. His elder brother, Ngo Dinh Thuc, appointed Archbishop of Hué, though later excommunicated by the Vatican, effectively took control of what became the state religion in all but name. His younger brother, Ngo Dinh Nhu, became Diem's closest adviser, as well as head of the regime's security forces, disguised as a political movement called the Can Lao; while Nhu's wife, always known as Madame Nhu, seemed often to be in charge of a state propaganda programme that fully matched the communists' in stridency. A third brother was allowed to become virtually a warlord in the southern

Mekong delta. In the army, promotions were made on the basis of loyalty and religious affiliation, not merit. The cabinet was largely disregarded and the President was jettisoned after just one year: in a national referendum, organized and comprehensively rigged by Nhu in October 1955, Diem vanquished Bao Dai by the margin of ninety-eight per cent of the votes cast to two. The former Emperor's public role in Viet Nam, after many stops and starts, was finally at an end.

Diem could brook no dissent, he could allow no tolerance. To the extent that the political landscape of South Vietnam was rife with factions, some of them armed, his instincts during the first years of his power were not altogether mistaken. Quickly, but often employing clandestine methods, he moved against the principal religious sects: the Cao Dai, the Hoa Hao and the Dan Xa. Resistance collapsed early in 1956, after the Hoa Hao's military commander, Ba Cut, was captured and publicly guillotined. Thereafter the sects were emasculated.

Diem's next move was against the Binh Xuyen, the former city gang that had become Saigon's unofficial police force. Egged on by Madame Nhu and her ambitious husband, Diem issued a series of edicts outlawing gambling and prostitution, the two activities that still furnished Binh Xuyen members with opportunities of graft. Attempts by Lansdale to mediate between Diem and Bay Vien, the leader of the forty thousand-strong Binh Xuyen force, failed, and soon there was skirmishing on the capital's streets. Government troops were barred from several quarters as the French, who still maintained a presence, sided against the President.

For a while it looked as though Diem would be ousted, but, mustering support in the army, he attacked Bay Vien's strongholds with mortars on 28 April. The Binh Xuyen fought back with small artillery, shelling the grounds of the presidential palace. Not for the first time in its history, Saigon became a battlefield. At one point elements of the government forces threatened to mutiny, and five hundred civilians were caught in the crossfire. In addition, many poorer dwellings were razed to the ground. But Diem and Nhu persevered, and after two days the Binh Xuyen capitulated. Bay Vien went into exile, but some hundreds of his followers scattered to the countryside where, along with others who had born arms for the Cao Dai and Hoa Hao, they subsequently joined the incipient Viet Cong.

Arguably, Saigon needed cleansing of the Binh Xuyen, and the Mekong delta of the sects, at least in their paramilitary incarnation.

But Diem's next target, far from reducing the fractious South to a manageable polity, created major and ultimately insurmountable problems for the Saigon government. During the second half of the decade Diem, Nhu and a clutch of mainly Catholic high-ranking army officers defined the narrow, élitist character of their rule by conducting campaigns against political 'dissidents' – almost anyone identified as a former Viet Minh member, or as having at any time sympathized with the Viet Minh.

This policy was disastrous in that it alienated large sections of a potentially biddable population. Viet Minh supporters could reasonably claim that, having fought for Vietnamese independence, either politically or militarily, they were true patriots in a way that the Diem clique was not. The communist creed had never sunk as deep roots in Cochinchina as it had in Tonkin or even Annam; but rather than work with this fact, Diem chose instead to assume that communism never could have a decisive appeal in the South. Yet if he had looked at communist methods, and in particular at the Viet Minh strategy of furnishing a broad umbrella beneath which a people could unite, then he might have understood that a policy of conciliation can achieve better results than a relatively crude form of authoritarianism.

Diem, however, was bolstered in the path he chose to follow by his own beliefs, Catholic and mandarin, and by continuing American support. As early as June 1954 Washington had secretly decided to fund, equip and help train a Vietnamese national army (the ARVN, or Army of the Republic of Vietnam), whose numbers were steadily built up by Diem until, by 1962, they had reached a quarter of a million. In the years ahead a growing body of US 'advisers', nearly all military personnel, would be posted to the southern republic to nurse, and sometimes cajole, ARVN officers through their campaigns against communist insurgents. Yet in the early stages of his drive to rid his country of both actual and potential opposition, though secure in his knowledge of the United States' friendship, Diem chose rather to rely on the Can Lao and the secret security methods spawned by his brother Nhu.

Now, in the summer months of 1956, Nhu's men moved systematically through the villages and hamlets of the Mekong delta and other parts of South Vietnam, rooting out former revolutionaries, their families and even their friends. Accordingly, an estimated fifty thousand individuals were imprisoned, and frequently tortured, while an even greater number, perhaps as many as seventy-five thousand, were unceremoniously slain.

This pogrom was Diem's alternative to the Geneva agreement's stipulation that there should be a general election in July 1956. It unsettled, and in many cases destroyed, traditional village rule in the South. Nhu's secret police and local military commanders took over government functions at the provincial and district levels, and the republic became, in effect, a police state. And with this sea-change in political organization also came a massive increase in levels of corruption. The mores of Saigon were spread throughout the land as senior ARVN officers sought to extract profits from their postings in the manner of traditional warlords. Among Nhu's many victims were those who refused to pay bribes to appointed officials, and those who were killed merely because others bore them a grudge.

Judicial processes were widely ignored. A man was lucky if he came up before an impromptu tribunal before being led away for an indeterminate period of detention. Newspapers were summarily ordered to shut down, and many journalists and intellectuals were added to the government's list of suspects. The net effect of such activities was to transform a climate of potential unrest into a climate of real revolt. Although Diem and Nhu succeeded in destroying a majority of former Viet Minh cells in the South, enough remained to begin orchestrating nationwide insurgency. And as more reprisals were instigated, so the clamour against the regime grew louder.

The pattern of violence that had marked and undermined the French occupation now began to repeat itself. At first there were only isolated terrorist incidents: a government official murdered here, a police station bombed there. Were these the work of criminal gangs, or the deliberate first notes of a score orchestrated by communist masterminds? The attacks began in late 1956, but for a while they never seemed to involve more than a handful of men. Then, in October 1957, a series of co-ordinated bomb-attacks took place at US installations in Saigon, and in January 1958 rubber and coffee plantations in the plains to the north of the city were assailed by armed guerrilla groups. The Viet Cong, as Diem disparagingly described communist militants, had arrived.

In North Vietnam, where the dream of reunification governed the hearts and minds of the new ruling élite, these events were followed closely; but the point at which Hanoi began actively intervening in the South's affairs remains uncertain. At least up until July 1956, the date of the promised election, the Central Committee was anxious to be seen to abide by the terms of the ceasefire signed at Geneva. If the North could project itself as the aggrieved party, then internationally it would command more support for any later actions. Even though, therefore, some communist units had been deliberately left behind below the Seventeenth Parallel, in itself a contravention of the Geneva ceasefire, and other commando-type units may have been introduced as early as late 1955, their orders were to lie very low; and it was not until October 1957 that Hanoi, again secretly, sent instructions to communist cadres in the South to organize some thirty-seven armed units based in the jungles and forests of the western Mekong delta.

Thereafter, for the next two years, there is reason to believe that, whatever preparations it may have been making for a larger conflict, the Central Committee still counselled restraint more than aggression. In March 1958, still hoping for political reconciliation, Pham Van Dong wrote personally to Diem proposing mutual troop reductions and trade relations between the two states. Predictably, South Vietnam's leader spurned the approach. But until it was absolutely apparent that Viet Nam could not be reunified by political means alone, the communist leaders, knowing that a resumption of armed struggle was likely to be a prolonged and bloody affair, were loath to commit themselves openly to a military solution.

But the Democratic Republic's initial mood of caution was not dictated solely by political expediency. When the French withdrew, the country was sorely in need of a respite in which to rebuild both a physical and a social fabric, as well as a state apparatus. A nation had to be created anew.

This task was far less of a problem for Ho Chi Minh and his politburo than it was for Diem in the South. Communism provided a ready-made blueprint of how a society should be structured; organizational skills had been acquired through long years of experience; the leadership was able, committed and sincere; and, critically, the sense of victory among the majority of ordinary people, whether peasants or urban proletarians, furnished social cohesion. The war against the French had been conducted primarily in Tonkin, and the Tonkinese could rejoice collectively in its success.

Just as there were dissident radicals in the South, however, so there were 'reactionary' subversives in the North, and in dealing with these the Central Committee could be every bit as authoritarian and ruthless as Diem. Those who had not supported the Viet Minh were rigorously excluded from public office. Worse, there was a bloody purge, amounting to a pogrom, against the wealthier landlord class, especially kulaks of the Red River delta. Partly this was an affair of ideological inclination, but partly too it was an economic matter. Northern Viet Nam had for a long while been reliant on rice and other foodstuffs grown in the south. In 1955, with this traditional supply cut off, a famine threatened. While the immediate crisis was averted by importing rice from Burma at a cost the government could ill afford, a long-term solution was sought in wholesale land reform. All arable land was collectivized and then divided into small family plots. The losers were those farmers rich enough to have employed others to work their estates. Now they were dispossessed; and it seems that, rather than create a class of potential dissidents, the Party decided simply to liquidate them. Accordingly, murderous henchmen were dispatched throughout the arable flatlands.

Estimates of how many North Vietnamese were killed as a result of these decisions vary dramatically. Some historians have placed the figure as high as a hundred thousand (out of a total population of fifteen or sixteen million); others as low as two and a half thousand. In addition, labour camps were established in several delta provinces, matching the concentration camps set up in the South by Diem. Again, though, precisely how many were interned in these remains unknown. What is certain is that an event or events of this sort did take place, for a year later, in August 1956, Ho Chi Minh admitted in public than 'errors have been committed'. Those who had been wrongly classified as landlords and rich peasants, he said, would be reclassified correctly, thus signalling an end to whatever bloodiness had occurred. But in at least one province, Nghe An, Ho's assurances went unheard. There, on 2 November, there was something akin to an uprising. Order was only restored after several battalions of regulars were deployed to the offending districts and further lives were lost.

Whether there was agitation in other areas is unknown. But although the government was forced to soften its line, and Truong Chinh, foremost among the hardliners, was obliged to resign as General Secretary of the Workers' Party, any changes were cosmetic. Truong Chinh still sat on the Central Committee, and the episode confirmed that communism, far from being merely the vehicle of national liberation in North Vietnam, was now firmly installed as the ruling, indeed the only, ideology.

This secondary victory, of state socialism over any other form of government, was, with or without its Stalinist trappings, to have the most profound consequences for Viet Nam. Principally, by perpetuating the idea of necessary struggle, it created political stability in at least one half of the country, while assuring instability in the other. To justify its backward economic methods, the communist leadership had of necessity to create a national goal to which all other goals could be subordinated; and, still fired by the patriotism that had triumphed over the French, its natural desideratum was national reunification.

Even before the crisis arising out of food shortages and land reform was fully resolved, the Central Committee set about focusing the public mind on what it perceived as Diem's perfidy. His refusal to call an election was, Prime Minister Pham Van Dong declared, 'a blatant violation of the Geneva agreement'. Slowly but surely the government prepared North Vietnam for a resumption of armed conflict. Side by side with ministerial statements came increasingly strident denunciations of the Saigon regime's corruption, and of American imperialism, as throughout 1958 the tension in South Vietnam mounted.

It was a vicious circle. As the number of terrorist incidents rose, and their scope widened, so Diem, relying more and more on his US-supported army, increased the level of repression. Nor were his efforts wholly ineffectual. In many cases Viet Cong guerrilla units, composed in the main of former southern Viet Minh, were forced out from the most populous areas either towards the fringes of the Mekong delta or away from the urban enclaves of the upper coastline into the hills and mountains of the Central Highlands. In a foretaste of the strategic hamlet programme to come, Diem also attempted to shield rural populations from communist infiltration by creating *agrovilles*, or tightly guarded farming villages. Similarly, the montagnards, or ethnic minorities living in the mountains, were herded into secure camps. But because the main thrust of his governmental policy continued fiercely to favour the Catholic élite and landlordism, such measures, coupled with an ongoing, seemingly indiscriminate campaign against the defenceless poor, were in the long term counter-productive.

Clearly, an opportunity for realizing the Central Committee's cherished dream of reunification under communist rule existed. In 1959, as the annual number of 'assassinations' of southern officials passed the thousand mark, two local but important uprisings revealed that the guerrilla movement potentially enjoyed the sort of popular support at the village level that would make a second 'people's war' practicable. The first of these was at Barum Carum, in the coastal province of Thuan Hai, in February. The second was further north, at Tra Bong, in Quang Ngai province, in August. In both cases government offices were seized by armed locals assisted by trained guerrillas. In both cases, too, units of the ARVN, or Saigon army, were dispatched to restore order. Since in effect this meant bloody reprisals, discontent was aggravated rather than defused.

A third, much larger uprising occurred in Ben Tre in January 1960, after Diem had promulgated further counter-terrorist measures in October. Now it was made official that not only were all Viet Cong and former Viet Minh to be executed, but so too were their friends, relatives and even 'associates'. Ben Tre, a delta province with only a very small Catholic minority, was particularly affected. As one revolutionary later put it, 'Unless we responded militarily, we stood to lose everything – our land, our chattels, our loved ones, and our lives.' It was do or die. On 17 January, at Dinh Thuy, a crowd assembled and stormed the local police station. A few rifles were seized. Other weapons were fashioned out of ploughs, hammers and knives. In due course an ARVN detachment arrived to quell the riot, but by then the unrest had spread throughout the district (Mo Cay). Further army units were dispatched, and more villages revolted. In Ben Tre city itself, the streets seethed with demonstrators, and it was not until twelve thousand troops had been dispersed throughout the province that calm was temporarily restored. And yet the moment the Saigon army unit left a pacified village, that village immediately reverted to guerrilla control. Thus the ARVN was shown for what in reality it was: an army of occupation staffed by native Vietnamese.

In fact, although nobody in South Vietnam realized it at the time, Ben Tre marked the true beginning of the second Vietnamese war, for the good reason that the uprising was the first of its kind to be sanctioned in advance by Hanoi. A significant detail was the enthusiastic participation of women activists. Working on both the military and political fronts, they organized demonstrations, appealed to Saigon army soldiers to lay down their arms and desert (which many of them did), portered weapons and supplies, and over the ensuing months sometimes turned themselves into soldiers.

These *toc dai*, or 'long-haired ones', were indicative not only of the depth of unrest in the non-Catholic South, but also of a greater planning, deriving ultimately from the North. The previous year Le Duan, a native of Quang Tri, now General Secretary of the Workers' Party and the man destined to succeed Ho Chi Minh as North Vietnam's leader, had travelled secretly from Hanoi to South Vietnam to 'assess the situation'. His itinerary included Ben Tre, where he heard at first hand the grievances of the people. The report and 'fifteen recommendations' he delivered to the Central Committee in November warned that unless communists in the South were supported by communists in the North, unless they reorganized and were encouraged to engage in the kind of protracted warfare that the Viet Minh had practised against the French, then there was every chance that Diem would crush them beyond any kind of usefulness.

Consequently, the Central Committee formally resolved to support the armed struggle in South Vietnam. Although this decision was not communicated to the outside world at the time, it effectively brought North Vietnam into the conflict, and the Ben Tre uprising was the first fruit of this development.

Vietnamese communist historians have insisted that up until the end of 1959 the Party in Hanoi had neither sanctioned nor encouraged terrorist activities in the South. Rather they were the doings of desperate comrades acting on their own initiative. Given that southern communists had always shown a certain independence from the Party at large, there is some reason to accept this analysis at least in part. Indeed, the Central Committee's November 1959 decision may even have been prompted by a desire not to lose control of a movement in which it considered it had a proprietorial right. On the other hand, prior to Le Duan's report, in May and July of 1959 two specialist units had been set up specifically to enable infiltration of men and weapons to the South. Group 559 was tasked to improve and enlarge the existing network of roads and paths through Laos and Cambodia – what in fact was to become the all-important Ho Chi Minh Trail; while Group 759 was instructed to study and prepare ways of transporting supplies by sea.

While these similarly secret measures fell under the heading of advance contingency planning, they showed that Defence Minister Vo Nguyen Giap had lost none of his meticulous attention to detail. In the fifteen years of conflict that lay ahead, this was not the least of the qualities that would bring the communists a second victory.

The disturbances in Ben Tre manifested the triple hallmark of organized communist insurgency. Military action, political protest and the involvement of something like a broad mass of the people were knit together in an onward rolling affront to the prevailing government. In this case military action had taken the form of terrorist attacks on police stations and other government installations; political protest consisted in demonstrations coupled with demands that Diem's government moderate its programme; and popular involvement was expressed in the sheer numbers who turned out to march not just through the streets of Ben Tre, but also through the countryside towards designated assembly places.

The specifics often varied according to circumstances. In particular the military struggle was to intensify out of all recognition, as guerrilla units were at first supplemented and then overshadowed by regulars operating out of mobile base areas, supplied down the Ho Chi Minh Trail with northern cadres and Chinese and Soviet hardware. But the interactive triangulation of initiatives remained the ideal of communist strategy right up until the final Ho Chi Minh Campaign, which delivered Saigon into Hanoi's hands in 1975.

For Diem, all this posed a set of intractable problems. An astute statesman would have analysed a palpably adverse situation into its constituent parts and then acted on every front to form an integrated solution. What was needed in South Vietnam, as some of his American advisers – including Lansdale – now began advocating, was a fundamental political reform that would effectively enfranchise a majority of the population, coupled with a softening of his government's security operations. But Diem was neither a statesman nor especially astute. He chose instead to stick obdurately by the narrow, closed character of his regime while demanding ever greater financial and military assistance from his Washington sponsors. The taunt that he was a puppet president, and his was a puppet government, gained rather than lost plausibility therefore, even though Diem himself was often suspicious of American motives and frequently resisted what he regarded as moves by the foreign power to take control of his country.

Diem's greatest fault, however, which guided his ineptitude as a leader and set him at a disadvantage in any comparison with Ho Chi Minh, was his disdain for his ordinary subjects. In the opening years of the new decade, and what proved to be the closing years of his regime, this was manifest in two policies carried out by his government: the 'strategic hamlet' programme, and a campaign against Buddhists. Both revealed a deep lack of understanding of or sympathy for the normative values of Vietnamese culture; and both swelled the rising tide of popular discontent.

The strategic hamlet programme, largely devised by Nhu and William Colby, Lansdale's replacement as CIA head of station, got properly into stride in 1962, although experiments in relocating rural populations into 'safe' compounds, including the *agrovilles* of the late 1950s, had been conducted for some years. Historically, there were two significant precedents. In the 1940s the French had tried isolating some Tonkinese villages from Viet Minh infiltration by maximizing the security around them; and in the 'bandit war' fought against Chinese communists by the British in Malaya during the 1950s, the protective resettlement of Malay populations in secure *kampongs* had proved outstandingly successful in combating Chinese insurgency. Indeed, Sir Robert Thompson, a British guerrilla warfare expert, was invited to Saigon to give his advice. But the South Vietnamese misapplied the lessons that Thompson had learned in Malaya. In the Viet Cong war, the 'bandits' were ethnically identical to the relocated villagers and under normal circumstances no great threat to them. In addition, the Vietnamese peasant had a relationship with the land of his village which went beyond ownership or tillage. He was bonded to it by the spirits of his ancestors. It was the bedrock of his culture.

Despite this, the Saigon government, deploying massive material and financial aid donated by Washington, embarked in March 1962 on a programme that aimed to uproot and resettle several million villagers, in those areas most affected by Viet Cong infiltration. Particularly along Route 1, connecting Saigon with the coastal cities of Qui Nhon, Quang Ngai, Da Nang, Hué and Quang Tri, the seaboard plains were emptied and the inhabitants regrouped along or near the highway, where they could be more easily observed. But the new encampments, although designed to fulfil the requirements of a broader 'pacification' programme, were more like prisons than homes. They were surrounded by ditches and barbed wire, and guarded by militiamen. A curfew was operated, and the enclosed families were sorted into groups of five. Inside each group, each family was made responsible for the security of the other four. And on each door of each hut the names of every occupant was posted.

By September of the same year, mainly to impress its American benefactors, the government boasted that some 4,322,034 individuals (nearly 25% of the population) had already been successfully and happily relocated. In reality, however, the strategic hamlets were already a shambles. Mainly this was because no one wanted to live in them; the majority of villagers vacated their new premises and returned to their ancestral homes within months or even weeks. But there were other reasons as well. Those relocated inevitably included some Viet Cong effectives: far from being isolated in a stripped countryside, these men and women now found themselves clothed and sheltered by their enemy, and with ideal opportunities in which to proselytize their cause. Many disgruntled peasants who had not listened to them before listened to them now. The programme also provided too much of a temptation for the ubiquitous corrupt official. Building materials, seed and funds went astray on an enormous scale, only increasing the resentment felt by peasant communities towards those who ruled over them.

Although over seven thousand hamlets were constructed along the coast and in the Mekong delta, most had been abandoned within two years of the programme's onset. Their fabric was vandalized and pillaged, until soon there remained little physical evidence that they had ever existed. But it was not entirely a matter of the regime scoring an own goal. The ball had been passed into the goalmouth by a communist agent, Colonel Pham Ngoc Thao. Thao was in many ways Nhu's right-hand man, and Thao it was who, knowing how unpopular the strategic hamlets would be, encouraged Nhu and his brother Diem to race ahead with the scheme.

Thus the regime unnecessarily alienated large swathes of the rural population. Alienation of sections of the urban population soon followed. Under French rule Buddhism, the traditional religion of Viet Nam, had been effectively disestablished. Its continuance was permitted, but public ceremonies were discouraged by a law requiring official licences before they could proceed. Diem, who not only favoured Catholics but aimed to create a Catholic state within the state, saw no reason to rescind this law. On 8 May 1963 in Hué, the centre of Buddhism in Viet Nam, crowds gathered to celebrate the anniversary of the Buddha's birth. Arbitrarily, the deputy provincial chief, a Catholic appointee, enforced a decree prohibiting the display of a multicoloured flag that, in Vietnamese Buddhism, enjoys a high iconic value. Angered by this, and by the fact that a week before the city had been hung with papal banners to mark the twenty-fifth anniversary of Archbishop Thuc's ordination, two to three thousand Buddhists convened in front of the provincial radio station to listen to a speech due to be broadcast by a senior monk, Tri

Quang. The speech, however, was cancelled. In its place several armoured vehicles rolled into the square. When the crowd refused to disperse the soldiers opened fire, killing one woman and eight children.

The sense of outrage throughout South Vietnam was immediate and profound. The government, by refusing to moderate its stance towards Buddhism, and doing nothing to salve the wound to popular pride, appeared by its inaction to welcome, or at the very least condone, what had happened – an analysis that seemed confirmed when, cynically exploiting the episode, Diem declared that the Hué incident was the work of the Viet Cong, while his sister-in-law, Madame Nhu, inclined the other way: it bore the hand, she said, of American agents. But in reality it was neither. Within days the Buddhist Church, taking advantage of its nationwide organization, rallied its followers in a series of demonstrations and hunger strikes.

Despite these, and despite the pleas of the US Ambassador, Frederick Nolting, and the official rebuke delivered by Deputy Ambassador William Trueheart, Diem, counselled by his brother the Archbishop, refused to relent. As a result there occurred a novel form of protest that was as memorable as it was macabre. On the morning of 11 June, Quang Duc, a monk in his early sixties, climbed out of a car at a crossroads in Saigon and sat cross-legged on the street. Around him were one or two nuns and a bevy of other monks. One of these poured petrol over his head, another ignited him and a third stood by with perfume to mask the smell of burning flesh. Without stirring, Quang Duc was consumed by flames and smoke.

It was not an individual act of protest, but a co-ordinated and desperate political gesture, and one that would be repeated in many other urban venues in South Vietnam. Malcolm Browne, a journalist working for the Associated Press newsagency, was present at the scene. Though he had had no idea what was to take place, he had brought his camera. Next day, his pictures adorned breakfast tables and television screens around the world.

'Let them burn, and we shall clap our hands,' was Madame Nhu's response. And still her brother-in-law, Ngo Dinh Diem, was obdurate.

Within five months the President's uncompromising attitudes had killed him. In every department his government was falling apart, and even before the clash with the Buddhists, his generals and other senior armed forces officers had begun plotting his overthrow. Indeed, attempts at a coup had been made as early as 1960 and 1961, and in February 1962 two fighter pilots strafed and bombed the presidential palace in an unsupported assassination bid. Most critically, the communists were being allowed to transform subversion into a full-scale civil war; and despite rapidly increasing US aid, expressed in terms of training, advisory manpower and *matériel*, it was the enemy who seemed to be calling all the shots.

With Hanoi now firmly behind it, the revolution in the South was taking large strides forward on both the political and the military front. In a move strongly reminiscent of the creation of the Viet Minh League in 1941, in December 1960 the communists set up the National Liberation Front, a supposedly neutralist body dedicated to the removal of the puppet regime, but in fact an umbrella organization ultimately controlled from Hanoi. With its field headquarters in Saigon, and its true identity carefully masked, it was able to focus discontent within the southern republic. In particular, its propaganda constantly exposed the country's lack of democratic institutions, while clandestinely it helped to co-ordinate the different aspects of the new people's struggle. Although chaired by the mild, bourgeois figure of Nguyen Hu'u Tho, a city lawyer who had been briefly imprisoned by Diem for 'leftist activities', the Front was run by communist cadres some of whom held commissions in the Liberation Army, as the Viet Cong were now sometimes called.

That army, though still of a predominantly guerrilla character, was expanding rapidly. At the close of 1961 US military intelligence estimated enemy strength to be in the region of seventeen thousand operatives. Cresting the wave of discontent induced by Diem's policies, a substantial recruitment drive coupled with the infiltration of political and military cadres from the North down the Ho Chi Minh Trail into the Central Highlands and even the Mekong delta led to the formation of the first regular units.

The Ho Chi Minh Trail was already developing into the strategic backbone of the communists' war. As an exercise in logistics, it rivals and even supersedes the spectacular efforts of the porters who had kept Giap's army supplied at Dien Bien Phu, for Dien Bien Phu was a one-off affair, while the Trail was manned, kept in repair and expanded over a fifteen-year period under conditions of the utmost adversity.

Since ancient times there existed a network of criss-crossing paths used by the montagnards, threaded through the eastern mountains of the Laotian panhandle and of Cambodia, providing an alternative connecting route between the Red River and Mekong basins that no one in ordinary circumstances would have contemplated travelling. In French times a few rough roads, mainly traversing the mountains from Annam to Laos, had been hewed, but in 1960 the Trail was still haphazardly planned and perilous to journey. It took up to six months to go from north to south, even with reliable guides. Weather conditions veered between the extremes of tropical jungle heat by day and, on the heights, freezing cold at night. Torrential and sometimes aseasonal monsoon rains were an added hazard, making supposedly shallow streams impossible to ford, and sweeping away all but the best-made pontoon bridging. Malaria, dysentery, dengue fever and other diseases were a perennial liability and claimed an estimated ten per cent of lives in the first few years. Venomous snakes abounded, and there were green blood-sucking leeches everywhere. In addition, foodstuffs were scarce, and supplies often had to be carried for hundreds of kilometres, thus slowing down movement and increasing exposure to the other risks. And all these hazards existed independently of the massive aerial bombardments that rained down on the Trail later in the war.

Yet the North Vietnamese took on this crude and dangerous system and made it their own, so that in time the journey to the South took only a month or six weeks, and the paths were turned into roads capable of bearing the heavy transports needed to carry all manner of artillery and ammunition. What prompted them was precisely the Trail's remoteness, and the fact that its entwined tendrils led mostly through Laos and Cambodia. Laos and Cambodia, at least until the time when their own communist guerrillas, backed by Hanoi, took control of all rural areas, were supposedly neutral, and therefore supposedly immune to South Vietnamese or American ground attack. From 1964 onwards the USAF flew unrelenting bombing and strafing missions against the Trail. Napalm and defoliants were used unsparingly to clear the hills and valleys of all their cover. Later, B-52s flew over the region in carpet-bombing forays; but while these operations damaged the Trail, they never severed it.

An enormous labour-intensive enterprise evolved. To ease the passage down the Trail, ammunition dumps, rest houses, fuel depots, miniature base camps, hospitals and clinics were built at regular intervals, often underground, and eventually connected by a field telephone system. All these had to be staffed, as did the quickly multiplying batteries of Chinese and Soviet anti-aircraft guns. But just as remarkable were the work gangs, composed of some fifty thousand youth volunteers, many of them girls. Living in concealed camps within walking distance of the Trail, they came out at night to fill craters and lay pontoons across the rivers. At dawn, the latter were removed and hidden to escape detection by reconnaissance planes.

It took time to build, and colossal manpower to maintain. But slowly new channels were cut through the mountains and forests into South Vietnam, feeding the Trail into different areas of the Central Highlands and then finally into the Mekong delta itself. During 1964 some ten thousand regulars were sent secretly into South Vietnam this way. In the winter of 1967–8, in anticipation of the Tet Offensive, 150,000 regulars could be thus routed, for the most part still avoiding the main trunks of the Trail, which were reserved for motorized transport travelling by night. Yet even in 1960, when the going was that much rougher, some five thousand cadres made the journey. They travelled in small groups to escape detection, often just five men and their guides. Casualties from natural causes were high. Yet they persisted. These were the political cadres who now took charge of the war and asserted Hanoi's authority.

Hardship, far from being a deterrent, acted as a spur to the communist warrior, whatever his specific duties. It imbued him with purpose, it purified his sinew. And the Trail was only one of the ordeals he might be expected to face. For many years the Viet Cong guerrilla had to live on his wits, and on the sufferance of villagers. In the far south, beyond the Mekong delta, in the mangrove swamp province of Minh Hai, on the run from ARVN patrols, even finding drinkable water was a perennial problem, for the canals were salted and rain came irregularly. In the delta itself living conditions were easier, but security was tighter. Here the guerrilla had to seek refuge in the underground rooms of friendly villages when patrols came by. At night he often slept under the raised floors of the peasants' dwellings. And in the mountains of the Central Highlands, where the first base areas were established, food again became a problem, and in particular salt, for which there was no natural source. The Saigon regime, copying the French before them, maintained as best it could an embargo against salt leaving the coastal plains. And yet there were guerrillas who managed, by dint of economy and abstinence, to make the small stocks of salt they took with them last for several years, until tendrils from the Trail found their rear.

Away from the hills, where the ground was firm enough, tunnels were burrowed in jungle and forest areas. Originally the purpose of these was to provide simple hiding places safe from enemy patrols. Then, when American aircraft began disgorging their fearful cargo of napalm and deadly herbicides, they became air-raid shelters. But as the war dragged on, the ingenious Viet Cong extended their use, so that in some cases, notably in the area around Cu Chi, some fifty kilometres north-east of Saigon, they became underground encampments. Vast complexes of tunnels, on as many as three or four levels, were hewed out of the substratum, stretching a hundred or more miles. Inside these systems were sleeping quarters, arsenals, offices, store rooms, meeting halls, dining places and kitchens. They were also carefully designed with false walls, hidden doors and booby traps to confuse, hinder and destroy intruders.

Men lived down these mineral-less mines for weeks, sometimes months on end, thirty or forty feet below the ground, without either adequate oxygen supplies or fresh food. Most famously, prior to the Tet Offensive of 1968, an army of some five thousand troops was carefully sequestered within striking range of the capital in the tunnels of Cu Chi, one of whose arms even encroached directly underneath an American base.

Such undertakings and experiences, far from denting morale, served to increase it. No one willingly endures such deprivations without good reason, so it had to be assumed that the reasons for them were good. In the Saigon army, by contrast, creating any kind of morale was problematic. Whereas among the Viet Cong and infiltrated northern regulars promotion and seniority were generally a matter of ability and service, in the ARVN what virtually amounted to a caste system operated. Between officers and the ranks there was very little rapport. Men joined, or were conscripted, for the least idealistic of reasons. With unemployment running high, they needed the meagre pay because their families could not afford to support them at home. Many joined for the simple reason that they were conscripted. In some years, desertion rates approached twenty per cent. Officers, on the other hand, joined to line their pockets. In Saigon commands were bought and sold, or dispensed as favours by the Diem regime and its successors. Catholics did especially well. Merit and ability were never more than secondary considerations. Corruption was endemic. Under a military dictatorship generals were rewarded with provincial governorships, and a provincial governorship was a chance to make money in a thousand different ways. American supplies arrived and were promptly returned to Saigon to be resold. Many preferred to sell arms clandestinely to the enemy rather than fight him. And casualties were ill-tolerated: not because the regime valued its serving men, but because it jealously counted the cost of their training. Therefore commanders, even when they had the enemy in their sights and on the run, were often reluctant to issue orders for their pursuit.

A classic example of the shortcomings of the ARVN occurred at Ap Bac, on the edge of the guerrilla-infested Plain of Reeds to the west of Saigon, on 2 January 1963. A Viet Cong radio transmitter had been identified in the village of Tan Thoi. Units of the ARVN's 7th Division were duly despatched to eliminate it. A plan, largely drafted by a senior American adviser, Lieutenant-Colonel John Vann, was meticulously prepared. An infantry detachment would be landed by helicopter to the north of the village, while two Civil Guard battalions would be brought up from the south, through the village of Ap Bac, supported by M–113 armoured vehicles. It was estimated that up to 120 guerrillas were guarding the transmitter. This, however, proved erroneous. There were in fact some 360 Viet Cong in the area, many of them dug into well-camouflaged foxholes in a paddy-bank to the west of Ap Bac. There were also Viet Cong camouflaged to the south, lying in ambush.

The ARVN should have been pleased rather than distressed by the false information supplied by its intelligence services. A main problem confronting Saigon resided in the difficulty of ever finding sufficient quantities of Viet Cong to make a successful attack meaningful, while because of a tendency towards over-deployment of ARVN forces there was still a significant superiority of numbers in the coming engagement. The battle itself, however, developed into a shambles, governed by the ineptitude and panic of those Saigon officers present. Nor, flying over the scene in an L–19 spotter airplane much of the day, was the presence of John Vann, a gifted tactician, of any advantage. His radioed suggestions were spurned, his orders countermanded.

The operation was supposed to begin at dawn. At 7.45 the Civil Guard made contact with the enemy, but no further advance was made. Instead frantic requests for reinforcements were signalled. Thick fog meanwhile had delayed the landing of the helicopterborne troops to the north of Ap Bac until 9.00 a.m., thus destroying any semblance of a co-ordinated surprise attack. What was supposed to be a quick-kill mop-up made the worst possible start. When reserves were airlifted in, their transporting CH–21 helicopters, piloted by Americans, landed too near the enemy line and suffered accordingly. Such reserves as were disembarked immediately headed for cover. Meanwhile a column of M–113 armoured vehicles, meeting a stream, ground to a halt. Only in the early afternoon could its Vietnamese commander be persuaded to resume his advance. Then, when the M–113s did finally lunge towards the enemy, they were beaten back with grenades. The Viet Cong held their positions while what remained of the afternoon was consumed by arguments between Vann and his ARVN counterparts. Finally, at dusk, it was agreed that further reserves should be airdropped to ensure that the enemy was at least surrounded. But these were deployed on the wrong side of Ap Bac, and under cover of darkness the Viet Cong withdrew, leaving behind eighteen dead. On the ARVN side eighty troops had been killed, along with three Americans.

Not every operation against the Viet Cong fared so badly. Indeed the previous year, armed with American equipment and accompanied by American supervisors, tolerably competent incursions against Viet Cong bases inside the Plain of Reeds itself had been carried out. But these were the exception rather than the rule. The battle of Ap Bac was altogether more paradigmatic, although few operations equalled even its modest scale; throughout 1962, 1963 and 1964 the government steadily lost ground in the delta and on the coastal plains, as the Viet Cong extended their control over more villages and more districts. By night, most highways had become impassable without serious risk of ambush, and increasingly, despite a vigorous pacification programme, the government's authority was being limited to the towns and cities.

It was against this background of military and political deterioration that American ground-troops were to be dragged into the war, and the United States itself into an ever greater involvement in South Vietnamese affairs. By the middle of 1963 it had become apparent to most objective observers that neither Diem's regime nor the ARVN's counter-insurgency campaign could succeed. The choice that faced American leaders, therefore, was whether to abandon the republic altogether or fight its war for it.

But it was not simply a matter of opting to bolster a client-state. It was far more a geopolitical consideration. The beginning of the 1960s saw an expansion of communist interests in many parts of the world, including Africa, the Middle East and South America. The 'security' of East Asia was also suspect. Although South Korea was fast developing into a strong bulwark against communism in the Far East, Red China nourished ambitions against Taiwan (Formosa); and in South-East Asia, where the British war against Chinese insurgency in Malaya was only now drawing to a close, there existed the real possibility of a communist takeover in General Sukarno's Indonesia. Not until his effective deposition in October 1965, and his replacement by the right-wing dictator Sueharto, would the prospect of a second Indonesian revolution begin to recede. In Thailand and the Philippines too there were signs of a guerrilla offensive, while in Laos the Pathet Lao, strongly supported by Hanoi, were engaged in an intermittent war against a 'neutralist' government. Meanwhile Mao Tse-tung, seeking to establish his leadership of Third World revolutionary movements, proclaimed his bellicosity in a series of shrill denunciations of the West, and in particular of America. And although there was a steadily widening rift between the Soviet Union and China, beginning in 1960 when Moscow ceased all its aid to Peking after ideological disagreements, this was for a long time unseen or ignored by those who chose to behold in communism a monolithic threat.

Such a man was John F. Kennedy, a Democrat elected by the slenderest of majorities to the American presidency in November 1960. Although commonly held up as the defender of liberal democratic values and a champion of free enterprise, he was also the inheritor of a more ambiguous political culture: a culture that was protectionist, and that in the preceding hundred years had involved his country in any number of gun-boat escapades. Indeed, American foreign policy may generally be regarded as being driven by two distinct motors: the one geared to disseminating the freedoms of the American Constitution and Bill of Rights; the other cogged by powerful vested economic interests.

On the face of it, South Vietnam offered an opportunity for synthesizing the two traditions. By combating communism, Kennedy could squarely claim to be protecting American interests at large, and to be defending the kind of ideology most Americans believed in. Yet even he sensed that there were serious contradictions in this pitch. One of them was the palpably illiberal nature of the Diem regime; another was the possibility of committing the United

States to an expensive and ultimately unwinnable colonial-type war that would undermine his country's international standing. There was also the concern that, by taking on the communists in Viet Nam, a much wider conflict might be precipitated.

By the time of his assassination in November 1963, there is evidence that Kennedy had fallen prey to those doubts, apropos of Viet Nam, that were to destroy the mental equilibrium of his successor, Lyndon Johnson. At the beginning of his term, however, there was a concerted revival of domino-theory thinking. Partly to reassure the American right, the speeches that Kennedy made both in his election campaign and in his first year of office heavily underlined a vision of a strong nation that would honour its overseas commitments and defend a liberal-capitalist world-order. And if there were any doubts in Kennedy's own mind as to the need for such a stance, these were dispelled during the Cuban Missile Crisis of October 1962, when Moscow was only prevented from installing nuclear weapons in the Caribbean by a staunch display of brinkmanship.

In these years there were very few voices in America that advocated either restraint or a retreat from perceived global responsibilities. Conversely, in the Pentagon and among the Chiefs of Staff there was a marked hawkishness. Those entrusted with defence and strategic planning were, when it came to escalating the United States' involvement in Viet Nam, regularly ahead of the White House, as the *Pentagon Papers*, originally published by the *New York Times* in 1971, were to reveal; and although some of these activities fell within the remit of sensible preparations against all contingencies, the apparent availability of ready-made military solutions throughout the 1960s was perhaps a decisive factor in turning the conflict in South Vietnam into America's war.

In 1954 the idea had been to create a bulwark-state in South Vietnam against possible encroachments by China into South-East Asia. To do this civilian and military aid would be channelled through the offices of the Military Advisory and Assistance Group (MAAG) in Saigon. In addition, the CIA was permitted to finance and control some clandestine activities; but the US Embassy was to keep a watchful eye on the participation of all American personnel. Thus by the end of 1959 the South Vietnamese Armed Forces, now approaching a strength of a quarter of a million men, enjoyed the services of approximately 320 accredited American advisers.

In 1960, as Hanoi ordered an increase in terrorist activities, the number of American advisers roughly doubled. By the end of 1961 the figure had risen to three thousand, among them three hundred pilots who now began flying bombing missions out of Bien Hoa, twenty-five miles to the north of Saigon and in time to become the site of a vast military complex. The following year Green Berets and Special Forces officers were introduced, as were helicopters, instruments of war that, on account of their mobility, initially had a considerable impact against the Viet Cong; and while all advisers were prohibited from combat except in circumstances of necessary self-defence, this rule was honoured more in the breach than in the observance.

Such increases in manpower were made by Kennedy under pressure. In April 1961 he established a 'task force', or policy advisory group, to look into ways and means of facing down the communist threat in South Vietnam. In October, confused by differing assessments of the actual situation, and in response to a request from President Diem for a security treaty, he sent his personal security adviser, General Maxwell Taylor, to Saigon to prepare a direct and confidential report. Taylor's conclusions included a recommendation that some eight thousand combat troops should be shipped immediately across the Pacific. Diem meanwhile had told the US Ambassador in Saigon, Frederick Nolting, that he too would welcome such a deployment. He also, at the end of the year, declared a state of emergency.

While Kennedy resisted demands to send ground forces, he continued to increase the advisory corps – up to sixteen thousand in 1963, after Ap Bac – and commissioned further studies and visits to South Vietnam by his top officials. But while opinions differed as to what military solutions would be most effective, on one point there was a rising chorus of unanimity. Maxwell Taylor (now Chairman of the Joint Chiefs of Staff), Secretary of State Dean Rusk and Defense Secretary Robert MacNamara all concurred that the central problem was Ngo Dinh Diem himself.

Nolting, soon to be replaced as Ambassador by Henry Cabot Lodge, was instructed to apprise Diem of Washington's fears for his country's security, and to force him to moderate his policies. But Diem, now openly antagonistic towards the hand that fed him, resisted. His policies remained unchanged, and by late August a further five Buddhist monks had immolated themselves in fire. Diem's, or his brother Nhu's, response to this was to have troops enter and seize the main Buddhist pagoda in Saigon, the Xa Loi.

Simultaneously, across the country, some fifteen hundred protestors were arrested and imprisoned. The new ambassador, Lodge, arrived in Saigon to find soldiers posted on every street and a curfew imposed.

Lodge, a Republican, had been given an unusually broad brief by Kennedy and the State Department. He was empowered to withdraw and cancel all forms of aid in a bid to coerce Diem into changing tack. But as events unfurled, Lodge played a different hand. Supported by William Colby, the CIA station chief for the Far East, he and the *in situ* CIA controller, Lucien Conein, now began a series of secret talks with a group of Diem's senior generals. The generals' principal grievance was the authority vested by Diem in his brother Nhu. They had learned that Nhu was planning a purge of senior army men. Unless Nhu were removed they had no option but to consider a coup. They had approached Lodge because they needed to know whether, in the event of a change of government, American aid would continue. Without it, South Vietnam would collapse in any case, and therefore there was no reason for them to risk their own careers and lives.

That coup was eventually executed on 1 November 1963. In the intervening period there was much dithering by all those party to the plot, including Kennedy. His administration was now confronted by the prospect of sanctioning the overthrow of a man whom it still purported to support. Kennedy himself gave out contradictory signals. The generals blew hot and cold. Lodge tried once more to reason with Diem. One by one Conein, under cover of visiting a city dentist, was introduced to the conspirators: General Tran Thien Khiem; General Duong Van Minh, Diem's personal military adviser; General Nguyen Khanh; Le Van Kim; Colonel Nguyen Van Thieu. They would only act, they said, if they knew they had Washington's approval. On Capitol Hill the National Security Council convened to discuss the issue, but the buck was passed back to Lodge. Then the generals prevaricated. They needed more time: the details of their planned attack had yet to be worked out.

In early September Robert MacNamara visited South Vietnam on yet another fact-finding mission, as a result of which Kennedy, on 2 October, proposed a compromise. Talks with the generals should cease, but Diem should be given an ultimatum. Either Nhu was removed from his several positions by the end of the year, or American aid, including military advisers, would be cut back. On 3 October the generals made another U-turn and told Conein that the coup was on. They wanted to know whether the United States would take any action against them if they succeeded. Referring back to Lodge, Conein was able to tell them that the United States would not intervene against them once a coup was under way. Suddenly, the local Chief of Staff, Tran Van Don, appeared to be in the picture.

'We are launched on a course from which there is no respectable turning back,' Lodge had cabled Washington as early as 29 August. In October the plans were finalized. More generals and other senior officers were co-opted, including Colonel Pham Ngoc Thao and, most critically, General Ton That Dinh, the commander of the Saigon military region. Nhu meanwhile, getting wind that a plot of some sort was planned against him, began vehemently denouncing the United States. Madame Nhu identified the Buddhist monks as 'hooligans in robes', after another had set fire to himself outside the central market. Day by day the temperature was rising.

And then it happened. All through the morning of 1 November there were 'unusual' troop movements in and around Saigon. But Diem and Nhu, believing that General Dinh remained loyal and was manoeuvring against their enemies, kept their composure. At ten o'clock the President even received the American Ambassador at the palace. It was not until the early afternoon that the fiction of normality was shattered. Suddenly, at around 1.30 p.m., the palace was surrounded, the police headquarters captured and the radio station seized.

Lodge, and then the rebel generals, telephoned Diem to offer him and his family safe conduct out of South Vietnam if he agreed to surrender. But Diem, obstinate to the last, refused. Instead the two brothers escaped the palace by a secret passage in the evening as their guard returned fire against units massed outside. They fled to a Catholic church in Cholon, the city's Chinese quarter.

In the morning, realizing that all was lost, Diem and Nhu, now bartering on the telephone for their lives, revealed their whereabouts to the generals. An armoured vehicle and four jeeps were detailed to pick them up. An hour later, probably on the orders of Duong Van Minh, they were dead, shot through with bullets and heavily stabbed.

Although the possibility of assassination had been sometimes mooted, and although Conein had been present at the generals' headquarters during the course of the coup, it seems unlikely that either he or any other American condoned the killings in advance. Kennedy, when given the news, was severely shocked. Nonetheless, Washington recognized the new government on 7 November 1963, two days after its composition had been announced in Saigon. Nguyen Ngoc Tho, Diem's vice-premier, now became Prime Minister of a civilian cabinet, in an effort to suggest the continuation of 'civilian' rule. But real power was vested in a Revolutionary Council made up of generals and colonels, and presided over by Duong Van Minh.

These changes, however, heralded no great political reform. Although the campaign against the Buddhists eased for the present, the new regime was in most respects as corrupt as its predecessor. Government remained concentrated in the hands of an élite who were generally out of touch with the broad mass of the people. Political and military appointments continued to be made on the basis of favour rather than of merit, and American aid continued to be siphoned off into private pockets. Nor was the new regime inherently stable. On the contrary, coups, albeit bloodless, now became the fashion. Over the next year and a half there would be ten changes of government, as the generals jockeyed among themselves for supreme power, and it was not until Nguyen Van Thieu became President in 1967, with Nguyen Cao Ky as his Vice-President, that a semblance of order was achieved.

But on one point the succession of ruling generals was unanimous: that the United States should be encouraged to participate more fully in the running of the war, even to the extent of taking over effective military command; and this was the real significance of the coup against Diem. Although backed by Kennedy's administration in the belief that it would enable South Vietnam to stand more squarely on its own feet, it in fact cleared the way for much greater American involvement. The generals, far more than the murdered President, were to be Washington's puppets.

But not Kennedy's. Three weeks after Diem's demise, on 22 November, the US President too was assassinated, the victim of a lone sniper shooting at his motorcade from a high window in Dallas. Henceforward ultimate decisions about Viet Nam would be made by Kennedy's successor, Lyndon Baines Johnson, the former Vice-President.

The military situation meanwhile showed no improvement, despite a fresh inflow of American advisers. Even as the generals plotted among themselves in the autumn of 1963, the first battalion-sized units of the NVA (North Vietnamese Army) were preparing to set out down the Ho Chi Minh Trail on the long journey south. Over the course of the coming year this infiltration was substantially to alter the balance of forces in the Central Highlands; while during the coup itself, the Viet Cong took advantage of the disorder in Saigon and a temporary withdrawal of ARVN regiments to extend their control over villages in the Mekong delta, attacking many police stations and military outposts, and also destroying many of the strategic hamlets that still remained.

The campaign climaxed at the end of November, with sizeable guerrilla assaults in and around Ca Mau in the extreme south, and on a US Special Forces camp at Hiep Hoa, west of Saigon. By the end of the year the total number of Americans killed in Viet Nam had risen to seventy-three.

No sooner had Johnson been sworn in as President than he was besieged by both the Joint Chiefs of Staff and by the Defense Department to consider escalating his country's role in South Vietnam. General Curtis Le May, commander of the United States Air Force, who would soon be recommending that North Vietnam be 'bombed back into the Stone Age', pronounced that present strategy amounted to 'swatting flies when we should be going after the manure pile'. Yet Johnson, even more than Kennedy, had reason to be reluctant. Far more than Kennedy he was a reforming politician, committed in his own mind to a programme of social progress inside America which, in his public statements, he referred to as the Great Society. He recognized immediately that to get involved in the kind of Indochinese war that the French had fought would undermine, perhaps cripple, that programme; but at the same time he was conscious that in order to govern at all he needed the support not just of American liberals, but of a broad cross-section of the American electorate. With a presidential election looming in the autumn of 1964, he could ill afford to risk giving ground to a Republican campaign (eventually led by Senator Barry Goldwater) that was likely to focus on the continuing 'need' to combat communism globally. If he was not heard to echo at least some of the same sentiments, then he would forgo whatever opportunity he had to enact his reforms.

Johnson's method for dealing with this problem was to rely on a fabric of committees that he hoped would provide a consensus for decisions about Viet Nam that at heart he did not want to take. A skilled political manipulator, he thus allowed himself to become boxed in by his own 'experts'. Yet because of his reluctance, escalation of US participation in the war was gradualized, to the extent that the military initiative was lost as often as it was seized. It was also, to an unnecessary extent, concealed from the public, giving rise over a period of time to a distrust in the government's handling of its foreign policy.

Johnson hoped, like Kennedy before him, that indirect and covert actions would swing the war in Saigon's favour. He therefore sanctioned operations that ironically, and in the wake of the Gulf of Tonkin incident, led directly to greater overt participation. Two days after taking office, he announced that the United States would continue its support for South Vietnam, currently running at a cost of one million dollars a day. A phased withdrawal of military advisers, mooted by Kennedy, was scrapped. He also elected to retain Rusk and MacNamara in their respective positions at the State and Defense Departments. For the hawks, it was business as usual. In March 1964, still struggling to gain a clear picture of what was happening in Saigon after a coup in late January that elevated General Tran Thiem Khanh to the prime ministership, Johnson ordered MacNamara and Maxwell Taylor to make yet another visit to South Vietnam and report back.

MacNamara's findings were particularly bleak. Although in public he expressed confidence in Khanh and declared that the 'war can be won', he told Johnson that in fact the Viet Cong were continuing to make progress, and that up to ninety per cent of some delta provinces was now in their hands. As a result, and after Johnson had consulted the National Security Council, American aid was increased towards a value of approximately two million dollars a day; and during the course of the same year the number of advisers climbed to twenty-three thousand.

But just as critical as these steps were provisions made at the beginning of 1964 to expand the clandestine war against both North Vietnam and the Pathet Lao. National Security Action Memorandum no. 273 specifically authorized a review of potential future actions, while an actual menu of actions, OPLAN–34A, was granted presidential approval at the beginning of February. At the same time the CIA was authorized to extend its bombing missions inside Laos to cover the Ho Chi Minh Trail.

None of this was vouchsafed the media, and the upshot was that when, six months later, North Vietnamese patrol boats skirmished with an American warship in coastal waters off North Vietnam, the affair turned into a public relations exercise which the 'hawks' exploited to their own maximum advantage.

Covert operations north of the DMZ had for some while been planned by Americans but, for obvious security reasons, were undertaken by South Vietnamese teams. Although some minor acts of sabotage were commissioned, the majority of these sorties were designed to furnish intelligence about North Vietnam's infrastructure and defence capability. In a report prepared for the Defense Department, completed on 1 March, plans to mine Haiphong harbour and bomb specific military and industrial targets in the DRVN (Democratic Republic of Vietnam) had been adumbrated by William Bundy, MacNamara's Assistant Secretary of State for Far Eastern Affairs and, as it happened, a former employee of the CIA. In particular, small South Vietnamese vessels were directed to survey coastal installations such as radar and anti-aircraft batteries. In late July, these missions were intensified to the point that the South Vietnamese were encouraged to execute actual raids against select coastal targets. Nor were they operating entirely by themselves. Rather the Saigon commandos were expected to co-ordinate their operations with two US Navy destroyers, the *Maddox* and the *C. Turner Joy*, which were patrolling the same waters with an array of sophisticated electronic surveillance equipment.

The inevitable occurred. The South Vietnamese raided two offshore islands. The North Vietnamese, on 2 August, responded to the provocation by attacking the USS *Maddox* with three motor torpedo patrol boats. Calling up air support from the carrier *Ticonderoga*, lying deeper to sea, the commander of the *Maddox* successfully saw off the threat. Indeed, he sank one of the North Vietnamese vessels and crippled another.

Two days later, during a storm on the night of 4 August, the *Maddox*, ordered to resume its patrol and now accompanied by the *C. Turner Joy*, was allegedly attacked again. As a consequence, on 5 August, Johnson authorized an immediate punitive bombing of naval installations at Quang Khe and Hong Gai, and an oil depot outside the city of Vinh – the first time that strikes of any kind were made north of the DMZ.

Controversy surrounds both North Vietnamese attacks. The second is widely believed never to have happened. Either it was the product of an overzealous imagination, or it was deliberately fabricated in order to provide a pretext for America's subsequent action, which had certainly been pre-planned, if only as a contingency. As regards the first attack, there was a dispute as to whether the *Maddox* had infringed the DRVN's territorial waters prior to the attack. Washington, recognizing a three-mile limit, said it had not; Hanoi, claiming a twelve-mile limit, said it had. And yet, on any broader view, such arguments were academic. The *Maddox* was scarcely a pleasure-cruiser that had drifted into the Gulf of Tonkin by some accident of misnavigation; rather it was actively engaged in seaborne espionage, even though at the time this could hardly be admitted.

Because of the time differential between Viet Nam and America, America's response began rolling on the morning of 4 August, Washington time. High-level meetings were held all day. Shortly before midnight, Johnson appeared on television to tell the American people about an 'unprovoked attack' on his warships, and to inform them that bombers had already been ordered to retaliate. But the most important consequence of the Gulf of Tonkin incident was the Gulf of Tonkin Resolution, passed virtually unopposed by both houses of Congress: by the Senate on 7 August, and by the House of Representatives on the 8th. This empowered the President 'as commander in chief, to take all necessary measures to repel any armed attack against the United States and to prevent further aggression'. It was the closest the United States would come to a formal declaration of war against North Vietnam, and it gave Johnson the green light to deploy ground combat units in South Vietnam.

It is possible, however, that the Resolution, or something like it, would have been enacted in any case, albeit in the framework of a less hectic schedule, for the *Maddox* episode coincided with a further deterioration of the situation in South Vietnam, where the government of General Nguyen Khanh was floundering badly. Washington had also attempted to open backdoor negotiations with Hanoi through a Canadian diplomat attached to the International Control Commission, Blair Seaborn; but imprecise warnings about what the United States would and would not tolerate, when put to the DRVN's Prime Minister Pham Van Dong, had fallen on deaf ears. Indeed, in late June the Viet Cong had again intensified their military campaign, frequently directing their activities against American personnel and installations. Most worryingly, the revolutionaries now appeared to be much stronger in the Central Highlands and adjoining seaboard; and the CIA had learned that China was increasing its aid to North Vietnam.

In fact, in Hanoi, measures that were the equivalent of the Joint Resolution had already been taken. A meeting of the Central Committee in December 1963 had passed a secret resolution calling for an intensification of the struggle in the South. As captured documents later revealed, this mapped out a comprehensive strategy, expressed in eight 'objectives':

1 The ARVN was to be worn down unit by unit.
2 The strategic hamlets were to be destroyed.
3 The size and the skills of the People's Liberation Armed Forces of South Vietnam were to be developed under Party guidance.
4 The political struggle was to be intensified, and the appeal of the NLF broadened to induce support from religious groups which might otherwise be used against the Viet Cong.
5 Particular efforts were to be made to subvert soldiers enlisted in the ARVN.
6 Existing base areas were to be expanded, and new ones created.
7 An international propaganda campaign aimed at building support in the Third World and among the 'masses' in America, France and Britain was to be launched.
8 The Party's leadership of the movement as a whole was to be strengthened.

At the same time, a propaganda campaign inside the DRVN itself was waged to harden public attitudes against the Saigon regime, coinciding with an assumed decision to send large detachments of the NVA down the Ho Chi Minh Trail.

This was followed in February by an agreement between Hanoi and the Pathet Lao to escalate guerrilla fighting in all parts of Central Laos. Concurrently, Le Duan made conciliatory noises towards Peking, as the Soviet Union and China moved further apart. In general, Hanoi endeavoured not to be caught out in the communist great-power rivalry, and even managed to play the one off against the other when it came to securing essential military supplies and other forms of aid. But in early 1964 China seemed the most likely benefactor, and the tone of the Central Committee's public statements was tailored accordingly. And indeed, on 2 March, after several appeals from the DRVN's Foreign Minister, Xuan Thuy, Peking pledged its support.

CIA surmises were therefore essentially correct. But for the Pentagon the truly worrying aspect of this was that North Vietnam was not alone in receiving Chinese help. Chinese communists were exerting increasing influence over their counterparts in Indonesia, and the ruler of 'neutralist' Cambodia, Prince Norodom Sihanouk, was also rumoured to be leaning towards Peking.

Under these circumstances, and with presidential elections only three months away, it was perhaps unlikely that Johnson could avoid deepening the United States' commitment to the defence of South Vietnam without a radical reversal of existing policies that in all likelihood would have been at this time unacceptable to the majority of his people. Equally, it had become desirable to seek congressional approval for any further actions. The Gulf of Tonkin incident therefore acted merely as a catalyst for decisions which in many cases had already been taken, or at least were firmly in the offing.

Johnson, however, remained in two minds as to what he should do, and about how far he should pursue his military options. Even as his bombers flew towards their targets in North Vietnam, he told America: 'We will seek no wider war.' Keenly aware that any single measure to escalate the conflict was unlikely to be decisive, but would risk antagonizing the communist giants, he delayed sending ground-troops until March 1965. In the interim, both sides, North Vietnam and the United States, tested each other's resolve, while the Viet Cong continued to make inroads upon Saigon's authority.

On the political front, it seems probable that the communists had a hand in fresh outbreaks of civil unrest inside Saigon and other cities. On 21 and 22 August 1964 the capital was once more rocked by demonstrations, as students and Buddhists protested against government policies. In October, Hanoi instructed the first whole regiment, the 325th Division's 95th, to deploy to the Central Highlands via the Ho Chi Minh Trail. On 1 November powerful guerrilla units attacked the US airbase at Bien Hoa, killing five Americans and destroying six B–57 bomber aircraft. On the 17th, in line with North Vietnam's policy of equal friendship towards the Soviet Union and China, the NLF opened an office in Moscow. On the 29th, Saigon was again seized by riots, and a month later, on Christmas Eve, the Brinks Hotel in the centre of the city, where American officers were billeted, was bombed, killing two and injuring a further hundred. But the most telling indication of Viet Cong strength was reserved for the New Year. The People's Liberation Armed Forces of South Vietnam had by now formed its first full division of regulars. At Binh Gia in the delta province of Phuoc Tuy two ARVN battalions were surrounded and annihilated in the largest battle of the war thus far. Saigon and the United States did their best to respond in kind.

While in May William Bundy had produced the most comprehensive plan yet devised for possible retaliatory actions against North Vietnam, in October US Special Forces were deployed in South Vietnam for the first time; simultaneously General William Westmoreland, recently promoted to run the US Military Assistance Command, Vietnam (MACV), organized units of the ARVN to conduct a programme of heliborne search-and-destroy missions aimed at flushing out Viet Cong guerrilla bands from their deeper jungle camps. In December the USAF began bombing the Ho Chi Minh Trail, as part of Operation Barrell Roll, dedicated against targets in north and eastern Laos.

Throughout 1964 the size of the ARVN had, with America's blessing, been steadily increased, so that by the beginning of 1965 more than half a million South Vietnamese were in uniform, out of a total population of between sixteen and eighteen million. In January, as well as yet more American 'advisers', a contingent of South Korean soldiers arrived to supplement these numbers. Yet every indication suggested that the communists were mastering the situation, and that unless very strong action was taken the southern republic would collapse within a year, if not sooner. Like the French before them, the defending forces were committed across the widest possible front, while the enemy could pick and choose where to strike at will.

This was made particularly apparent in February, when on the 7th and 10th, following a general campaign of small terrorist attacks against US installations, large attacks, perpetrated in part by NVA regulars, were mounted against American–ARVN bases at Pleiku in the Central Highlands and Qui Nhon on the Annamese coast. At the same time it was rumoured that General Khanh was preparing to negotiate directly with Hanoi, possibly to form a 'neutralist' government in Saigon which would include representatives of the NLF (National Liberation Front).

As before, Washington responded by immediately ordering retaliatory air-strikes against North Vietnamese targets. Operation Flaming Dart One, on 7 and 8 February, hit Vinh Linh and Dong Hoi, while Flaming Dart Two, on 11 February, went for other areas to the immediate north of the DMZ. But these were tokens of intent rather than decisive ripostes. At the end of January, in a new series of high-level talks in Washington, it had already been conceded that either the United States must use main force to meet the communist threat in South Vietnam, or seek a negotiated withdrawal of its many thousands of advisers and cease its support for the Saigon government altogether.

The main concern was China. If the war were to be escalated, how would Peking react? Would the Red Army suddenly sweep through Indochina as it had once swept across the Yalu River into Korea? Did the United States really want to find itself engaged in another major land-war in Asia? The answer to this was no. On the other hand, it was not just Viet Nam, Laos and Cambodia that were threatened. Intelligence reports indicated that the Red Army was once again massing units on the mainland directly opposite Taiwan, as it had done in 1950 and again in 1958. There was also clear evidence of a major China-backed initiative in Indonesia. Indeed, during the course of February, Jakarta was regularly given over to anti-American riots, and Sukarno's government, bowing to pressure from the PKI (Communist Party of Indonesia), seized control of all American-owned plantations and businesses.

Under these circumstances it really did seem that the security of the whole of East Asia was in jeopardy. There was also the narrower issue of whether or not the United States should honour its pledges to the South Vietnamese nation.

MacNamara and the Joint Chiefs of Staff forcefully advocated strong measures. Secretary of State Dean Rusk and the newly appointed ambassador to Saigon, Maxwell Taylor, counselled restraint. Then came the attacks on Pleiku and Qui Nhon. On 21 February General Westmoreland urgently requested a shipment of combat troops. The Pentagon, which had authorized large-scale military exercises in the two Carolinas as early as October the previous year, had all the necessary plans to hand. The arguments of the 'hawks' seemed right to Johnson. Even though in November he had won a landslide victory against Goldwater in the presidential elections, he was acutely aware that he could not afford to appear soft on communism. Accordingly, on 24 and 25 February 1965, he authorized the two military initiatives that decisively transformed the struggle into an American war. An intensive, open-ended bombing campaign against North Vietnam, code-named Operation Rolling Thunder, designed to interdict supplies to the South, was to be launched; and two battalions of Marines were to be dispatched.

Rolling Thunder began on 2 March, and on 8 March soldiers from the 3rd US Marine Division waded ashore at Da Nang. Although initially they were tasked only with the defence of Da

Nang airfield, on 6 April Johnson positively authorized offensive operations by US combat troops inside South Vietnam.

4

The American War

Whilst I was walking around in the rubble, I noticed an old woman piling up bricks. I went to talk to her. She wasn't as old as she seemed – fifty-seven. Her name was Nguyen Thi Sang, a peasant, and she told me that her entire family of ten – from her four-year-old grandchild to her son and daughter-in-law – had been killed in the December 14 raid. 'I saw it happen from the field over there,' she said. 'The planes flew above us three or four times, then dived. One of the bombs hit the shelter where my family was.' I asked her why she was picking up the bricks. 'My house was destroyed. I have to rebuild it.' Asking her to forgive my cruel question, I prodded: 'Your family is gone, the Government will take care of you now, why do you want to rebuild your house?' She smiled sadly, closed her eyes, then replied: 'Well, I may live for a while still and I want my own home. . . . No, that's not why. I guess it's because I know that after I'm gone, someone else will come here and live in my house. That's the way we go on. The only way to live is always to start again. . . .'

John Gerassi, *North Vietnam: A Documentary* (1968)

Within three years of the Da Nang beach landings there would be upwards of half a million US servicemen on duty in South Vietnam. In the eight years that America was directly involved in ground combat in Indochina, from 1965 until the beginning of 1973, over three million military personnel passed through South Vietnam. The majority of these were not engaged in battle, although a demographically disproportionate number of blacks were. All were subject, during what was usually a one-year tour of duty, to the fear of the surprise terrorist attack. The vast majority returned home alive. However, 57,690, according to official statistics, did not. Of these, 47,244 died as a result of enemy actions. The remaining 10,446 deaths resulted from disease, accidents and other causes. Over two thousand men were lost in helicopter mishaps alone. A further 153,329 soldiers received wounds that required hospitalization, while over half a million are estimated to have suffered from 'post-traumatic stress syndrome'. But an even more telling statistic perhaps is the fact that by 1988 suicides among 'Vietnam veterans' had actually exceeded war fatalities. These had occurred overwhelmingly among men who had taken part in actions against the enemy, in particular among those who had participated in forward units of search-and-destroy missions. No comparable statistic exists for any other army in any other war.

Set against these figures are the far greater casualties sustained among the Vietnamese, both military and civil. An estimated half-million Viet Cong and regulars sent down from the North perished in battle. Many thousands also died on the Ho Chi Minh Trail, as a result either of disease or of aerial bombardment. On the Saigon side, over a quarter of a million ARVN soldiers were killed by their enemy. But an even greater tally of civilian deaths accrued from the USAF's bombing raids against North Vietnam, unpacified areas of the South, and Cambodia and Laos. To these must be added other forms of reprisal that also fell on the civilian population. All told, it is thought that between two and three million Vietnamese lost their lives as a direct result of hostilities between 1960 and 1975.

Morale among American soldiers in the beginning was high, the more so as, for a while, US tactics seemed to have an impact on the enemy, and only well-trained professionals were used. Throughout the eight years the US Marines especially performed well even under extreme duress. The same was less true of the ordinary infantry, and far from true of the growing number of draftees, whose only real concern was to survive Vietnam and return to the United States alive. The average age of the US infantryman was just nineteen. As American motives for fighting in Vietnam, seldom explained in any detail to the ranks, became progressively muddled, and opposition to the war inside the United States became more vociferous, discipline was severely dented. By 1971 up to a third of American troops were using drugs, including heroin. Meanwhile a new word had been introduced into the military lexicon: 'fragging', or the deliberate elimination of unpopular officers, usually by means of a fragmentation grenade. Between 1969 and 1973 there were 730 reported incidents, with eighty-three officers actually murdered by men under their command.

Bifurcated living standards had something to do with this. At base camps like Bien Hoa and Da Nang, the soldier's every need was catered for. He ate well and drank well in air-conditioned barracks, and the host nation laid on a seemingly endless supply of cheap and playful prostitutes. But on a jungle sortie all this changed dramatically. The soldier had then to cope with the constant threat of ambush, with an alien physical environment, with venomous snakes, mosquitoes and leeches, with extremes of heat and with an enemy whose ubiquity and elusiveness constantly made him distrustful of the local peasant population.

The same circumstances that steeled the Viet Cong guerrilla, or the NVA regular army man, in lesser doses ground down his American counterpart. Partly this was because there was no lasting identity between the latter and the land he was fighting in, not even the identity of a colonial stewardship. The American soldier was never more than a visitor fighting somebody else's war. Partly it had to do with an over-reliance on far superior weaponry. Because of the sheer, sodden might of their air-power, the Americans in Vietnam never lost a major battle. But partly too, where the ranks were concerned, the malaise stemmed from higher up. Junior and middle officers were often no more experienced than the men they commanded, and sometimes much less so. And above them, there was neither a coherent command structure nor a compelling grand strategy.

The Military Assistance Advisory Group (MAAG) was established in Saigon as early as September 1950, after President Truman had authorized funds and *matériel* to be meted out to the French. After 1954 it oversaw the deployment of aid and advisers to the Diem regime. In 1962, however, when the need for closer co-operation with the ARVN became paramount, a new body, the Military Assistance Command, Vietnam (MACV), was formed in Saigon under the command of General Paul Harkins. In 1964 MAAG was absorbed into MACV and ceased to exist as a distinct entity. Thereafter MACV became the effective field headquarters for American ground operations in Viet Nam. But its remit was significantly constrained. Its relationship with South Vietnam's own armed forces continued to be advisory, and joint operations were carried out on the basis of agreement rather than of command. Further, being subordinate to the Commander-in-Chief of the Pacific Command in distant Honolulu, MACV had no direct authority over naval and air-force operations, so that again joint operations had to be based on mutuality.

In theory this latter arrangement presented no great problems; in practice, however, it led to bitter wrangling between the different participating forces. A strong commander, of the stamp of a Patton or a MacArthur, would have seen the need for, and demanded, a unified command to take account of both American and South Vietnamese services. But William C. Westmoreland, who took over at MACV from General Harkins in July 1964, lacked ultimate independence. A fine and sometimes bewilderingly professional soldier, who had served as an artillery and infantry officer in Europe during the Second World War, and as commander of an airborne regiment in Korea, he has been described by one commentator (Stanley Karnow) as 'a corporation executive in uniform, a diligent, disciplined organization man who would obey orders'. In short, a higher species of yes-man. Although Westmoreland persistently requested ever greater manpower, and was not above making strategic recommendations, he failed to master the bureaucracy that corseted him in far-away Washington.

And yet, for two and a half years at least, Westmoreland did manage to make headway against an increasingly dangerous enemy. Against Giap's protracted warfare he evolved the tactics of attrition, and he secured South Vietnamese defences sufficiently for it to be realistic to think about staging a counter-offensive. His search-and-destroy operations, combining air mobility, aerial fire and ground combat teams, provided an effective counter to guerrilla warfare, or would have done had they been able to take place in a sealed environment, rather than in an environment ventilated by the Ho Chi Minh Trail.

But what finally stymied Westmoreland was the unwillingness of Washington to permit the ground war to be carried into North Vietnam or, until it was much too late, into Laos and Cambodia. While Johnson seemed prepared to sanction any amount of bombing, such secondary attrition, though frequently costly in human lives, had only a limited material effect on a rural economy whose few factories produced very little of the weaponry that travelled south along the Ho Chi Minh Trail and were, in any case, widely dispersed. Rather, North Vietnam's armaments came from China and increasingly from the Soviet Union, which alone could provide the sophisticated surface-to-air (SAM) missiles to combat the United States' jet-planes.

An invasion of North Vietnam might well have secured the outcome that Saigon and the Americans were looking for. It is possible that, after twenty years in government, Hanoi's leadership would have balked at the idea of having to resume a guerrilla struggle once driven out of its cities; and Ho Chi Minh might therefore have accepted a negotiated settlement in which he agreed not to succour revolutionary forces in the South. But the perceived risk of Chinese, even Soviet, intervention ruled this option out of court; and the United States was therefore committed to lesser, and ultimately unsustainable, strategic goals. On the one hand it hoped to force Hanoi into submission through Operation Rolling Thunder; and on the other it hoped simply to defeat communist insurgency south of the Seventeenth Parallel.

The bombing of North Vietnam lasted, in its first phase, three and a half years, with only short intermissions during which attempts were made to bring Hanoi to the negotiating table. Operation Rolling Thunder began on 2 March 1965 and finished on 1 November 1968. Some 350,000 sorties were flown, disgorging 655,000 tons of bombs, for the loss of 918 aircraft. Civilian casualties averaged a thousand per week. Factories, military installations, bridges, roads and railway tracks, but not the life-supporting system of paddi-dykes, were the preferred targets, chosen not by the MACV but by the Pentagon, and ultimately by President Johnson himself. Certain areas, such as Hanoi, Haiphong and the Chinese border, remained 'off-limits' for fear of causing the war to escalate 'unnecessarily'. USAF fighter-bomber aircraft such as F–100s and F–105s were sent out from airbases in South Vietnam and Thailand; US Navy F–8 Crusaders and Skyhawks from a fleet of five carriers stationed permanently in the South China Sea. In addition, long-range B–52 strategic bombers were deployed against the area immediately north of the DMZ. Napalm and cluster-bombs were used as well as conventional high-explosives.

In September 1966 alone some twelve thousand strikes were initiated, while the cost of the programme in that year topped $1.2 billion. Although the Soviet Union supplied SA–2 and SA–3 surface-to-air missiles, the most effective form of defence was radar-guided anti-aircraft artillery, operating from camouflaged batteries. Even rifles and machine guns were fired from fixed emplacements. A single bullet, striking in the right spot, could bring an enemy aircraft down and add to the tally of pilots killed or taken prisoner of war. In addition, from 1966 onwards the NVAF (North Vietnam Air Force) was able to strengthen air defences with fighter planes supplied by Peking and Moscow. These included Soviet-made MiG–21s, equipped with air-to-air missiles. Care was also taken to disperse fuel and petroleum supplies, so that even direct hits on supposed dumps caused relatively little damage to either the country's war effort or its economy.

Thus in 1966 the USAF was authorized to target oil depots on the perimeters of Hanoi itself, but no more than an estimated seven per cent of North Vietnam's strategic petroleum reserves were destroyed. A more telling target would have been the Soviet tankers moored in Haiphong harbour, but attacks on these were also prohibited, underlining the fact that Rolling Thunder was a blunt instrument incapable of being directed where it might have hurt the most.

Far from discouraging the people of North Vietnam, the blitz united them and increased their ire. In the area to the immediate north of the DMZ, entire villages were created underground. Under such siege conditions, people shared whatever they possessed for the common good. Food shortages led to frequently severe rationing, which in turn bonded the population. As more and more of the menfolk were called up to serve in the NVA, more and more of the womenfolk undertook home defence tasks. Unseen in his high-altitude war-machine, the individual enemy represented a collective terror.

Westmoreland, who was subordinate to Ambassador Maxwell Taylor as well as to command headquarters at Honolulu, had no hand in either the planning or the execution of Rolling Thunder, although he did condone it. For him the real war was to be conducted inside South Vietnam, and his strategy, with its demands for ever greater numbers of combat troops, did have an important bearing on decisions made in Washington. Broadly, he sought, in the first instance, to secure US air and military bases against communist attack, and to block the passage of NVA regulars exiting the Ho Chi Minh Trail through the Central Highlands, thus offering further protection to the coastal enclaves. Thereafter he would go on the offensive. Guerrilla units would be subject to the kind of search-and-destroy operations he had endeavoured to teach the South's armed forces, except that now they would be undertaken by American airborne infantry, while larger enemy formations would be confronted in a series of set-piece battles. At the same time outlying rural areas would be 'pacified', using a combination of military measures and civilian aid packages.

By the end of 1964 communist strength in South Vietnam had doubled from the previous year's figure to an estimated 170,000 men. Of these, thirty thousand were organized into approximately fifty battalion-sized units of regulars recruited mainly from inside the country, but 'stiffened' by the presence of northern veterans, including General Tran Do. An operational headquarters, called the Central Office for South Vietnam (COSVN) was believed to be sited somewhere in the western Mekong delta. Now armed with modern AK–47 rifles, mortars and even rocket-launchers, infiltrated across the Seventeenth Parallel by sea and down the Ho Chi Minh Trail, the Viet Cong could anticipate engagements with the ARVN with confidence.

Thus, in a series of typically well co-ordinated nationwide attacks beginning on 11 May 1965, the Viet Cong launched a fresh offensive during the course of which they succeeded in annihilating two ARVN battalions in Quang Ngai, while inflicting substantial casualties on regiments ensconced at Dong Xoia in the province of Phouc Long. Song Be was also overrun.

By mid-June it was widely conceded that the communists had hobbled the ARVN's best mobile units, making a mockery of Washington's declared military aims. The Marines who landed at Da Nang were, in the first instance, committed for defensive purposes, to guard US airbases and thus 'release' ARVN units for mobile, offensive actions. Yet as early as 6 April, following a White House meeting on the 1st, Johnson authorized the use of US ground combat troops for offensive purposes – although this was not made public until June. At the same meeting, responding to urgent appeals from Westmoreland, he agreed to the deployment of a further two Marine battalions and eighteen thousand 'logistical' troops.

From such small beginnings grew the vast US military presence in South Vietnam. Even by the end of 1965, 185,000 American servicemen found themselves there. By the same date 636 had been killed in action and the first draft card had been burnt in protest. In July MacNamara, returning from another trip to Saigon, had advised Johnson that Westmoreland's requests fell short of what was required, even though Johnson had just sanctioned a further deployment of forty thousand, and a 'Free World Military Force', comprising South Korean, Australian, New Zealander, Filipino and Thai battalions, was already being assembled *in situ*.

Substantial bases at Da Nang, Chu Lai, Quang Ngai, Qui Nhon, Nha Trang, Cam Ranh Bay and Vung Tau on the coast, and at Bien Hoa and Long Binh outside Saigon, were either already operational or under construction when, on 27 June 1965, airborne forces mounted the first major US offensive: a search-and-destroy operation in Military Zone D, to the north of Saigon. Simultaneously, B–52 aircraft began striking at Viet Cong targets on the perimeter of the Mekong delta, inaugurating a process that was eventually to denude a land Washington had chosen to defend.

And yet, as the Americanization of the war proceeded, it became quickly apparent that Johnson's army had arrived not a moment too soon. The Viet Cong were poised to deliver a mortal blow to the ARVN, and only the superior fighting skills and morale of the first Americans prevented it. In the upper reaches of the republic, both around the coastal enclaves and in the Central Highlands, marine and infantry patrols encountered large bodies of Viet Cong regulars, trained and reinforced by NVA officers and NCOs infiltrated from the Ho Chi Minh Trail.

Two campaigns, in August and October–November 1965, demonstrated the scale and nature of the crisis, as well as the ability of the men and weapons under Westmoreland's command.

As General Wallace M. Greene, the Commandant of the Marine Corps, famously quipped during an early visit to his troops, 'You don't defend a place by sitting on your ditty box.' No sooner had US Marines landed at Da Nang than it was realized that passive protection of military installations would contribute very little to the war, for this simply enabled the Viet Cong to gather strength in any surrounding hills or forest. This was dramatically brought home on 1 July, when a large guerrilla force gained entry to the US airbase outside Da Nang and destroyed two C–131 transport aircraft and an F–102 fighter-bomber. Already, from the middle of April, the Marines had mounted reconnaissance patrols into the surrounding countryside. On 22 April one such patrol clashed with a company-sized enemy unit near the village of Binh Thai. In the ensuing skirmish, one Viet Cong soldier was killed, officially the first victim of American ground involvement. At the beginning of August a search-and-destroy operation, codenamed Blastout One, was directed against the village of Cam Me. But as this was under way, an intelligence report indicated that some fifteen hundred Viet Cong regulars had massed at Van Tuong, twelve miles from Chu Lai, a second airbase to the south of Da Nang.

Another, larger operation, codenamed Starlite, was now devised to trap and destroy what in fact was the 1st Regiment of the People's Liberation Armed Forces of South Vietnam, thus pre-empting any assault on Chu Lai itself. Three bodies of Marines were taken by sea, land and helicopter to strategic points around Van Tuong at dawn on 18 August. Within hours the main force of Marines found themselves ambushed and pinned down by Viet Cong fire. Relief came only in the evening, in the form of a naval bombardment and called-up air-cover. The fighting, however, continued for another three days, and Van Tuong was only entered on 21 August, by which time the main Viet Cong force had disappeared, 'melting' into the forest.

In a variety of ways Operation Starlite was to be paradigmatic of America's war in South Vietnam. The proportion of those killed on each side, later expressed as the 'kill ratio', was in excess of ten to one: 614 Viet Cong, as opposed to 45 US Marines. Critically, enemy regulars were temporarily prevented from launching a major assault on an identified target, but they proved to be finally elusive. Nonetheless, however many of them were destroyed or captured, sufficient numbers survived to create ambushes in the same locality or elsewhere at a later date, once they had been reinforced from the North. And perhaps most significantly, they had shown themselves capable of sustaining a fire-fight against US forces at least until such time as the latter were able to make their air supremacy tell.

The second campaign, called the battle of the Ia Drang Valley, or Operation Silver Bayonet, was an altogether larger affair that took place in the Central Highlands. Since the late 1950s, US Army Special Forces personnel had worked to build up and train small counter-insurgency units in Pleiku, Kon Tum and other mountainous provinces. These were made up of ARVN Special Force counterparts and of montagnard, or tribal, fighters, and their role had been to oppose Viet Cong guerrilla groups. As the Ho Chi Minh Trail came on line, however, the security of South Vietnam's upland regions was progressively threatened. There was a growing likelihood that large formations of NVA regulars would seek to come out of Laos and, by driving eastwards to the South China Sea, divide the country in two. By eradicating the ARVN from this area, General Giap's commanders could then bring as many divisions as they pleased over the Seventeenth Parallel and claim the bulk of old Annam for the communist cause.

The evidence was that, in the summer and early autumn of 1965, just such an operation was being concocted. Not only was there increased activity in and around the coastal enclaves, but in the mountains southern communist regulars were working alongside NVA regulars. And in fact at least one base area, under the command of General Chu Huy Man on the eastern slopes of Mt Chu Pong, straddling the Cambodian frontier south-west of Pleiku city, had been established. Here no fewer than three NVA regiments were encamped with a battalion of the People's Liberation Army.

The Americans stumbled on this almost by accident. For General Man the problem was that, in order to sweep down on the coast along Route 19, he had first of all to seize Pleiku itself; and he could not seize Pleiku unless he also overran, and obliterated, two protecting Special Forces camps, at Plei Me and Duc Co. Accordingly, in late July, he surrounded Duc Co. An armoured ARVN relief column was ambushed and badly mauled. Then, on 20 October, he also laid seige to Plei Me. A second relief column was also ambushed, on the 22nd, but on this occasion it was spared annihilation by US air support.

In due course, the Plei Me camp was relieved, after stout resistance by a section of Green Berets. But this was done not by a ground force, but by a battalion of the 1st US Cavalry Division (Airborne).

The use of helicopters as an integral feature of battle tactics had been strongly promoted inside the United States since 1962. Against the communists in South Vietnam, it was often to prove a powerful weapon, since it gave America a mobility that the French had never had. In principle, heliborne infantry could be deployed almost anywhere, including close behind enemy lines, once an LZ (landing zone) had been found and secured. It was no longer necessary for companies of infantry to spend weeks slogging through the jungle in search of the enemy. Rather, once the enemy had been identified, either by air reconnaissance or by small jungle-trekking units, relatively fresh combat troops could be immediately deployed against them.

Yet even at this early stage, before the concept of airborne infantry had been properly tested in battle, a further refinement had been made: the idea of an air *cavalry*. Using an array of differentiated helicopters – the OH–13 Sioux, for reconnaissance; the AH–1 Huey gunship, for assault; the UH–1 Iroquois Huey troop carrier, also used for close support; the CH–47 Chinook transport craft; the Sikorsky CH–54 Tarhe Flying Crane, for transporting artillery and light vehicles; the OH–6A Cayuse Loach, for light reconnaissance; as well as 'Medevac' craft, for airlifting the wounded – an unprecedently integrated mobile commando-style field force had been created.

When the 1st Cavalry Division (Airborne) arrived in September

1965 at its new base at An Khe, inland from Qui Nhon, it was just four months old. It had been preceded, in April and July, by two Airborne Brigades, which mixed infantry and helicopter transport in a less innovative manner. Together, they now demonstrated the efficacy of heliborne attacking manoeuvres against insurgents in what had traditionally been regarded as near-impregnable terrain.

Following the attacks on Duc Co and Plei Me, it became clear that the communists had a concentration of forces somewhere to the south of Pleiku city, and the 1st Cavalry was ordered to assist in a large-scale search-and-destroy operation. But it was not until after several skirmishes between American forces and detached NVA units that, as the result of captured documents, the base area on Chu Pong mountain was pinpointed. Accordingly, beginning on 14 November, an entire air cavalry battalion was airlifted into the region across from the Ia Drang River.

The fighting lasted until 27 November. Repeatedly platoons and whole companies of American troops found themselves ambushed and pinned down by gruelling communist fire; and repeatedly the enemy attacks were beaten back by powerful air support (including fixed-wing squadrons). At the end of the day, a total of 1,519 NVA and southern communist regulars were confirmed dead, at a cost of 157 US lives, approximating to the kill ratio of ten to one that became an average for the war.

Once again, the communist main force, numbering up to ten thousand, rather than commit itself to an all-out, potentially ruinous engagement, withdrew, on this occasion over the Cambodian border. There, because of Cambodia's formal neutrality, it was safe for the time being at least, and its losses in manpower were quickly replenished by the North.

The Viet Cong, like the Viet Minh before them, believed they had time on their side, and were not easily to be drawn into battle. An important point had, however, been established: the revolutionaries could no longer infest the more remote and awkward regions with absolute impunity. The United States' use of the helicopter, both as a means of transport and as a wickedly mobile battlefield weapon, a flying tank indeed, dramatically demonstrated that a new kind of warfare had arrived.

The 1st Cavalry Division (Airborne) showed that the crisis was manageable. Pleiku had been saved, and with it the coastal enclaves.

Impressed by the seeming success of the tactics employed during the Ia Drang campaign, Westmoreland, Defense Secretary MacNamara and the Pentagon chiefs opted to pursue the war by the same search-and-destroy methods. So long as battlefield returns showed a consistently high kill ratio, the belief, or illusion, that American armed forces were winning the war could be sustained. Over the coming three years there were to be over three hundred such missions. Ironically, the ARVN, which it had been Washington's original policy merely to support, played little part in these. It was relegated instead to providing security in areas already subjected to Westmoreland's programme of attrition, and to overseeing an ongoing programme of pacification.

In the Central Highlands, a network of fortified hilltops, or 'firebases', was built. Instant sites were created by 'Daisy Cutter' bombs, turning the heights into blunted cones. On to these Sikorski helicopters lowered 105mm howitzers. Foot patrols worked the valleys and jungle below, signalling back the co-ordinates of any discovered enemy to the gunners above.

In the Mekong delta and coastal flatlands, the same tactics prevailed, though with different means. Instead of firebases, much greater emphasis was put on airborne artillery and precisely targeted bombing. Foot patrols, sometimes referred to as 'dangling the bait', fanned out through the jungles, forests, plains, elephant grass and, in the extreme south, mangrove swamps. The delta's many rivers too were patrolled by armoured boats, some of them amphibious. In all cases, radioed messages could unleash swift and devastating reprisals against Viet Cong infestations.

The build-up of troops continued unabated. By mid-1966 there were three hundred thousand US servicemen in South Vietnam; by the end of 1967 half a million. Costs and casualties also escalated. In January 1966 it was projected that in the year ahead the United States would have to spend $12.7 billion in South Vietnam, and even this fell short of the actual expenditure; while in the financial year 1967–8 the war cost the American treasury $21 billion, or three per cent of the gross national product. In the same year, an average one million tons of supplies a month were being shipped into South Vietnam from the United States. Meanwhile the number of Americans killed rose from five thousand in 1966 to sixteen thousand in 1967.

But the number of communists killed also rose, fifteen thousand to fifty thousand for the same two years. And it was this body-count that reassured the White House that progress of sorts was being made. On paper, the war was being won.

Yet the reality increasingly failed to conform to the statistics. Although the communists were prevented from launching major attacks, although they suffered from a lack of competitive mobility and although the proportion of southerners among them was steadily eroded, there was a near-inexhaustible supply of NVA regulars coming into the country from Laos and Cambodia. By early 1965 there were some three hundred bombing sorties a day targeted on the Ho Chi Minh Trail: eventually more ordnance would be dropped on Laos than was dropped anywhere in the Second World War; but the impact on infiltrators was seemingly negligible.

A seething stalemate developed. Troop increases on the two sides kept pace with each other as the means of combat became more and more deadly. The communists learned how to booby-trap the jungle and shoot down helicopters and airplanes, while the United States resorted to using more napalm, and then herbicides and defoliants – agents Orange, White and Blue – in an attempt to deprive the enemy of natural cover.

An equally sinister development, and concatenate with the use of chemical weapons, was the designation by MACV of 'free fire zones': unpacified areas of South Vietnam that, because they were believed to be supportive of the revolutionaries and their cause, became open targets. Both the material and the human fabric of the hamlets and villages within these districts became fair game. Any person could be killed, and any building razed to the ground, without subsequent inquiry.

In moral terms, this resort to hi-tech barbarism represented an absolute degeneration of the war. It created a climate in which atrocities, on both sides, became commonplace. Most notoriously, at the hamlet of My Lai, in the village of Son My in Quang Ngai province, some five hundred old men, women and children were cold-bloodedly butchered on 16 April 1968 by a company of GIs led by Lieutenant William Calley during a search-and-destroy operation that had failed to locate enemy effectives. Yet at another village, Binh Hoa, in an adjoining district, a massacre of similar proportions had been perpetrated in December 1966 by South Korean mercenaries. Again, some five hundred old men, women and children had been wantonly killed.

This earlier episode went unreported until 1991, probably because, on the face of it, it was an intra-Asian affair and therefore of less intrinsic interest to western media than My Lai. But while such selectivity on the part of journalists was indicative of an at least unconscious racism among some of those whose job it was to report the war, mirroring the overt racism of many Americans who fought it, both massacres were symptomatic of a greater desuetude. American and communist commanders alike were aware of the extraordinary punishment meted out on the civilian population. Either side could have put an immediate stop to it by ordering a unilateral ceasefire. But neither side did. The political imperatives – of nationalism and neo-imperialism, of communism and anti-communism – simply overrode humanitarian values.

Yet political imperatives also contained the war. Although Ho Chi Minh skilfully avoided having to choose between Moscow and Peking, instead relying on both communist superpowers for civil as well as military aid, he had nonetheless to respect their views. In 1965, when the United States began deploying ground-troops in South Vietnam, there were rival tendencies within the DRVN's leadership. Pham Van Dong and Vo Nguyen Giap leaned towards the Soviet Union, while Truong Chinh, Foreign Minister Nguyen Duy Trinh and Le Duc Tho leaned towards China. But cutting across these affiliations was another debate about how the war itself should be pursued. General Chi Thanh, a senior commander, argued for a large attack across the Seventeenth Parallel in an all-out campaign. Giap, mindful of American air supremacy, and of the crushing defeats he had suffered in 1951, argued for a continuation of protracted warfare. Ironically, it was the Chinese who helped the Defence Minister's views to prevail. In Peking in 1965 Lin Biao had published a speech cautioning restraint. The implication was that, unless Hanoi conducted its war to China's taste, military aid would be scaled down or even halted.

Many years later Hanoi was to claim that China had acted deceitfully in this, that China had long-term hegemonic ambitions over its southern neighbour. Yet at the time the picture was vastly more complex. On both sides of the Sino-Soviet border large armies were being massed in anticipation of a potential conflict. Simultaneously Mao Tse-tung, threatened by internal dissent, was preparing the Cultural Revolution. While it suited him for the United States to be kept at bay in South-East Asia, prudence dictated that he farmed his empire's resources carefully. An attack by the DRVN across the DMZ might very well result in a counter-attack on the

DRVN itself. He would then have to decide whether to send his own Red Army to Hanoi's rescue.

Washington's strategy meanwhile remained firmly predicated on the assumption that China would move troops into North Vietnam if the war were escalated beyond a certain point. There was also a perceived risk of Soviet intervention, either in Viet Nam or at some other hot spot of the cold war. Johnson, beginning to come under intense pressure from a burgeoning anti-war movement at home, therefore resisted pleas from Westmoreland and sections of the Pentagon for an 'enlarged war' that would have meant sending ground-troops into Cambodia to destroy communist sanctuaries and either invading North Vietnam or using nuclear weapons against its cities.

The net beneficiary of these constraints was the National Liberation Front in South Vietnam. The sudden influx of American forces had undoubtedly blunted the Viet Cong's armed struggle, but the struggle was only blunted. While Operation Rolling Thunder paradoxically guaranteed the DRVN's continuing support, Cambodia remained a safe haven for increasingly large formations of regular troops, the majority of whom were now northerners, whenever the need might arise.

But of equal importance to the fortunes of the NLF was the fact that the internal South Vietnamese political situation continued to favour revolution. Although several years had passed since the overthrow of Diem, nothing much had changed in Saigon. At regular intervals coups and reshuffles among the ruling generals furnished perennially endemic corruption with a new leadership. In January 1964 General Nguyen Khanh had emerged as *primus inter pares*, but his one-year rule was spattered with plots and counter-plots. At the high point, in August and September, coups had come at the rate of one a week. These Khanh survived, but at the end of December he lost out to a military 'purge' staged by Air Vice-Marshal Nguyen Cao Ky and (as he now became) General Nguyen Van Thieu.

Ky became Prime Minister and Thieu Chief of General Staff. For the next two years, however, they jockeyed between themselves for pole position, with the issue only finally resolving itself in a 'general election' of September 1967, from which any candidates sympathetic to the NLF were rigorously excluded. Thieu won, became President and sportingly gave Ky the vice-presidency. But for all the difference it made, the result might just as easily have gone the other way. What was lacking in South Vietnam was a constitution, or a clear political programme that offered any prospect of meeting the needs and aspirations of the broad mass of the people. Instead Thieu, Ky and their closest associates allowed themselves to become over-reliant upon Washington, whose munificence filled the junta's pockets to overflowing.

Although the strategic hamlet initiative had shown itself incapable of securing its objectives, large tranches of the population were still being regularly relocated in order to clear areas heavily infested with Viet Cong soldiers, particularly those that were about to be designated free-fire zones. Apart from the frustration and anger caused to affected villagers, this policy also created urban drift. In 1960 the population of Saigon had been little above one million. Now it had risen to between three and four million. Insanitary living conditions and a substantial army of rats meant that typhoid, bubonic plague and rabies were rife. On the outskirts, shanties proliferated like spores on rotten meat. Prostitution, drug-trafficking and black-marketeering flourished. And in many quarters, criminal gangs openly held sway.

All this contributed to an atmosphere of destitution and violence. But there was also a violence engendered by the government. South Vietnam remained a police state run by and for the narrow interests of a Catholic minority in which the unruliest elements were often the highest placed. In August 1964 the city had once again erupted in riots as students protested against the corruption and warlordism of the ARVN outside the ARVN's city headquarters. Simultaneously, there were clashes between Buddhists and armed Catholic gangs. As a result of these disturbances, and the strong action taken by the National Council to quell them, a reported 449 deaths occurred.

The regime's response was never magnanimous. In 1965 there was renewed agitation as the Council once more sought to impose laws forbidding freedom of assembly. Again, newspapers were quashed and people who had little or no sympathy for the activities of the NLF found themselves imprisoned, usually without trial.

A far more serious situation arose the following March when a non-Catholic lieutenant-general, Nguyen Chanh Thi, who held command of ARVN forces in Hué and Da Nang, began insisting publicly on a purge of corrupt officers, including some of his superiors. Marshal Ky, instead of listening, dismissed him. At once Hué and Da Nang were enflamed. Tri Quang led his Buddhist followers on to the streets. But now these were joined by mutinying army men. A second civil war threatened.

The crisis was only averted by US intervention and mediation. Even so, there were several hundred deaths and many thousands of arrests. Ky had sought to make his point by dispatching some twenty thousand of his troops to Da Nang.

And these were the soldiers whom Washington equipped and paid to fight the communist insurgents. Not surprisingly, Westmoreland and the Pentagon pursued the war with less and less reference to either the Saigon government or their military counterparts, thus giving dissidents further cause of complaint. Through 1966 and 1967 one Viet Cong stronghold area after another was subjected to search-and-destroy missions. Thus, in April 1966, Operation Masher/White Wing blitzed much of Binh Dinh province, to secure Qui Nhon. In May and June, Operation El Paso moved against Loc Ninh. In a prolonged battle between September and November – Operation Attleboro – twenty-two thousand marines and infantry-men scoured Tay Ninh, to the north of Saigon. In January 1967 the 'Iron Triangle', closer to the capital but in the same direction, and the seat of a Viet Cong regional command was similarly swamped by Operation Cedar Falls; while between February and May Operation Junction City, deploying twenty-five thousand men, sought out COSVN (Central Office for South Vietnam) in the same broad sector.

In each of these engagements, as in many others, the pattern was the same. Small detachments of Marines or infantry, advancing from improvised firebases, provoked or trapped the enemy into showing himself. At once, as the American detachments in turn found themselves trapped, reinforcements were sent in by helicopter and communist concentrations were subjected to artillery and aerial bombardment. But, with very few exceptions, the People's Liberation Army declined the invitation to throw more men forward. Instead they either retired to Cambodia or melted into the terrain.

At the end of every engagement the bodies were counted. Two hundred Viet Cong here, a thousand there, as against twenty or a hundred GIs. Patently Westmoreland was inflicting substantial casualties at a relatively small cost to his own forces. But equally in every case, as soon as the American task force withdrew, the enemy seeped back into the evacuated area.

It was victory and it was not victory. In a bizarre development the Pentagon tried to circumvent the prohibition on sending ground-troops to Laos to interdict the Ho Chi Minh Trail by commissioning an 'electronic fence' that would detect communist infiltrators heading south and cue in pinpointed, computerized bombing sorties. Known as the MacNamara Line, this comprised air-dropped seismic, acoustic and even olfactory sensors which, as often as not, directed US ordnance against dogs and stray bullocks instead of human beings. Treated with contempt by Giap's cohorts, it was never fully completed. Meanwhile, inside South Vietnam, American mobility meant a maximum diffusion of the conflict, but little else. In the absence of anything remotely resembling a front line, Pentagon statisticians consoled themselves with body-counts that, because of the inclusion of civilian casualties, or even the fabrication of local units, frequently misrepresented the actual situation.

In turn, government spokesmen in Washington, and on occasion the President himself, sought to reassure an increasingly sceptical public that all was well, that communism in South Vietnam was backing off. But it was not really so, as the siege of Khe Sanh and the Tet Offensive demonstrated with shocking force in the early spring of 1968.

In the latter half of 1967 aerial reconnaissance, intelligence reports and the sensors that MacNamara had ordered dropped into the jungles of Laos all indicated that the number of troops and supplies on the Ho Chi Minh Trail was multiplying. In September several hill bases, mainly manned by US Special Forces and trained montagnards, over a wide area of the Central Highlands, came under attack from small to middling NVA units. The largest assault was against Dak To, to the north of Pleiku, lasting twenty-two days. But none of these actions remotely approached the scale of either the attack upon, or the defence of, Khe Sanh.

In French times Khe Sanh, a one mile long, half a mile wide raised plateau in a valley equidistant from the Seventeenth Parallel and the Laotian border, had been converted into a 'hedgehog', complete with an airstrip and underground bunkers. In the days before the division of Viet Nam, its strategic importance had rested in the fact that it overlooked Colonial Route 9, the best of the roads connecting the Annamese coast and southern Laos. Its proximity to the DMZ and the Ho Chi Minh Trail gave it added significance in American eyes, and during 1967 Khe Sanh was turned into the largest firebase in a network of firebases in this extreme north-western sector of South Vietnam. But more than this, Westmoreland intended that, as soon as he gained permission from Washington to conduct a ground campaign against the Trail inside Laos, Khe Sanh would be used as a forward operations base.

To this end, the airstrip was refurbished and reinforced with aluminium strips, enabling it to take C-130 transport planes; 146 heavy field guns were emplaced at all points around the plateau; and a sizeable ammunition dump, weighing in excess of fifteen hundred tons, was accumulated. In addition, several surrounding hilltops were also fortified, being supplied by helicopters either from Khe Sanh or from supply bases nearer the coast.

From the communists' viewpoint, Khe Sanh represented a formidable obstacle on the most serviceable road out of Laos into South Vietnam. If it could be reduced, then not only would Route 9 fall into their hands, but so too would the fortified western end of the DMZ. This would enable an assault to be made on Quang Tri, to the north of Hué, and then on Hué itself. It would also reduce the risk of interdiction to the Trail.

Whether, at this stage of the war, it was in Hanoi's mind to strike at Quang Tri, or whether, as has usually been claimed, the NVA's attack on Khe Sanh was a diversionary tactic, to concentrate American forces in one area before the Tet Offensive, is uncertain. Given that the concept of flexibility was deeply ingrained in Giap's tactical thinking, most probably it was both. At any rate, during January 1968 Khe Sanh was effectively surrounded by two of the NVA's most distinguished divisions, the 304th and the 325th. In a logistics operation reminiscent of Dien Bien Phu, a quantity of artillery was stealthily hauled into and out of Laos, and installed in concealed positions on such hills in the vicinity of Khe Sanh as had not been fortified by Westmoreland.

With these guns also came an equal quantity of modern Soviet hardware: rocket-launchers, anti-aircraft batteries and powerful mortars. The NVA infantry was also better armed than previously. Each man had a semi-automatic, and each company a flamethrower. Back-pack radios were also supplied for the first time.

MACV, aware of the unusually large movements on and off the Trail, had taken the precaution of increasing Khe Sanh's garrison from one Marine battalion to six mixed Marine and ARVN Rangers; but the sheer scale of the NVA barrage, when it came, caused embarrassment as well as alarm.

It began at dawn on 21 January 1968. Without warning, Khe Sanh was deluged with rockets and artillery fire from several points of the compass. An early missile, hitting the ammunition dump, caused an explosion that lit up the whole valley for several minutes. Seventeen Marines were killed, and the engagement clearly had the makings of a major débâcle.

But if the communist attack was unprecedentedly severe, then so too, over the ensuing seventy-seven days of the siege, was the American riposte. Within twenty-four hours Westmoreland had activated Operation Niagara, originally planned as a softening-up aerial bombardment against the Trail. The area around Khe Sanh and its adjacent 'satellite' hills was utterly flattened. In the most concentrated aerial bombardment of any war, B–52s and Skyraider and Skyhawk fighter-bombers flew three hundred missions a day, dropping thirty-five thousand tons of bombs a week. Using computerized targeting techniques, the USAF quickly obliterated the NVA's anti-aircraft installations, despite poor visibility. The communists' artillery remained largely undamaged, however, and Khe Sanh, under the command of Colonel David Lownds, continued to soak up punishment.

The persistence of the NVA was phenomenal. Not only did they withstand the napalm, herbicides and conventional explosives raining down on them from the sky, but they even endeavoured to move in on their targets. On 5 February one of Khe Sanh's satellites, Hill 861, was almost overrun. Two days later a Special Forces camp at Lang Vei was successfully assaulted. Nine hundred montagnards and a handful of Americans were killed. Trenches were built to within thirty metres of the base of the plateau. But in the increasingly barren landscape around Khe Sanh, and confronted by the Americans' unassailable air supremacy, the main attack gradually died on the vine. The siege was officially lifted on 8 April when a relief force – Operation Pegasus – made contact with Lownds' beleaguered Marines. But the issue had been decided well before then.

During the battle, both sides had become mesmerized by the attention it attracted in the world's media. Reporters and television cameras flew in with the morning supply planes and flew out again in the evening. With scant regard for meaningful military comparisons, they turned Khe Sanh into 'America's Dien Bien Phu'. Because Lownds' men held the high ground, and because of the awesome capabilities of the American air force, the analogy was entirely wrong. It was also wrong in terms of the outcome. The Marines were not dislodged, and though Lownds lost 205 of his troops, this figure was as nothing compared to NVA casualties. After the battle, 1,602 enemy corpses were found, but these were probably a small fraction of the actual number of men lost. Under the drenching bombardment of Operation Niagara an estimated eight or nine thousand men may have been entirely blown away, making for the highest kill ratio in America's favour of any major engagement during the war.

Yet for all this, or because of it, Khe Sanh entered history not just as an exemplar of Marine grit, but also as a badge worn on the lapels of the rapidly burgeoning anti-war movement in the United States. Even before mid-June, when the decision was taken to abandon the most hotly disputed firebase of the war, Khe Sanh had become synonymous with the futility of America's involvement. This was because Khe Sanh was not an isolated phenomenon, but, as Hanoi intended, an element of a much larger campaign: the Tet Offensive, so named because it coincided with Tet, the Vietnamese New Year.

At the end of January 1968, as the siege of Khe Sanh moved into full gear, there was a sudden burst of communist activity in the Central Highlands. On the 30th, the cities of Kontum, Pleiku and Ban Me Thuot were each subjected to mixed guerrilla and regular attacks. To Westmoreland this confirmed that the communists had decided to concentrate their offensive operations in the mountains. In fact, the three strikes were a day early. They were supposed to happen on the 31st, Tet, as part of a countrywide chain of military actions planned by Hanoi from July 1967 onwards, after the Central Committee had convened to discuss what was an increasingly adverse situation in the South. But far from alerting MACV to the impending conflagration, the premature Central Highlands campaign merely induced complacency. Through diplomatic channels in Europe the DRVN had hinted that it might now be prepared to negotiate a settlement with the United States, and this too had served to lower tension in Saigon.

As well as a quasi-religious movable New Year festival in which the whole mass of the people participated, in previous years Tet had been a period of unofficial ceasefires. Many ARVN soldiers took leave to visit their families, or drank alcohol in their barracks. Saigon and other towns and cities were also, for several days before Tet, generally aswarm with holidaymakers and peasants coming in from rural districts to sell various festival treats. In 1968 the communists took advantage of this temporary slackening of security and infiltrated both weapons and men into nearly every major conurbation in South Vietnam. Then, without warning, in the early hours of the 31st all hell broke loose. Quang Tri, Hué, Da Nang, Quangnai, Qui Nhon, Nha Trang, Dalat, Vinh Long, Ben Tre, My Tho, Can Tho, Ca Mau and a score of other centres were rocked by explosions and rifle fire as the insurgents took over public buildings, shot at contingents of the ARVN and assassinated local officials.

In Saigon, where an estimated four thousand out of eighty thousand Viet Cong and People's Liberation Army regulars who took part in the Tet Offensive had gathered, havoc swept across the centre of the city. The ARVN's Joint General Staff Command building, already shaken by bombs that had been planted beforehand, came under rocket and mortar attack. Several police stations were overrun, as was the national broadcasting station. The presidential palace came under fire, and the perimeter of the United States Embassy itself was breached by a 'suicide' squad of nineteen guerrillas – all of them killed, along with seven Americans.

The purpose of all this was threefold: to cripple the ARVN, to provoke a general uprising and to damage American prestige. For once, however, the ARVN snapped out of its torpor and gave US forces real support in crushing the terrorist revolt nearly everywhere that it had occurred. Largely because of this, but also because the populace at large was not as committed to a revolution as southern cadres had led Hanoi to believe, the general uprising failed to materialize. In Saigon, as in many other cities, order was effectively restored by the evening of the following day. Thereafter combined US and ARVN operations sortied against the sixty-four district capitals that had also been attacked.

In two cities, however, the communists held firm: Hué and Ben Tre. In the event Ben Tre, always a communist stronghold, was levelled to the ground by artillery fire and aerial bombardment, prompting an American officer to remark: 'We had to destroy it to save it.' In Hué, prolonged resistance gave rise to the bloodiest close battle of the war.

In the initial attack the equivalent of a division of NVA regulars, having successfully penetrated through the Central Highlands, first fired rockets on Hué, then invaded it, setting up their headquarters on the ancient citadel to the north of the imperial palace. Importantly, Route 1, the main highway connecting North and South, and passing through Hué, was severed. Then, having established control of the city, the communists inaugurated a terror. In the largest single atrocity of the war, between three and five thousand civilians – officials, professionals, Catholics and anyone thought to sympathize with the Saigon regime – were killed. Well before Tet secret lists had been compiled by agents living inside Hué, and these now furnished the addresses and identities of those deemed enemies of the liberation movement. The victims perished inside their homes, or at designated sites along the Perfume River. Most were shot, but some were stabbed to death or buried alive.

These reprisals were executed swiftly and exactly. It was a bloodbath, but it was not, like the atrocities on the other side, a random bloodbath. And even as they were carried out, Hué itself was turning into a grim battleground. To the south of the river, within the confines of the 'new' city, an MACV office building was in the process of being relieved by a battalion of Marines. Over the next three weeks, as further American and Saigonese arrived, the whole city was engulfed by fire-fights that were as intimate as they were intense. Every street, every block, every building, even every floor of every building, was contested. Where they could, the Americans advanced behind tanks and armoured vehicles; but many of the city's lanes were too narrow for even this protection, and the only effective manoeuvres in what had become a sniper's paradise were stealth and quick reaction.

By 14 February the new city had been reclaimed. On the 24th the communist flag was finally removed from the south wall of the citadel, after the citadel itself had been blasted to smithereens. Thus the battle finished. For political reasons, in the closing stages units of the ARVN Airborne Infantry were invited to advance on the last remaining communists. But by then most of the surviving enemy, ordered to retreat, had abandoned their posts; and much of old Hué, including the imperial palace, had been reduced to rubble. Ten thousand houses had been destroyed, creating some 116,000 refugees. 5,113 communist troops were known to have died, as against 147 Americans and 384 ARVN soldiers. Once again casualties had approximated to the ratio of ten to one.

In the Tet Offensive as a whole it was officially recorded that thirty-seven thousand communist insurrectionaries had lost their lives, as against six thousand allies, including two and a half thousand Americans. In addition, the communists were driven out of every city, town and village that they had attempted to seize.

Briefly it seemed that the military deadlock had been broken, in the United States' and Saigon's favour. The initiative, however, had come from Hanoi, although the exact strategic purpose of Khe Sanh and Tet remains unclear. An important consideration was the demoralization of the Viet Cong resulting from the efficacy of American air mobility, which gave Westmoreland's search-and-destroy operations far more edge against guerrilla units than any campaigns fought against them by the French in the first war. There was therefore a need to reassert revolutionary vigour. It is also possible that Hanoi believed it could win the war by delivering a decisive knock-out blow, augmented by a nationwide uprising. That, after all, was a familiar theme of Vietnamese revolutionary literature: the *idea* of a glorious, brilliant coming-together of all the elements. With Giap still at the helm, however, such a plan seems unlikely, even though he had written much of that literature himself. He was too good a strategist, too good a tactician, to underestimate his enemy's fire-power. More probably Hanoi sought to demonstrate to the United States that the war was unwinnable, that all its efforts and expenditure were a waste of resources; and so bring Washington to the negotiating table on terms acceptable to the DRVN's leadership.

If this was the strategic thinking behind the Tet Offensive, then in the long term Hanoi gained its objectives, despite the immediate semblance of high military miscalculation. However, at the end of Tet the morale of communist forces in South Vietnam, far from being lifted, sank to new depths. Henceforward, the revolutionary struggle was increasingly to be waged by NVA regulars infiltrated through Laos and Cambodia; and it is conceivable that, left to their own devices, the southern communists would gradually have been annihilated by their foes.

Ironically, the compelling evidence of the superiority of US arms manifest in the outcome of the Tet Offensive was interpreted by a growing number of Washington officials, and by the American media at large, in quite another way. If, as Westmoreland and the Pentagon claimed, America was winning the war, then Tet should never have been allowed to happen in the first place. Instead what it evidenced was an enemy more numerous, more diffused and better armed than in 1964. Thus, while Westmoreland and the Chiefs of Staff pleaded for additional reinforcements with which they believed they could inflict permanent humiliation on the Viet Cong, as well as interdict the Ho Chi Minh Trail, public opinion in America turned decisively against the war in Indochina.

Unlike the media in North Vietnam, which were rigorously controlled by the Workers' Party and its Ministry of Propaganda, and were therefore unlikely to affect the course of the war, newspapers, television and radio in the United States could and did inhibit a strictly military assessment of the conflict's progress. In addition, there was the democratic process of national presidential elections, held once every four years – always a test of a government's performance against public opinion, and something else to which the DRVN were immune. In 1964, particularly in his handling of the Gulf of Tonkin crisis, Johnson had had to keep one eye on the polling booths. Now, in 1968, he faced a similar ordeal. Once again elections would be held in November, and once again 'Vietnam' would be a major issue. Indeed, all the portents suggested that it would be the only issue.

The American anti-war movement, a socio-political phenomenon of enormous complexity, long predated the Tet Offensive, yet Tet gave it critical momentum. The opposition of only two Senators in the whole of Congress to the Gulf of Tonkin Resolution in August 1964, betokening the political establishment's resolve to face down communism in the world at large, rapidly became an anachronism. Significantly, Senator J. William Fulbright, who had steered the legislation through both chambers on Johnson's behalf, had by late 1967 become a force of opposition to the war on Capitol Hill. In his capacity as Chairman of the Senate Foreign Affairs Committee he had voiced criticisms of the government's Vietnam policy during televised hearings in 1966. At Johns Hopkins University he also spoke out against 'that arrogance of power which has afflicted, weakened and in some cases destroyed great nations in the past'. Now, early in 1968, he conducted closed sessions of the Committee in a bid to discover whether in fact the Gulf of Tonkin incident had been deliberately engineered in order to hasten American involvement in the defence of South Vietnam.

In Washington other voices joined in a rising chorus of dissent, not just against the way in which Johnson was pursuing the war, but against the war itself. Dean Acheson, a main architect of Truman's global anti-communist strategy, was one of many surprise gainsayers.

Earlier, in November 1967, Senator Eugene McCarthy had announced his decision to contest the Democratic Party's presidential nomination against Johnson on an anti-war ticket. Now that challenge gained substance. And behind McCarthy loomed the far larger threat of Senator Robert Kennedy, determined to carry his assassinated brother's torch back into the White House, and soon to announce his own candidacy.

Johnson particularly feared Kennedy, whom he guaged to have sufficient popular appeal to win the nomination. Yet a more immediate problem had arisen within the ranks of his own close followers. The inter-departmental consensus on which he had relied to carry through his war strategy was itself now breaking down. The man who began opposing him most insistently in cabinet was Secretary of Defense Robert MacNamara. MacNamara's doubts about 'Vietnam' had originated at some point in the spring of 1967. In May of the same year he recommended scaling down the bombing of North Vietnam. In November he profferred his resignation. In December, when North Vietnam's Foreign Minister, Nguyen Duy Trinh, had intimated to diplomats in Hanoi that his government would be prepared to open peace negotiations once the bombing missions stopped, he signalled approval. The United States, he told Johnson, should stop the bombing missions at once and start talking.

Eventually that is exactly what Johnson did. On 31 March 1968 he appeared on television to announce that henceforward bombing of North Vietnam would be restricted to below the Twentieth Parallel. At the same time he authorized Averell Harriman, a State Department official, to open negotiations with Hanoi whenever Hanoi was ready. But he also announced that he would not be seeking re-election as President in November.

By then MacNamara had been replaced. Clark Clifford, a lawyer whose inexperience in either military or international affairs Johnson hoped would make of him a biddable subordinate, took over as Secretary of Defense on 1 March. Yet within days of entering the Pentagon, Clifford had convened an advisory group and delivered a report to the White House in which he urged a reduction of the role of US forces inside Viet Nam, to the extent that they should be allowed only to defend Saigon and the coastal enclaves. Westmoreland and General Earle Wheeler (the current Chief of General Staff) meanwhile were clamouring not only for reinforcements, but for authority for American ground-troops to pursue communist forces into their Laotian and Cambodian sanctuaries.

While militarily these requests made good sense, politically they confronted Johnson with an insoluble dilemma. A further escalation of the fighting would undoubtedly split his party and so lose him the presidency. Yet even in the wake of the Tet Offensive, public opinion against the war had not so crystallized that he could afford to display any weakness in the anti-communist struggle; for it was still almost a maxim of American politics that the Democrats could only win an election when they espoused traditional values and vowed to uphold America's global standing – as both Truman and Kennedy had done. In the New Hampshire primary McCarthy had come within an ace of beating him. But while many of the Democrat votes which McCarthy attracted were anti-war, the Senator had also reaped the benefit of a different kind of protest: those who thought that Johnson's measures were not tough enough.

Thus Johnson opted not to seek a second full term in the White House. In reality he was a broken man. But it was not a sudden crisis that had humbled him. Rather the whole of his first, and only, full term as President had been accumulatively poisoned by the Vietnam factor. What had begun as marginal dissent, normal in any democracy that finds itself at war, had gradually burgeoned into turmoil. Vietnam, far from synthesizing the historic liberal and hegemonic strands of American foreign policy, made manifest their contradiction, and in so doing divided the country.

Groups protesting against the United States' involvement in Vietnam had been organized as early as 1963. Mainly these were peopled by those who had an abiding devotion to the simple idea of peace. But once ground-troops had been committed in 1965, and young men began being drafted into the war in accordance with standing legislation, the movement spread, so that in time it touched nearly every sector of American society. It was also underpinned by a cultural revolution characterized by anti-establishment values. Younger Americans were no longer prepared to accept unques-tioningly the dictates and programmes of their elders.

Yet while university campuses remained an important arena of dissent throughout the war, the anti-war movement spread far beyond the bounds of collegiate gates. Religious congregations, parents whose children had died in Vietnam, or might be about to die, draft dodgers, black-power leaders, teachers, writers and artists, many eminent intellectuals and eventually a substantial proportion of Vietnam 'veterans' all contributed, for a variety of sometimes contradictory motives, to the swelling tide of objection. Some maintained an ideological love of peace, some thought Vietnam the wrong war in the wrong place, believing it to be 'neo-imperialist' in tone, some objected to the increased tax burden, some were afraid to die, some simply had better things to do than join the army, some protested for narrow political purposes, while a small minority sympathized with the revolutionary aims of Vietnamese communism. But the very diversity of views contained within the movement assured its nationwide character, and therefore its impact.

As early as October 1965 co-ordinated anti-war rallies had been held in over forty American cities, as well as in several foreign capitals. These were peaceful occasions, in most cases not attended by more than a few thousand protesters, although at the end of November a crowd of thirty-five thousand, organized by SANE (Committee for a Sane Nuclear Policy), marched with commendable discipline on the White House. The burning of draft-cards in public places became commonplace, and there were isolated acts of even greater individual derring-do: at the beginning of November Norman Morrison, a Quaker, set fire to himself outside the Pentagon in an imitation of the Buddhist self-immolations that had so shocked Saigon; and he in turn was copied by Roger Allen La Porte, a Catholic, outside the United Nations building in New York a week later.

During the course of 1967 the pattern began to change, towards far larger demonstrations and an increased level of militancy. Violence, particularly in resisting arrest, became more common as an increasing number of young men refused to be conscripted into the military, preferring either imprisonment or voluntary exile. At the same time an 'International Tribunal', led by European intellectuals including Jean-Paul Sartre and Bertrand Russell, was established in Stockholm, specifically to investigate American 'war crimes' in Indochina. In April and again in October there were massive rallies, in New York, San Francisco and Washington; and in December further demonstrations tied in with a nationwide 'Stop the Draft Week'.

Public agitation continued throughout 1968, the showpiece coming in Chicago during the Democratic Nominating Convention held in late August. Yet according to opinion polls, America was still evenly divided for and against the war, and apropos of Johnson's direction of it. In October 1967 polls even suggested that three-quarters of the population believed that the anti-war movement was positively 'hurting' the country. The government was therefore as secure in pursuing the war as it would have been in abandoning it. But for Johnson the telling blow came from what he saw as the desertion of the media. Such opinion-forming newspapers as the *New York Times* and *Washington Post* were no longer prepared to toe the government line, as they had broadly done before the Tet Offensive.

The new mood was inadvertently summed up by Walter Cronkite, a venerated television reporter, when on 1 February 1968 a CBS studio microphone picked up an aside never intended for broadcast: 'What the hell is going on?' Cronkite snapped. 'I thought we were winning this war.' 'If I've lost Walter Cronkite,' Johnson is alleged to have remarked in the White House shortly afterwards, 'I've lost Mr Average Citizen.' More to the point, Johnson's administration could no longer realistically aspire to having its views put squarely in front of the average citizen. Hence, in large measure, Johnson's withdrawal from the presidential race. As the black civil rights leader Martin Luther King had expressed it in a slogan the year before, 'The Great Society has been shot down on the battlefield of Vietnam.'

Ironically, however, this great upheaval led not to the triumph of the liberal wing of the Democratic Party, but to the triumph of the conservative Republicans. In November the presidential election was won by Richard Nixon. By then Robert Kennedy had, like his brother, been assassinated, as had Martin Luther King. In early June, Westmoreland had been replaced as commander of US forces in Vietnam by General Creighton Abrams, and in Paris the first round of peace talks that were to last five years had been held between Harriman and Xuan Thuy, an equally middle-ranking DRVN official. On 31 October Johnson, in a vain attempt to win support for the compromise Democrat candidate, his own Vice-President Hubert Humphrey, had ordered the complete cessation of the bombing of North Vietnam. But by then Richard Nixon's star was firmly in the ascendant.

Nixon took office in January 1969. During his election campaign he had stolen the Democrats' thunder by declaring his determination to withdraw American troops from Vietnam. Simultaneously, he had promised tough negotiations with Hanoi. Peace with honour was his motto, and his presidency was very largely consumed in an attempt to reconcile these two seemingly contradictory ambitions.

But while, like Johnson before him, he soon discovered that the realities of the conflict inhibited his activities, Nixon's political approach was radically different. Seldom stinting on anti-communist rhetoric, he nonetheless purposefully sought dialogue with both Moscow and Peking, albeit in a bid to derive whatever benefit was to be had from tensions that now pitted the two communist powers against each other. He was also less inclined than his predecessor to be cowed by public opinion. Indeed, his illegal application of the techniques of electronic surveillance on some of those who opposed the war – most notably Daniel Ellsberg, the man who passed the *Pentagon Papers* to the *New York Times* – started him on a road that led ultimately to Watergate, and his downfall.

Most critically perhaps, as regards Vietnam, Nixon introduced a radically different system of leadership. Whereas Johnson had relied upon his cabinet, and even more upon inter-departmental committees, Nixon relied upon his own counsels and those of one other man, Henry Kissinger, his National Security Adviser. His chosen Secretary of Defence, Melvin Laird, was regularly frozen out of decision-making, while Secretary of State William Rogers was responsible for very little of America's foreign policy during the Nixon era. Rather Nixon opened up a direct channel between the White House and the Joint Chiefs of Staff; and Nixon and Kissinger, a Harvard professor of international relations, between them accounted for most political and diplomatic initiatives.

The advantage, and disadvantage, of this system run by a gang of two was that it allowed for considerably more secrecy than had ever obtained under Johnson, even though Nixon was ill-disposed towards the CIA and other clandestine state agencies. There were correspondingly fewer restraints on potentially unpopular decisions. Yet that same secrecy had to be protected, and when it was not, or could not be, as in the case of the secret bombing of Cambodia, public anger served only further to disintegrate American society.

By instinct and in practice the least democratic of modern American Presidents, Nixon nonetheless endeavoured to attain a solution to the Vietnam problem that would satisfy both wings of American opinion: those who thought that the war's aims should be pursued, whatever the domestic political cost; and those who thought that US forces should be withdrawn entirely, however humiliating this might appear in the eyes of the world. His and Kissinger's strategy was threefold: in fact to begin the withdrawal of American troops from South Vietnam; to continue the war forcefully with what means remained, relying especially on the existing heavy concentration of air-power, in the hope of wresting concessions from Hanoi in the Paris negotiations; and to carry forward the 'Vietnamization' of the war (begun by Johnson). In other words, the ARVN and other Saigon forces were to be gradually built up until the point was reached when, with no more than advisory assistance, of the sort that the NVA received all along from the DRVN's Soviet and Chinese allies, they could reasonably be expected to conduct the war themselves. In the meantime no ground was to be yielded to the communists. On the contrary, in several key respects the war against them was to be widened.

The Paris peace negotiations became deadlocked almost as soon as they were started, and effectively remained so for the next four years. The United States, presenting in May 1968 a common front with President Thieu, insisted that in return for the withdrawal of American troops the DRVN must recall all its forces from the South. This was unacceptable to Hanoi. Hanoi, on the other hand, insisted that any military agreement must also contain a political settlement: that Thieu should be removed, and that the Saigon government should be replaced by a coalition that would include members of the NLF. This was unacceptable to Washington.

Unknown to the Secretaries of State and Defense, however, and following a private letter from Nixon to Ho Chi Minh, on 4 August 1969 Kissinger held the first of many secret meetings with Le Duc Tho which did eventually lead to an agreement, in January 1973. Through the exercise of 'personal diplomacy', the main sticking points on both sides were overcome.

Yet despite some changes in the diplomatic and political climates, the war itself continued unabated. Indeed, the Paris talks inspired rather than restrained military activity, since strength on the battlefield could be translated into strength at the negotiating table. Paradoxically, in light of the waning of public support for the conflict inside America, the period immediately after Tet was generally the one of greatest setback for the communists, and of greatest success for Saigon and its allies.

Under what remained of Westmoreland's command, and then under the beginning of General Abrams', search-and-destroy operations continued to be mounted. Simultaneously Thieu and his fellow generals pursued a new pacification campaign – called the Phoenix Program – inside the Mekong delta and other low-lying regions. Originally conceived by the CIA in 1967, this involved infiltrating agents into peasant communities in order to identify and root out subversives and revolutionaries. Its impact was considerable, even though its methods were violent and its victims often innocent. By 1969 it was claimed that some 19,534 Viet Cong had been 'neutralized' this way, of whom 6,187 had been summarily executed. Thereafter the numbers continued to rise. An untoward element of the Phoenix Program, however, was its 'quota' system. Agents and their henchmen were told in advance how many of the enemy they were expected to net, and they duly complied. It is also thought that up to seventy per cent of actual Viet Cong succeeded, once they had been apprehended, in regaining their freedom with bribes. Nonetheless, Phoenix substantially impaired the political and military capability of indigenous communism; and it became one more in a growing list of factors that was to give the communist victory, when eventually it came, its distinctively northern character.

The NVA regiments sent south to take advantage of the general uprising that Hanoi hoped the Tet Offensive would provoke had, with the exceptions of the fighting at Khe Sanh and Hué, generally avoided the actions of the earlier part of 1968. They therefore remained a threat and became the main target of US operations. An abiding, and finally elusive, objective was to find and destroy COSVN, the Central Office for South Vietnam, or communist headquarters, believed to be somewhere near the Cambodian border to the north-west of Saigon.

But concentrations of enemy regulars also existed in other parts of the country, particularly in the Central Highlands. It was here, in the A Shau valley, close up to the Laotian border to the south-west of Hué, that the next defining engagement took place. The valley itself was twenty-five miles long and two miles wide, and was known to be an NVA base area for units coming off the Ho Chi Minh Trail. It had been held by the communists since December 1965. Westmoreland, in one of his last significant actions as MACV commander, ordered the 1st Cavalry Division (Airborne) to retake it. Operation Delaware commenced on 24 April 1968, but was abandoned on 11 May. Abrams decided to give the A Shau a second shot in August, but again nothing much was achieved. One problem was that the floor of the valley was pitted with small, densely foliaged hills, making assault by helicopter difficult.

But Abrams did not give up. Immediately after the second attempt, he ordered his engineers to begin building a road that would connect Route 1 to A Shau itself, thus solving the problem of how to keep his ground assault teams supplied. By December this road had reached the eastern end of the valley, and in January 1969 Operation Dewey Canyon set off to secure the entire channel. Once this was done, Operation Massachusetts Striker was launched against the communist camps. This, however, only succeeded in driving the NVA

battalions towards a group of taller hills at the western end of A
Shau. In particular, the communists sought refuge on Hill 937,
known variously as Ap Bia or 'Hamburger Hill'.

The bid to reduce Ap Bia duly became another epic landmark in
the futility of the American war. For nine days, between 11 and 20
May, a mixed force of American airborne and ARVN infantry, five
battalions strong and led by Lt.-Col. Honeycutt, assaulted nearly
every face of the hill. Above them were an estimated 1,200
communists, mainly entrenched in concrete bunkers that rendered
air and artillery support largely redundant. In a sense it was Khe
Sanh in reverse. On this occasion the enemy occupied the seemingly
impregnable higher ground. Nevertheless, by dint of intense fire-
fights and hand-to-hand combat, backed up by savage aerial
bombardment – one million pounds of ordnance, including 152,000
lbs of napalm – Operation Apache Snow (as the attack on Ap Bia was
designated) succeeded in its mission. An estimated 633 enemy-kill
was recorded, against seventy Americans.

And yet what was a strange and extraordinary feat of arms served
only to fuel domestic opposition to the war. On 5 June Hamburger
Hill (so called on account of 'what it did' to those who fought it) was
abandoned, along with the rest of the A Shau valley, prompting
Senator Edward Kennedy to call the operation 'senseless and
irresponsible'. Like Khe Sanh, Ap Bia proved quixotic. As they had
done in every other major engagement in the Central Highlands, the
communists, once they realized an immediate victory was beyond
them, retreated into Laos. They could be defeated, but they could
never be vanquished.

But even as it was fought, the battle of Ap Bia, marking perhaps
the high point of American gallantry, was an anachronism. While
Abrams was ordered not to deploy US forces in any further such
campaigns, the process of Vietnamization was already under way.
As early as June 1968 President Thieu promulgated the 'general
mobilization' law, rendering all South Vietnamese males aged
between sixteen and fifty liable to military service. By the end of the
year Saigon's combined forces totalled 643,000 men; by 1971 over a
million. To underwrite this expansion, US financial and material aid
to Thieu was massively increased. At the same time Nixon embarked
on his promised, election-winning troop withdrawals. In early July
1969 a battalion of the US 9th Infantry Division was brought back
home, the first of a twenty-five thousand troop reduction. Then in

September and December Nixon announced the withdrawal of a further ninety-one thousand by April 1970.

This scaling-down of American forces continued for the next three years. Having reached its peak of 549,000 after Tet – Johnson had actually agreed to an increment of some 10,500 troops – the number of American servicemen in South Vietnam declined steadily. Thus by December 1970 there were fewer than 300,000, and midway through 1972 fewer than 125,000. But to balance these developments, and to maintain pressure on North Vietnam, in other ways Nixon widened the conflict, particularly in regard to Laos and Cambodia.

In both countries supposedly neutralist governments were finding it hard to contain communist movements. The Pathet Lao, closely allied to the North Vietnamese and controlling nearly all the land close to the Vietnamese borders, had reduced their country to a state of civil war for several years. Thus although the infiltration of NVA units down the Ho Chi Minh Trail technically violated the Geneva agreements, there were innate difficulties in effecting any kind of rebuff. The CIA had long conducted a 'secret war' more or less on behalf of the recognized government, mounting relatively small-scale operations against the communist guerrillas; but without a commitment of the same proportions as its commitment to South Vietnam, Washington could do little more than conduct a holding operation.

In Cambodia the situation was, superficially, more salutary. The ruler, Prince Norodom Sihanouk, faced a lesser threat from Cambodian communists – or the Khmer Rouge, as he called them. On the other hand, the regular incursions of Viet Cong and then the NVA into his eastern territories, as they sought sanctuary from American operations, were a significant threat, both in themselves and in the encouragement they might give to native Cambodian guerrilla groups.

The question of whether or not to carry the war into Cambodia had exercised White House, State Department and Defense Department officials throughout the latter stages of Johnson's administration. So long as Vietnamese communists could find safe shelter across the border, there was little likelihood that the war in the South could be brought to a satisfactory conclusion. On the other hand, to extend American military activities into Cambodia risked not only public outcry in the United States, but greater support for Hanoi from Moscow and Peking.

Nixon resolved this dilemma, or sought to resolve it, by carrying the war into Cambodia secretly. As early as late February 1969, and with the complicity of both Kissinger and Sihanouk, he authorized the bombing of Viet Cong and NVA base areas. Operation Menu, subdivided into operations Breakfast, Lunch, Dinner, Supper and Snack, began on 16 March and continued for fourteen months. In the main it was carried out by B–52s, and it caused the same kind of damage on its target areas as the USAF had already wreaked on parts of the South Vietnamese landscape. Rightly Nixon adjudged that the DRVN could scarcely object without drawing attention to its own violations of Cambodian neutrality. At the same time, he sought to exploit the differences between the Soviet Union and China. To Moscow he offered talks on the limitation of strategic nuclear weapons, while to Peking he offered friendship.

These high and dangerous policies paid only partial dividends. While a much publicized visit by Nixon and Kissinger to Peking in February 1972, and a summit with Brezhnev in May, did much to stabilize the cold war, now a quarter of a century in the making, attempts to influence Hanoi through Hanoi's allies were less auspicious. At heart neither the Soviet Union nor China wanted to withdraw its support for North Vietnam for fear of letting the other hold sway in Indochina. Both communist powers therefore continued to supply Hanoi with arms and other valuable aid.

The Cambodian dimension of Nixon's grand strategy proved even less satisfactory, and for Cambodia ultimately disastrous. The net effect of Operation Menu, far from destroying communist sanctuaries, was to drive the Vietnamese deeper into Cambodia, towards the capital Phnom Penh. The unleashing of American bombs also considerably enhanced the appeal of the Khmer Rouge, who were therefore able to expand their forces. Now there was revolutionary insurrection in the whole of Indochina. As Sihanouk's government wavered, greater American involvement in the affairs of Cambodia became a necessity. In the spring of 1970, with Washington's connivance, Sihanouk was ousted by his own Deputy Prime Minister, Lon Nol. Sihanouk, a consummate self-server, promptly found himself in Peking, where he pledged his support for Pol Pot, the Khmer Rouge leader. In 1975, when the Khmer Rouge finally entered Phnom Penh to inaugurate their reign of terror, the fact that they were associated with the erstwhile monarch greatly enhanced their legitimacy in the eyes of ordinary Cambodians.

Lon Nol, by contrast, was distinctly the United States' man. No sooner was he installed in the presidential palace than, by prearrangement, he made urgent appeals for American aid. With Washington's help, he set about transforming himself from a capable soldier into an unpopular 'puppet' ruler. In particular, he sanctioned incursions by American and Saigon units on to Cambodian soil. While Sihanouk had at least attempted to preserve his kingdom's integrity, Lon Nol appeared to many of his people willing to sacrifice it. Worse, as the US air force inevitably directed its missions further westwards, uninvolved peasant communities were subjected to aerial bombardment.

The bombing, begun in March 1969, remained secret for just two months. It was exposed in May by William Beecher, a journalist, in the *New York Times*. While this dramatically fuelled a fresh wave of anti-war protest, Nixon responded by asking the FBI to place a tap on Beecher's telephone line. In the autumn he took steps to repair his credibility with the public, both by his announcement of further troop reductions and, on 3 November, by a televised address to the nation in which he shrewdly appealed for the support of 'the silent majority' in pursuing what he projected as a necessary war. Opinion polls showed that there was indeed a narrow majority still prepared to back the government's policy. On 30 April 1970, however, such credit as Nixon had managed to recoup evaporated when, following the fall of Sihanouk, he announced that a joint US–ARVN task force, numbering up to twenty thousand men, was being sent into Cambodia to attack communist bases.

This immediately triggered another flurry of nationwide anti-war demonstrations, particularly at university and college campuses, where sit-ins became the order of the day. At Kent State University, on 4 May, tragedy struck when National Guardsmen, unwisely called in by the Governor of Ohio, James Rhodes, opened fire on a large body of recalcitrant students, killing four of them. Loss of life as a result of the Vietnam war, it seemed, was no longer confined to Indochina. At once a massive army of demonstrators, around a hundred thousand individuals, marched on Washington.

But while Nixon did what he could to placate his opponents, apologizing to the nation for what had happened, his more purposeful response was to set up a secret surveillance team, answerable directly to himself and having nothing to do with existing state security agencies. In the first instance this illegal 'internal espionage' unit, sometimes dubbed 'the plumbers', directed its attentions towards those 'subversives' who were at the forefront of the anti-war movement. During the course of 1971, however, it broadened its scope to spy on the congressional opposition, in the form of the Democratic Party's campaign headquarters, housed in the Watergate building. Thus, out of America's involvement in Vietnam, was born the scandal that not only brought down the President, but also constituted the gravest domestic political crisis to affect the United States in the modern period.

The incursions into Cambodia had little strategic impact on the course of the war, except that their relative failure was one of several factors that provoked the Senate to repeal the Gulf of Tonkin Resolution, on 24 June 1970. Two main operations were staged, in May and June, against the two areas of Cambodia – nicknamed the Parrot's Beak and the Fish Hook – where its borders bulged into Vietnam, to the north-west of Saigon. But although some sizeable ammunition and supply dumps were found and either seized or destroyed, no large concentrations of enemy troops were located. Nor was there any sign of COSVN.

A worrying aspect of the campaign was the apparent unwilling-ness of ARVN units, who made up the bulk of the twenty thousand strong expeditionary forces, to expose themselves or push deep into the jungle. Some US commando, or Special Forces, units conducted independent forays, as indeed they had been doing covertly for several years, but with little more success; and in August, mindful of the mood of Congress, Nixon ordered that all combat troops be withdrawn from across the frontier.

Originally these operations, and the bombing of eastern Cambodia, had been conceived as an alternative to a renewal of the bombing of North Vietnam for bringing pressure on Hanoi at the Paris peace talks. They were also designed to test the efficacy of 'Vietnamization'. But neither objective was gained. In Paris, time was already beginning to run out for Kissinger. In August he intimated to Le Duc Tho that the United States might be prepared to compromise if the DRVN would do the same. In essence he proposed what came to be known as a 'standstill ceasefire': that Washington would no longer require the withdrawal of NVA troops from South Vietnam, on condition that Hanoi dropped its insistence on a coalition government that excluded President Thieu. This trade-off Le Duc Tho refused. He knew that, unless Nixon reversed his own troop-withdrawal policy, the day would come when the communists would have nothing more to fear than a straight fight with the ARVN.

On the latest showing the ARVN was no match for the NVA. But while the Pentagon was disappointed by the performance of Saigon's military, the Vietnamization programme continued. The great hope of Nixon and Kissinger was that, by enabling South Vietnam to defend itself, they would escape censure for selling out to communism in South-East Asia, while placating the 'peaceniks'. Towards the end of 1970 MACV began planning a further operation – Lam Son 719 – that would again test the ARVN's mettle, as well as widen the war against the communists. The objective this time was to attack NVA troop concentrations in Laos and, if possible, cut off the Ho Chi Minh Trail. And while ARVN units would enjoy the full support of American forces on the Vietnamese side of the border, beyond it they would be on their own.

Lam Son 719 was preceded, at the end of January 1971, by Operation Dewey Canyon II. A South Vietnamese mechanized infantry brigade was to clear Route 9 from the coast to Khe Sanh. There, a series of firebases close to the frontier were to be reactivated, so that the ARVN column, when it advanced into Laos, could do so under artillery cover. A detachment of the US 101st Airborne Division meanwhile created a diversion further south, in the A Shau valley. All this part of the campaign went according to plan, as did the initial stages of Lam Son 719 itself. On 8 February the ARVN commander, Lieutenant-General Hoang Xuan Lam, advanced his infantry and armour towards the Laotian township of Tchepone, which was quickly occupied by forward units. The South Vietnamese air force and air infantry meanwhile, adopting their tactics copybook-style from earlier American operations, created landing zones on either side of Route 9, to enable airborne reinforcements to be brought in.

At Tchepone, however, thirteen miles inside Laos, the operation halted. Although the plan had been to advance on NVA concentrations, or at least as far as the main artery of the Trail, General Hoang was loath to risk either his men or his equipment. The NVA meanwhile gathered themselves in the hills on either side of Route 9 between Tchepone and Khe Sanh. Fearing that he would now be cut off, Hoang ordered his column to retreat from Tchepone on 19 March. It did so in grave disorder, and was only spared annihilation by called-up American air-strikes at communist positions in the hills.

Even so, Hoang lost over fifteen hundred men, with another five and half thousand wounded.

Clearly the ARVN had a long way to go before it could be entrusted with the running of the war. Nor perhaps was that prospect much enhanced when, on 3 October, a single-candidate election confirmed Nguyen Van Thieu, a vain, uncritical and unassured leader, as President of the southern republic.

For the communists, after the military reverses of 1968, and the death of Ho Chi Minh on 2 September 1969, the tide of war was once again turning in their favour.

Although the Tet Offensive of 1968 had been followed in May of the same year by a 'Post-Tet' offensive, the latter was but a pale imitation of the former. The same was true of a 'Mini-Tet' campaign in February 1969. Disruptive guerrilla attacks had been organized throughout the towns and cities of the South, but they had scant impact on either US forces or the ARVN. Their purpose had been little more than to remind their opponents that the communists were still 'alive'. Thereafter, as Hanoi sought to replenish the depleted ranks of its armies and rebuild damaged political command, military initiatives were few and far between. Efforts focused mainly on creating enlarged base areas in Cambodia, Laos and the Central Highlands, and on expanding the Trail.

By the middle of 1971 much of their former confidence had been regained. The continuing political turmoil in America, and the hardening of worldwide opinion against the United States' continued involvement, augured well – as did Nixon's announcement towards the end of the year of a further reduction in American troops. With another 45,000 men ordered home, that left a mere 139,000 on Vietnamese soil. In addition, Australia and New Zealand had withdrawn all their troops. And then, of course, there was the proven ineptitude of the Saigon army.

Although, after Ho's demise, the presidency of North Vietnam had passed to Ton Duc Thang, the effective new leader was Le Duan, General Secretary of the Lao Dong (Workers' Party) since 1959. Like Ho Chi Minh he was an Annamite (born in Quang Tri province in 1908), and he had a similar aptitude for forging unity among those around him. He also had a particular interest in seeing the conflict through to a successful conclusion, since it had been his recommendations to the Central Committee in 1959 that had led North Vietnam to sponsor their southern counterparts.

The problem that faced Le Duan and his senior colleagues – chief among them Prime Minister Pham Van Dong and Defence Minister Vo Nguyen Giap – was whether to wait until Nixon had withdrawn all his men, or to force the issue sooner.

The first course was attended by two risks. It was uncertain whether Nixon intended withdrawing all his men before a peace had been concluded in Paris; and the longer Hanoi delayed, the better armed and better trained would Saigon's indigenous forces become. Already three-quarters of South Vietnam's provinces had reverted to Saigon's control; and the resolve and capacity of the Viet Cong to continue the struggle was necessarily questionable. There was also the nagging question of how long both Soviet and Chinese military aid, indispensable to any NVA campaign, would be forthcoming when the two communist powers were so clearly at odds with each other.

The second course risked depletion of men, equipment and morale. Tet had set Hanoi's war effort back by perhaps two years, and a similar reversal would only buy more time for Saigon. On the other hand, a reminder that the communists were once again capable of staging a large-scale offensive might very well persuade Kissinger to make more concessions to Le Duc Tho. 1972 was also election year in the United States. The American public's unprecedented reactions against the war in the wake of Tet, largely unexpected by the DRVN, had not been forgotten.

Having weighed the pros and cons, the inner core of the Central Committee, under Le Duan's guidance, decided in favour of a general offensive in the early part of 1972 – what in fact became known as the Spring or Easter Offensive. One factor that enabled this outcome was a substantial package of military aid gleaned from Moscow during Le Duan's visit there in the spring of 1971. Fearing that China would rule the roost in East Asia, the Kremlin had promised Hanoi a broad shopping-bag of more or less modern weapons, including T–34, T–54 and PT–76 tanks, 130mm long-range artillery and the latest in mobile surface-to-air missiles.

In due course Giap presented what would be his last strategic battle plan. There were to be three main thrusts: one across and along the DMZ, aimed at Quang Tri; one coming out of Cambodia towards Saigon through Tay Ninh and Binh Long provinces; and a main attack out of Laos through Kontum in the Central Highlands towards the coastal province of Binh Dinh.

It failed, partly because Giap had over-estimated his own strength; partly because he had taken insufficient account of the United States' continued air-power; and partly because he was unable to incorporate an element of total surprise – from November 1971 onwards US reconnaissance missions picked up the increased number of convoys moving down the Trail, including tanks, armoured vehicles and mobile batteries. Over 250 of his newly donated tanks were destroyed by American planes. Also the ARVN, in some quarters, showed an unexpected willingness to fight.

The offensive got under way on 10 March 1972. Firebases south of the DMZ, manned by the ARVN, were attacked and largely neutralized by long-range artillery guns positioned in the North. Simultaneously, three NVA divisions advanced across the Seventeenth Parallel in the direction of Quang Tri. The overwhelmed ARVN 3rd Division retreated untidily south of the smaller town of Dong Ha, leaving it to some US advisers to organize the destruction of bridges across the Mieu Giang River in their rear. The NVA divisions, however, merely diverted westwards and crossed the Mieu Giang at Can Lo. There they joined up with a fourth division that had moved eastwards from Laos along the A Shau valley. After two weeks' hard fighting, the communists broke through their enemy's lines, pushing the ARVN back towards Quang Tri itself on 2 April. On 27 April a secondary ARVN defensive line was also breached. Quang Tri now came under siege, yielding on 1 May. The routed Saigon army retreated in full panic southwards along Highway One, only to be shelled mercilessly by the NVA's powerful artillery.

Nixon, recognizing that this attack heralded an all-out onslaught against the southern republic, which if at all successful would further strengthen Le Duc Tho's hand in Paris, ordered a resumption of bombing missions against North Vietnam. This was the first time since November 1968 that American planes – other than reconnaissance aircraft – had entered Hanoi's airspace.

The initial targets were the road and rail passes behind the enemy's lines. At first only Phantom F–4 fighter-bombers, using both conventional ordnance and laser-guided 'smart' bombs, were deployed in a narrowly defined section to the north of the DMZ. But from 5 May onwards, B–52s were authorised to attack a much greater range of targets, including the port facilities at Haiphong and strategic infrastructure (such as the Paul Doumer bridge) in and around Hanoi. At the same time, in an effort to cajole the North Vietnamese delegation in France, he let it be known that he was not averse to considering the use of nuclear weapons. This he called the 'madman theory'. Deliberately, he sought to project the impression that if pushed too far he might lose control and unleash whatever came to hand on the DRVN.

The actual bombing, though effective in terms of destroying equipment, causing casualties and – particularly once the Ham Rung bridge across the Ma River had been taken out – disrupting communist supply lines, did not, in the northernmost sector of the campaign, succeed in blunting the offensive; while low cloud-cover reduced the USAF's opportunities for inflicting heavy damage on the divisions massed around Quang Tri.

Elsewhere, however, conditions were more favourable to the aerial interception of Giap's forces. The second advance, out of Cambodia, began on 2 April, when the communists launched a feint towards Tay Son city, drawing off a large detachment of Thieu's forces. The main attack commenced on 5 April, when the mixed NVA–Viet Cong 9th Division assaulted Loc Ninh, on the road to the capital. Loc Ninh capitulated the following day, and now the communists advanced up Route 13 towards An Loc.

An Loc, however, had been heavily reinforced by the ARVN's 5th Division, as well as by four Ranger battalions. There now began, on 7 April, a finally unsuccessful siege that was to last ninety-five days. An Loc was subjected to withering artillery bombardment, and on 13 April six NVA T–54 tanks even entered the town's main street. These, however, were swiftly incapacitated by anti-tank weapons. For once the ARVN defended its position well. But the battle was effectively turned by a massive intervention of American air-power. B–52s at one end of the scale, and Cobra helicopters at the other, devastated communist positions. By 11 July, when the last of the badly battered besieging forces melted away in the direction whence they had come, the immediate threat to Saigon had been seen off.

The third prong of the Easter Offensive, conducted in the Central Highlands, fared no better, despite initial victories against ARVN outposts. On 12 April a firebase overlooking Dak To to the east of Kon Tum came under NVA attack. Eleven days later the communists opened fire on a number of other ARVN outposts. In nearly every case they easily overran their targets. Even in entrenched positions occupying high ground, Saigon troops were no match for their northern counterparts. But while the communists sought to march their divisions to the coast, in May they were held up outside Kon Tum itself. Preparing to lay siege to the city, they were once again heavily punished by the full panoply of American air-power.

This failure to break through to Route 1 spelled the end of the campaign. Under their new commander, Ngo Quang Truong, the ARVN corps that had been driven from Quang Tri formed a new defensive line twenty-five miles north of Hué. Had Kon Tum fallen, then its rear would have been severely exposed to the enemy. Instead a slow counter-offensive, strongly aided by US fighter-bombers now able to operate effectively under clearer skies, was mounted; and although Quang Tri was not retaken until September, following an unusually desperate battle, by the end of May the Easter Offensive had all but petered out.

Communist losses for the whole campaign were put by MACV at around a hundred thousand men – two or three times those sustained during Tet four years earlier. Set against these were some fifty thousand ARVN killed. Once again Giap had shown an almost incredible willingness to expend the lives of his troops, all to little avail. And yet, at critical moments in each of the three theatres, reserves had been unavailable. Except on the fringes of the Mekong delta, where some villages and districts were returned to Viet Cong rule, and in an area stretching ten miles south of the DMZ, where the NVA dug in and held their ground, nothing had been gained.

On the other hand, it had been made abundantly clear that, without American air-cover, the Saigon regime was vulnerable. Both the morale and the skills of its troops were suspect. Having gained concessions from the United States in Paris, therefore, Hanoi could contemplate making at least one concession in return. Soon Le Duc Tho would drop his insistence that President Thieu be removed. The important thing was to get rid of America's air force.

During the offensive, some seven hundred US warplanes had been on permanent 24-hour call, out of a total of 1,200 bombers, fighters and reconnaissance craft based in South-East Asia. Despite the greater sophistication of North Vietnam's air defences, B–52s could still fly over enemy territory with relative impunity. Operation Linebacker, launched on 8 May 1972, combining elements of the USAF and naval and marine air forces, and escorted by F–4 and F–105 fighters, caused widespread damage. In the five months of its continuance, some 155,000 tons of bombs were dropped on nearly every military and strategic target conceivable. In addition, mines were released into Haiphong harbour; and American planes continued to destroy both the Cambodian and the Laotian forests.

The more troops he withdrew, it seemed, the more damage Nixon was able to inflict. Yet it was all to a purpose: to win the forthcoming November presidential election by finally disentangling America from Vietnam. Both Washington and Hanoi therefore wanted an agreement; and so, at last, an agreement was reached.

On 1 August 1972 Le Duc Tho intimated to Henry Kissinger that his government's reconsideration of President Thieu's status. This, combined with Nixon's earlier decision not to press for the withdrawal of the North's troops from the areas they held in the South, was the essential breakthrough. The details of a document could now be worked out.

On 21 October, amid international rejoicing, it was announced in Paris that a draft treaty acceptable to both Hanoi and Washington had been prepared. On 23 October, Operation Linebacker was halted. On 7 November, Richard Nixon won a second term of office in a landslide victory against his Democrat rival George McGovern.

'Tricky Dicky', the manipulative, devious genius of American politics, had, with Kissinger's help, pulled not so much a white rabbit as a dove out of his hat. Yet one problem remained. On 24 October President Thieu had denounced the terms of the agreement. The substantive parts of the peace deal had been negotiated behind his back. Without his signature there could be no treaty; at least, not one that would hold up in the eyes of the still considerable conservative, anti-communist American electorate.

Nixon astutely rode this problem until after the election. Then, on 14 November, he pledged Thieu that he would 'take swift and severe retaliatory action' should the communists fail to honour the ceasefire clauses. He also promised an additional and immediate military aid package worth in excess of one billion dollars. Thieu wavered. Then in December he presented Kissinger with a long list of amendments to the agreement which Kissinger duly pushed at Le Duc Tho. The latter, who had conducted his side of the negotiations largely without reference to the wishes of the NLF, insisted on abiding by the terms that had already been achieved.

Once again the peace talks were deadlocked. On 13 December Le Duc Tho angrily left Paris and returned to Hanoi. Nixon responded on the 18th by authorising Operation Linebacker II: the most intense bombing campaign against the North of the entire war. For thirteen days, with a brief pause over Christmas, the DRVN was subjected to an unrelenting air assault. Twenty thousand tons of ordnance were dropped, mainly on Hanoi, Haiphong and the arterial road connecting them, in a series of three thousand sorties. Nor were any restrictions as to the nature of their targets given to the pilots and bombardiers.

Although some twenty-six US aircraft were shot down, including fifteen B–52s, Linebacker II had its desired effect. On 8 January 1973 Kissinger and Le Duc Tho resumed the Paris talks, and the following day a fresh agreement was reached. Yet it was not Hanoi that now made new concessions. Rather it was Nixon who gave Thieu an ultimatum: either accept the terms thrashed out in October or forfeit all further US aid whatsoever.

Thieu capitulated. He had no choice. The Paris Peace Agreement was initialled by Kissinger and Le Duc Tho on 23 January, and formally signed by all parties on 27 January. Its terms were easily recognizable. Although fifty US military advisers would continue to assist the Saigon government, all other American military personnel, including air pilots, would be withdrawn from South Vietnam within sixty days. A ceasefire, with immediate effect, was to allow troops on both sides – North and South Vietnamese – to remain in the positions they already occupied. And a full exchange of prisoners was to take place.

Although Nixon and Kissinger recommended it to the American public as the 'peace with honour' they had always sought, the Paris Peace Agreement was in reality an even looser document than the Geneva Accords of 1954. It made no provision whatsoever for any kind of political settlement. There was not even the promise of an election. Instead, in a 'leopard spot' arrangement, communists and non-communists, still heavily armed, were to be left breathing down each other's rifle barrels in a thousand different locations. Nor had anything been done to reduce the still sizeable communist base areas in Cambodia and Laos.

While across the United States the settlement, so long awaited, was greeted with near euphoria, nobody in a position to know thought that the ceasefire would or could last. In Kissinger's haplessly memorable phrase, a 'decent interval' before hostilities resumed was the best that could be hoped for. Yet notwithstanding this, Kissinger and Le Duc Tho were jointly awarded the 1973 Nobel peace prize. Kissinger accepted it. Le Duc Tho declined.

The fighting resumed almost at once. Neither Saigon nor the communists could afford to be complacent. Thieu, apprehensive about the continuing presence of an estimated 150,000 NVA regulars and Viet Cong guerrillas inside his country, immediately set about tightening national security. Within weeks there was something like a return to the draconian measures of the Diem regime. By the end of 1973 he had clawed back some fifteen per cent of the territory disputed between the two sides. He also ordered his army to obstruct the communist occupation of the area immediately south of the Seventeenth Parallel. For their part, the communists defended wherever they were attacked, and sometimes made small-scale pre-emptive sorties.

For a while the military balance continued to stand in Saigon's favour. As an earnest of Nixon's pledge of continued support for the southern republic, Washington had delivered some $2 billion worth of military aid in the period leading up to the Paris Peace Agreement. In addition, the American armed forces deliberately left behind much of their equipment. Thieu now commanded the fourth largest air force in the world. But this bonanza was not to be repeated. The political mood in the United States not only swung sharply away from even the idea of renewed military intervention, but also balked at further hand-outs from the public purse. On 4 June 1973 the Senate approved a bill blocking funds for any further US action in Indochina. On 1 July Congress voted to end the bombing of Cambodia. And on 7 November it again acted, to reinforce the War Powers Resolution, drastically limiting the President's prerogative to commit American forces abroad. In 1974 aid to Saigon, originally proposed at $1.6 billion, was slashed to $700 million.

The effect of these measures, and of Richard Nixon's forced resignation as President on 9 August 1974, was fatal. Obliged to stand on its own feet, the Saigon regime had neither the skill nor the temperament to survive. The population of South Vietnam was once again subjected to heavy taxation, rising unemployment, rampant inflation, escalating corruption and all the rigours of an arthritic police state. The relative affluence induced by the spending power of the American servicemen evaporated, but in the cities the people still hankered after bygone luxuries. Desertion rates among the armed forces once again soared, while the donated equipment fell into disrepair. In particular, spare parts became hard to obtain. The economy was simply unable to sustain a weaponry designed for use by a world power. Militarily, Saigon began losing its edge.

Hanoi watched these developments with the eyes of a vulture. Le Duan and his colleagues never once wavered from their collective intention to conquer the South as soon as circumstances permitted. The reunification of Viet Nam was, after all, the great project of a movement born over forty years before. But for a while caution was necessarily the order of the day. Neither Moscow nor Peking was immediately willing to underwrite the cost of a final campaign. When Pham Van Dong visited the Chinese capital in the spring of 1973, Mao Tse-tung told him: 'I do not have a broom long enough to reach Taiwan, and you do not have a broom long enough to reach Saigon.'

But the Central Committee was not to be denied. Throughout 1973 and 1974 the communists worked to rebuild the army that had been so badly bruised during the Spring Offensive of 1972. By September 1974 nineteen divisions were fully operational, twelve of them located in base areas south of the Seventeenth Parallel. Work was carried out to improve further the Ho Chi Minh Trail, no longer the target of aerial attack; special care was taken to maintain the existing arsenal of Soviet equipment; and a new base area, under the command of General Tran Van Tra, was created at Loc Ninh, seventy miles north of Saigon in the foothills of the Central Highlands.

Le Duc Tho, having returned from Paris, resumed his former duties, which were to oversee the development of the revolution in the South. Always conservative in his thinking, he considered that perhaps a general uprising could be engineered sometime in 1976. Tran Van Tra, now able to drive back up the Trail in a few days, arrived in Hanoi to confer with his leaders. In his opinion an offensive could be staged much sooner, and he pressed Le Duan to bring communist plans forward. Typically, Le Duan steered a middle course. He told Tran Van Tra that military actions in the South should be stepped up, but that 1976 remained the likeliest date for completion of the Revolution.

Back in Loc Ninh, Tran Van Tra at once began an offensive against Phuc Long province, to his east. This he launched on 13 December 1974. Without warning, ARVN positions came under intense communist fire. On 6 January 1975 the provincial capital, Phuoc Binh, fell easily into his hands.

The inherent weakness of the Saigon army, and Thieu's inability to deploy effective air-cover, suddenly suggested to Hanoi that Tran Van Tra had been right all along. The southern republic was there for the taking. In addition, Moscow now declared its willingness to renew assistance. Not to be outdone, Peking promised rice and bullets. General Van Tien Dung, Giap's Chief of Staff, was given operational command and quickly prepared a strategic battle-plan. In several of its details this resembled the Spring Offensive. Most notably, a wedge was to be driven through from the Central Highlands to the coast, cutting South Vietnam in two, and hopefully isolating Thieu's northern corps.

Accordingly, four NVA divisions moved out of Laos at the end of March. On 10 March an artillery barrage opened up against the provincial capital of Ban Me Thuot, a hundred kilometres or so to the north-west of Nha Trang. By noon of the 11th, NVA tanks were rolling down Ban Me Thuot's main street. Once again Saigon's forces, numbering some four thousand, had surrendered without offering any serious resistance.

This swift victory created nationwide turmoil in South Vietnam and, once it became apparent that the United States had no intention of mounting a rescue operation on behalf of its threatened ally, convinced Hanoi to press ahead for immediate reunification. It had been Dung's intention to make further assaults on Pleiku and Kon Tum, to the north of Ban Me Thuot. But now these cities were abandoned, by both their military and civilian populations. Vast trains of self-made refugees began moving towards the coastal enclaves. Route 7, connecting Pleiku to Tuy Hoa, became especially congested. NVA artillery units happily homed in upon what became known as the 'Column of Tears'.

President Thieu, experiencing an absolute loss of nerve, ordered all his forces, including the Airborne Division stationed near Quang Tri, to withdraw to the perimeters of the Mekong delta, which alone was to be defended.

In the face of this bewildering pusillanimity, and with upwards of a million refugees converging on Da Nang, on 23 March General Dung revised his strategy. Instead of bisecting South Vietnam, he decided to focus his attack on Saigon itself. The Ho Chi Minh Campaign, as it was christened, had begun.

It took just over a month. In the north, NVA divisions swept down from the DMZ along Highway 1. One by one the coastal towns fell to the communists, including Hué on 25 March and Da Nang on the 29th. Meanwhile, all around the Mekong delta, NVA regiments and such battalions of the indigenous PLA as still survived prepared to encircle and close in upon the capital.

On 9 April Le Duc Tho arrived by motorcycle at the Loc Ninh headquarters, to help co-ordinate the final thrust, and to ensure that the Central Committee's authority was stamped on the impending victory. As he did so, NVA divisions descended from the Central Highlands, while other units advanced eastwards out of Cambodia.

From the extreme south, Minh Hai, Viet Cong guerrillas and regulars marched north.

Meanwhile the communist army advancing down Highway 1 had reached as far south as Cam Ranh Bay and Phan Thiet. Only at Xuan Loc, to the north-east of Saigon, did the ARVN, in the shape of the 18th Division, stage a proper fight, inflicting heavy casualties on Dung's forces. But on 18 April Xuan Loc too gave up; and by 25 April the battle for Saigon had begun.

By then Thieu, despairing of American help, had resigned the presidency and fled, with his family and his wealth, to Taipei. After several days his place was taken by General Duong Van Minh, the leader of the coup against Diem in 1963, and the only senior Saigon figure who did not attempt to flee what was widely perceived as an imminent communist terror. Instead he remained inside the presidential palace, patiently awaiting the arrival of his adversaries.

That moment was not far off. Within four days, from nearly every direction, communist troops had advanced to the outskirts of the city. Rockets, artillery shells and even air-strikes rained down upon the suburbs. On 29 April, as Dung directed his artillery fire on Tan Son Nhut airport, the United States, having delayed evacuation of its few remaining personnel in order to sustain the myth that American aid would be to hand in the final crisis, activated its last mission in Vietnam: Operation Frequent Wind. Sixty CH–53 helicopters began ferrying some eight thousand individuals (including high-ranking Saigon officials and their families) from pre-selected landing sites to ships of the 7th Fleet standing offshore in the South China Sea.

Some seventy thousand South Vietnamese, unable to fly out, took to the sea in boats. The last helicopter left the roof of the US Embassy shortly after dawn on 30 April. Simultaneously, NVA T–54 tanks crossed over the Saigon River and entered the city proper. Other units entered the capital by other routes, but it was one of these tanks, commanded by Bui Quang Than, that at around 11.00 a.m. knocked down the gates of the presidential palace and motored up to the porticoed steps.

Inside, Duong Van Minh immediately surrendered power. Within the space of a few short weeks South Vietnam had collapsed in the face of an impeccably organized communist onslaught. The country had at last been reunified under the rule of native Vietnamese.

Over the course of the next two to three years small 'reactionary' groups offered token resistance in some of the southern provinces, and as late as 1984 a former ARVN officer, Colonel Mai Van Hanh, attempted to re-establish the southern republic by leading a pitiably small force of volunteers, disguised as People's Army regulars, through Cambodia into An Giang. But the new national leadership, masters of control as well as of discipline, in general assured a minimum of opposition to their rule.

In the wake of the fall of Saigon the widely feared bloodbath did not materialize. There were relatively few killings. Duong Van Minh himself was placed under arrest, but released a year later. On the other hand, some four hundred thousand employees of the erstwhile Saigon regime were imprisoned in re-education camps, while some one million city and town dwellers were forcibly resettled in rural areas. Although for the majority of unfortunates re-education lasted only a year or two, a minority were held far longer. A new bureaucracy was also staffed very largely by northern cadres.

This perhaps was to be expected. But even the voices of southern communists, when they raised criticisms, were sometimes silenced. Notably a book written by General Tran Van Tra, in which he expatiated on the contribution made to the Revolution by his southern comrades, was withdrawn almost as soon as it was published.

Simply because the wars had lasted so long, the final outcome was always likely to reflect the triumph of one half of the nation over the other. In a sense, the Trinh had vanquished the Nguyen.

5

Reunification and Beyond

Marxist revolutionaries in the twentieth century found that their 'historical mission' was not so much leading the working class in advanced capitalist societies, but state-building in underdeveloped countries. It is, therefore, hardly surprising to find that they are among the most strident promulgators of nationalist ideology.

Grant Evans and Kelvin Rowley, *Red Brotherhood at War* (1984/90)

We should promote socialist economy in three respects – systems of ownership, of management and of distribution – so as to make the State-run economic sectors bring into full play their major role and, together with the collective economy, hold their decisive position in the national economy. With regard to the small commodity production economy and private capitalist economy (small capitalists) in some branches of production and servicing domains, they are controlled according to the motto: 'Use them for transformation, and transform them for better use'.

Nguyen Van Linh, *Vietnam: Urgent Problems* (Hanoi, 1988)

The communists achieved victory in 1975 for the same broad reasons that they achieved victory in 1954: during a long and arduous struggle they had, with some outside assistance, been able to mobilize and motivate sufficient numbers of Vietnamese people against an unpopular government; and in Marxism-Leninism they had an effective means of promoting and unifying political and military strategy. However, the fall of Saigon did not usher in the harmonious socialist state prophesied by Ho Chi Minh when, shortly before his death in 1969, he wrote:

> Our mountains shall always be,
> Our rivers shall always be,
> Our people shall always be;
> The American invaders defeated,

> We shall rebuild our land
> Ten times more beautiful.

Rather Viet Nam has remained, literally as well as metaphorically, embattled.

The reasons for this have been external as well as internal. 1975 marked an end neither to the era of warfare nor to Viet Nam's status as a pawn in geopolitical power contests. Eighteen days before the fall of Saigon the Khmer Rouge, led by Pol Pot, marched into Phnom Penh, the capital of neighbouring Cambodia, which now became the Democratic Republic of Kampuchea. In the same month, April, the Pathet Lao entered into a power-sharing arrangement with the official, neutralist (monarchist) government of Laos. By the end of the year, they had taken over completely. But whereas the existence of like-minded, seemingly fraternal regimes in Hanoi, Phnom Penh and Vientiane should have provided some guarantee for the future stability of Indochina, in fact the reverse was true. The Khmer Rouge, far from respecting their former Vietnamese mentors, turned on them, as Pol Pot inaugurated a reign of terror that accounted for the lives of between twenty-five and thirty-five per cent of his own people.

From 1976 onwards the Khmer Rouge regularly raided across the Vietnamese–Cambodian border, sometimes with horrendous consequences. In an assault directed against the western Mekong delta in April 1978, for example, an alleged four thousand Vietnamese villagers were wantonly killed. At Ba Chuc alone, seventeen hundred men, women and children were slain.

The motives for Khmer Rouge aggression were various. On the one hand, there was a historic rivalry between the two peoples, often expressed in territorial disputes. This perhaps was compounded by a resentment on the part of the Khmer Rouge leadership at the master–pupil relationship assumed by the Central Committee in Hanoi. Then there was the sheer absolutism of the Khmer Rouge creed: the will to total power, and the embracing of any means to achieve it. On the other hand, there was a geopolitical dimension. The Khmer Rouge were strongly backed by Peking, and Pol Pot allowed himself to be used by China to pursue the latter's regional ambitions.

Peking had no desire to subjugate Viet Nam directly, but it did seek to be the dominant regional power and to contain the Soviet Union. The Ho Chi Minh Campaign had been carried out with an arsenal of Soviet weapons, and China now feared that, through Hanoi, Moscow would assert its authority in South-East Asia. At the least, therefore, the Khmer Rouge's incursions are likely to have been undertaken with Peking's connivance.

Hanoi, aware that Pol Pot represented the sharp end of Chinese policy in Indochina, for a while eschewed reprisals. The day came, however, when national security considerations had to be put first. On 25 December 1978 Viet Nam invaded Cambodia with an army of 120,000, partly armed with American weapons left over from the previous war. In the face of superior Vietnamese fire-power and military organization, the Khmer Rouge, having lost whatever popular support they had once enjoyed inside Cambodia, disintegrated.

Phnom Penh fell on 7 January 1979. But this, for Viet Nam, was the beginning, not the end, of the fray. Peking, now seemingly thwarted in Indochina, launched its own punitive expedition. On 17 February, in order, as Deng Xiao Ping put it, 'to teach Viet Nam a lesson', two hundred thousand Chinese Red Army troops swept into the north-eastern provinces of Hoang Lien, Ha Tuyen, Cao Bang and Lang Son, destroying whatever was in their way: hospitals, schools, roads, bridges and crops.

The Vietnamese People's Army responded strongly, decimating the invaders, who in true Red Army tradition allowed their supply lines to become over-extended. On 5 March Peking began withdrawing its storm force. But the conflict with China endured on several fronts. Security along the Sino-Vietnamese border had to be maintained against occasional Chinese probes. In several places, Chinese emplacements remained embedded on the Vietnamese side of the border. Peking also contested various territories, most notably the Paracel and Spratly islands in the South China Sea. But most critically, China continued to back the Khmer Rouge.

Having been driven out of eastern and central Cambodia, the Khmer Rouge fell back westwards, against the Thai border. That frontier, however, having previously been closed to them, now opened up; and Pol Pot, escaping annihilation, was able to build up new bases, some of them disguised as refugee camps. In time his army began counter-attacking the Vietnamese. This was made possible by a concert of interests involving Thailand, China and the United States. Having in effect 'lost' Indochina to Moscow, Peking feared encirclement by its Asian neighbours. A deal was therefore struck with Bangkok in 1980 whereby, in return for Thailand turning a blind eye to Khmer Rouge activities inside its territories, China would henceforward cancel the aid it had been giving to communist insurgents inside Thailand.

This eminently suited the United States. In the Pentagon the domino theory had given rise to fears that Thailand, to all intents an American client-state, was next in line for a communist takeover. This threat was now seen to recede. But more than that, by underwriting continuing hostilities between the Khmer Rouge and the Vietnamese, Washington could underwrite the Sino-Soviet division within the communist world. The State Department therefore signalled to Bangkok that the arrangements newly proposed by the Chinese were in accordance with US interests, just as, indeed, it had indicated to Peking in February 1979 that a punitive raid against Viet Nam would not incur American displeasure.

In order to preserve its own security, and a Cambodian government amenable to its wishes, Hanoi was obliged to maintain an army of occupation inside Cambodia. Backed by both the United States and China, and enjoying Thai complicity, Pol Pot would certainly seize any opportunity to reassert Khmer Rouge power.

The effect of this, and of the 'border war' with China, on Viet Nam's economy was in itself severe. But coupled with the daunting tasks of having to care for many thousands of wounded soldiers and civilians and rebuild the fabric of a country devastated by thirty years of war, it was traumatic. Nor, with the important exception of the USSR and its East European satellites, was there much help forthcoming from the international community at large. The United States maintained a strict embargo, under the terms of the Trading with the Enemy Act of 1970, which even extended to a prohibition against the sale of medicines. Thus therapies developed in America to counter contamination by chemical weapons used during the war were denied those who needed them most. Washington also persuaded many of its allies to pursue a similar policy, and worked clandestinely to curb loans and aid packages from both the World Bank and the International Monetary Fund.

Under these circumstances Viet Nam was largely isolated, as China and the United States intended it should be. Hanoi became increasingly dependent on the Soviet Union and the Warsaw Pact countries for aid. But such aid, despite avowals of socialist solidarity, was seldom free. Complicated multinational bartering systems operated by Moscow usually meant that, in real economic terms, Moscow was the net beneficiary. In addition, there was a tranche of war debts that had been accumulated by North Vietnam. These included some $500 million owing to Iraq, on account of oil supplied during the period 1964 to 1975. In 1990 this was still being paid off by the simple expedient, amounting almost to a form of slavery, of utilizing Vietnamese labour inside Iraq for heavy construction work. At the end of their two- or three-year contracts, Vietnamese workers could expect to return home with no more than $100 in their pockets. Following Saddam Hussein's invasion of Kuwait in August 1990, some twelve to sixteen thousand of these workers were stranded in Iraq, their evacuation causing Hanoi further expense.

Meanwhile the physical fabric of Viet Nam had been recovering but slowly. On both sides of the Seventeeth Parallel the successive wars had caused great damage to the country's infrastructure. Ironically, in 1975 no road inside Viet Nam was in as good repair as the main trunk of the Ho Chi Minh Trail. But an even greater ecological destruction had been perpetrated, particularly in the South. An estimated 2.2 million hectares of forest had been blown away by eighteen million gallons of napalm and chemical defoliants, reducing South Vietnam's natural forest-cover by an estimated sixty per cent. The widespread use of arsenic-based Agent Blue had also made up to forty per cent of South Vietnam's farmlands temporarily uncultiveable. Permanent 'Agent Orange Museums' were created at such sites as Khe Sanh and the A Shau valley, while hundreds of thousands of bomb craters left a legacy of largely unwanted and poisonous fish ponds.

There were, in addition, serious knock-on effects. Deforestation created untimely flooding in many areas, washing away significant quantities of valuable topsoil. In a destabilized environment, diseases such as cholera and typhoid flourished. There was also the need to strip what forests remained, in order to furnish wood to rehouse those whose homes had been destroyed by bombs and napalm.

For what was, and always had been, primarily an agricultural economy, such privations would have created near-insoluble problems at the best of times. But an important obstacle to recovery and reconstruction inside Viet Nam was political. Hanoi's insistence on implementing a socialist economy inhibited renewal. The collectivization of peasant holdings in the south considerably sapped the individual farmer's willingness to restore the productivity of the land. Some even deliberately killed their livestock, rather than raise it to be 'stolen' by northern bureaucrats sent to manage co-operatives that bore little resemblance to traditional village social structures.

Annual harvests of rice, the staple food of a rapidly expanding population, consistently fell below their targets. Thus in 1983, a year of drought, typhoons and some famine, the actual national rice-product was sixteen million tons, against a projected twenty-one million tons.

Other sectors of the economy were equally retarded. A contributing factor was the exodus from Viet Nam of a large number of its skilled and professional persons. Many became 'boat people', in the eyes of the outside world a symptom of internal repression and malfunction. From 1976 onwards those wishing to leave Viet Nam, but unable to obtain official permission, set out on the surrounding seas in a variety of medium- and small-sized vessels to seek freedom and prosperity in foreign lands. In the initial stages of this refugee migration, most were southerners, and many of them Chinese, fleeing an anti-Chinese repression brought about by the war of 1979. But increasingly boat people also emanated from the north.

Exactly how many boat people there have been remains uncertain. Many did not survive, victims either of sea-storms or of marauding Thai pirates. Probably the total number of departures is in the region of one million individuals. In 1988 alone some forty-five thousand reached safe havens. Only now, instead of being called refugees, they were termed 'economic migrants', a label that enabled the British government, responsible for some fifty-five thousand Vietnamese held in detention centres in Hong Kong, to seek their 'enforced repatriation'.

For Hanoi, however, the boat people were only a problem insofar as they tarnished the government's image. On the up side, they represented so many fewer mouths to feed. But such was the economic stagnation inside Viet Nam that, in 1986, even the Central Committee was forced to relax its posture. At the Sixth Party Congress the new General Secretary, Nguyen Van Linh, introduced a package of reforms, called *doi moi* (or 'renovation'), designed to stave off national bankruptcy. Henceforward farmers would be able to lease the land they worked and sell their produce in a free market; joint-ventures with foreign companies, of any nationality, were to be encouraged, with tax concessions offered; and some restrictions of indigenous 'capitalists' (entrepreneurs) were lifted.

By 1991, however, it was still touch and go whether *doi moi* would work. While Saigon (renamed Ho Chi Minh City) appeared to be on the brink of a vigorous commercial recovery, prompting the tantalizing prospect of a 'reverse reunification', elsewhere in Viet Nam the economy remained beset with difficulties. Even though the national rice-product for 1989 had risen to twenty-two million tons, making the SRVN a net exporter of rice for the first time in its history, relatively few joint-ventures with foreign companies had been set up. Partly this was due to the continued economic hostility of Washington, but partly it had to do with uncertainty about Viet Nam's political future. Like Deng Xiao Ping's reforms in China, *doi moi* aimed only at economic, not political, renovation. In several key respects Viet Nam continued to embody a repressive regime. There was no freedom of the press, the legal system allowed for no genuine defence of the accused, and there was evidence, produced in an Amnesty International report, that Vietnamese gaols continued to house many purely political prisoners, among them some Buddhist leaders. No clear business code had been promulgated; and, in the face of the collapse of communism in eastern Europe, Nguyen Van Linh had repeatedly announced that Viet Nam would remain a one-party state.

Marxism-Leninism, reinforced by the traditional authoritarian tenets of Confucianism, had, it seemed, placed Viet Nam in a straitjacket from which its ordinary citizens could only look out, when the state-run media permitted, in despair and envy at the prosperity of other East Asian nations: of Japan, South Korea, Taiwan and Singapore in the first rank, and of Thailand, Malaysia and Indonesia in the second. The system that had enabled Viet Nam's national liberation now stymied its political, economic and social development; but because of its past achievements, it set itself above criticism.

Yet to insist on such an analysis is in itself ideologically and culturally specific. There is no universal law that states that all nations should pursue the freedoms promulgated and goals set by the West. Nor is it clear that there is an innate long-term advantage in the liberal-capitalist programme. Indeed, the unrestrained exploitation of the natural environment may yet prove the undoing of not just the West, but the whole planet. In terms relative to its own history, Viet Nam can boast some success. Against considerable odds, its people have achieved national independence, and the great majority of them are better off, and even enjoy more rights, than under either French colonial rule or pre-colonial mandarin rule. A rudimentary democracy exists where there was none before, even though this is limited to the election of Party officials. Material considerations are not the governing factor in the average individual's psychology, especially in the north of the country. A traditional respect for and responsibility towards nature have been preserved. And the necessary process of state-building has, however crudely, been largely achieved.

In September 1989 Hanoi withdrew its army from Cambodia. The Soviet Union could no longer afford to underwrite its cost, the United States had insisted on withdrawal as a precondition for normalizing relations with Viet Nam, and Vietnamese army men were showing signs of mutiny. Since 1978 some fifty to sixty thousand of them had died in Cambodia, as many perhaps from malaria as from Khmer Rouge bullets. But despite the multiplicity of causes behind this move, the net effect was to enhance Viet Nam's standing in the community of nations. It was simply no longer possible for anyone reasonably to argue that Viet Nam represented an aggressive factor in Indochinese politics.

At the same time it became apparent to some observers that the traditional unity within the Central Committee was undergoing a process of erosion; that there was indeed a significant division between 'hard-liners' and reformers.

This was manifest in Viet Nam's relations with China during 1990. Following the break-up of the communist bloc in Europe, Hanoi began leaning once more towards Peking, despite the Tiananmen Square massacre of May 1989. Yet in December 1990 it was reported that a comprehensive, strings-attached aid package offered by China in September had been turned down. Evidently there was a majority of Central Committee members who believed that Viet Nam's future prospects would be better served by keeping its doors open to the West.

That, after all, was the best hope of securing the capital necessary to begin the exploitation of Viet Nam's considerable natural resources, which include significant oil deposits in the coastal waters of the South China Sea. Meanwhile the existence of a political machinery that reaches down through the whole population at least makes possible the kind of command economy that, in previous decades, launched other East Asian states which share the Confucian heritage – Japan, South Korea and Taiwan – on the road to visible prosperity.

For the Vietnamese people, then, wars spanning five decades have vouchsafed national independence and a particular style of government. By way of conclusion, however, it is appropriate to ask: what has been the broader significance of the Viet Nam Wars?

First and foremost perhaps has been the effect on Third World liberation movements. In this context the Viet Minh's victory over the French was of peculiar importance. After Dien Bien Phu it was acknowledged that armed struggle against First and Second World powers could succeed. Similarly, the Vietnamese communists' denial of American war aims in the 1960s and early 1970s indicated that confrontation with a military superpower does not mean automatic humiliation. This too has been a lesson cherished the world over.

The success of the north Vietnamese has contributed to the demise of two related strands in western political behaviour that, a hundred years ago, were the mainsprings of geopolitical activity: colonialism and racism. Rule by crude military conquest is no longer a realistic option for the leaders of the white races.

It has to be remembered, however, that the Vietnamese did not vanquish France, and then America, without outside help. China and the Soviet Union provided much of the military hardware that was the *sine qua non* of taking on the might of the French Expeditionary Force and of the United States.

Conversely, as the Americans themselves discovered, with their much greater arsenals, weapons alone do not guarantee victory. The key external input perhaps was a style, or system, of war and government that enabled Ho Chi Minh, his colleagues and his successors to organize, wield and even exploit their largest manpower resource: Viet Nam's peasantry.

This system commonly goes under the name of communism. Its two most effective schools have been Marxism-Leninism and Maoism, both of which can be said to have influenced the Viet Minh and the Viet Cong at the pragmatic level. As a tool of change in the twentieth century its advantage has been that it gives equal weight to military and political strategy. Its politics, in an adverse situation, are geared towards maximizing not only the intake of rank-and-file military personnel, but also, in a labour-intensive industry, the efficiency (discipline) of that workforce.

Without question, the political- and war-management skills that were learned directly and indirectly from the Soviet Union and China gave the Viet Minh a decisive advantage over other nationalist parties in the 1940s. The battle for the hearts and minds of the

Vietnamese people had to be won before the resident colons could be tackled. When added to the Viet Minh's own abilities to improvise effective military tactics on and off the battlefield, these skills created a formidable force: a force which demonstrated, not for the first time in the modern era, that the armies of the West, despite their continuing technological superiority, are not the same arbiters of destiny as they had been in the three preceding centuries.

Conversely, communism's military character always tends to influence its politics. The insistence on discipline, on selflessness, so essential to maintaining the morale of a fighting force, once carried over into bureaucratic, social and economic structures, is apt to become a liability. To many observers, Viet Nam is a paradigm of the poilitical and social deadweight created in the wake of a successful Marxist revolution; and the decline of indigenous communism in many Asian countries in the period since 1975 incorporates this perception.

That communism did not make greater advances in Asia, however, also had much to do with the United States' willingness to make a military stand in Indochina. Though unsuccessful in Viet Nam, it is probable that America in fact achieved its wider geopolitical ends. By 1975 the threat of successful communist revolutions in Malaysia, Thailand and Indonesia had largely vanished.

Nonetheless, inside the United States the inability of American forces to defeat decisively the Vietnamese communists was read as a cautionary tale and had profound consequences for future foreign policy. The 'Vietnam Syndrome', as it came to be called, manifested itself through successive administrations as a distinct unwillingness to commit American troops overseas. Opportunities for overt military intervention in Angola, Iran and Ethiopia were spurned.

There was instead a greater reliance, particularly during the two administrations of Ronald Reagan (1980–8), on covert operations. In South and Central America what had traditionally been achieved by a show of force was now sought by backdoor means, as the histories of Nicaragua, El Salvador and Guatemala testify. Only in the state of Panama was main force used to achieve a desired political outcome.

The timidity of American policy in the years between 1973 and 1990 was a direct result of American involvement in Viet Nam. Two factors were of special importance: the realization by politicians and defence chiefs that superiority of arms does not necessarily translate into military success; and a reluctance on the part of the American people to sanction the expenditure of the nation's human and material resources in foreign wars. In addition, the morale of the United States' armed forces at large was considered to have been seriously undermined, and with it those forces' ability to fight.

It was not until Iraq's seizure of Kuwait in August 1990, with its attendant threats to western oil supplies and such stability as there was in the Middle East, that the effects of the Vietnam Syndrome began to wear off. Yet even in those circumstances Congress displayed a marked disinclination to debate the question of American involvement until the very eve of hostilities; and when hostilities did break out, on 16 January 1991, President George Bush, in a televised address to the nation, made a specific allusion to Viet Nam when he said that 'this time' American soldiers would not be obliged 'to fight with one hand tied behind their backs'.

Paradoxically, however, the Vietnam Syndrome had helped Washington to achieve many of the cold war objectives that had originally led to the deployment of American troops in South Vietnam. No longer able or willing to rely on force, the State Department had to depend on other means to overcome the perceived threat of communism. A series of diplomatic initiatives on both sides led to meaningful arms limitation agreements between the United States and the Soviet Union in the 1980s.

While the preservation of a strategic nuclear capability during the same period undoubtedly contributed to this peace process, the lessening of America's military posture worldwide helped to convince the Kremlin that talks were worthwhile. At the same time, the relaxing of cold war tensions enabled political reforms within the European communist bloc.

These in time led to the promulgation of *glasnost* and *perestroika* within the Soviet Union, and to the de-communization of eastern Europe. Whether these same events would have occurred had American forces triumphed in South Vietnam, and had there never been a Vietnam Syndrome, is necessarily an open question. But the possibility exists that they would not.

Further Reading

As stated in the Preface, there is a vast literature on the military conflicts that have taken place in Viet Nam in the modern period. Much of this is of a specialist nature. The books suggested below are aimed to provide a balanced list for the general reader. Most contain their own bibliographies.

Anon., *History of the August Revolution* (2nd edn), Hanoi, 1979.

Anon., *Uncle Ho*, essays and reminiscences, Hanoi, 1980.

Bodard, L., *The Quicksand War: Prelude to Vietnan* (translation), New York, 1967.

Burchett, W., *Vietnam: Inside Story of the Guerrilla War*, New York, 1965.

Buttinger, J., *Vietnam: A Dragon Embattled*, 2 vols., New York, 1967.

Butler, D., *The Fall of Saigon: Scenes from the Sudden End of a Long War*, New York, 1985.

Cameron, A. W. (ed.), *Viet-Nam Crisis: A Documentary History*, 2 vols., Ithaca, 1971.

Caputo, P., *A Rumour of War*, New York, 1977.

Dickson, P., *The Electronic Battlefield*, Indiana, 1976.

Dung, Van Tien, *Our Great Spring Victory*, New York, 1977.

Dunn, P. M., *The First Vietnam War*, London, 1985.

Evans, G. and Rowley, K., *Red Brotherhood at War: Vietnam, Cambodia and Laos since 1975* (2nd edn), London, 1990.

Fall, B. B., *Street Without Joy: Insurgency in Indochina 1946-63*, Harrisburg, 1963.

Fall, B. B., *Hell is a Very Small Place: The Siege of Dien Bien Phu*, New York, 1966.

Fenn, C., *Ho Chi Minh: A Biographical Introduction*, London, 1973.

Fitzgerald, F., *Fire on the Lake*, New York, 1972.

Giap, Vo Nguyen, *People's War, People's Army* (translation), New York, 1967.

Giap, Vo Nguyen, *Dien Bien Phu* (4th edn), Hanoi, 1984.

Halberstam, D., *The Making of a Quagmire*, New York, 1972.

Hellman, J., *American Myth and the Legacy of Vietnam*, New York, 1986.

Herr, M., *Dispatches*, New York, 1978.

Hersh, S. M., *Cover-up: The*

Army's Secret Investigation of the Massacre at My Lai 4, New York, 1972.

Hodgkin, T., *Vietnam: The Revolutionary Path*, London, 1981.

Karnow, S., *Vietnam: A History*, New York, 1983.

Kemf, E., *Month of Pure Light: The Regreening of Vietnam*, London, 1990.

Lacouture, J., *Ho Chi Minh: A Political Biography* (translation), New York, 1968.

McCarthy, M., *Hanoi*, London, 1968.

Maclear, M., *Vietnam: The Ten Thousand Day War*, London, 1981.

Mangold, T. and Penycate, J., *The Tunnels of Cu Chi*, London, 1985.

Mason, R., *Chickenhawk*, New York, 1981.

O'Ballance, E., *The Indo-China War 1945–54*, London, 1964.

O'Brien, Tim, *If I Die in a Combat Zone*, London, 1973.

O'Neill, R. J., *General Giap: Politician and Strategist*, Melbourne, 1969.

Pimlott, J., *Vietnam: The Decisive Battles*, London, 1990.

Robbins, C., *The Ravens: Pilots of the Secret War of Laos*, London, 1989.

Shawcross, W., *Side-Show: Kissinger, Nixon and the Destruction of Cambodia*, New York, 1979.

Sheehan, N., *A Bright Shining Lie: John Paul Vann and America in Vietnam*, New York, 1988.

Smith, R. B., *An International History of the Vietnam War*, 2 vols., London, 1985.

Snepp, F., *A Decent Interval: An Insider's Account of Saigon's Indecent End*, New York, 1977.

Summers, H. G., *Vietnam War Almanac*, New York, 1985.

Summer, H.G., *On Strategy: A Critical Analysis of the Vietnam War*, California, 1982.

Todd, O., *Cruel April: The Fall of Saigon*, New York, 1990 (translation).

Westmoreland, W. C., *A Soldier Reports*, New York, 1976.

Wintle, J., *Romancing Vietnam: Inside the Boat Country*, London, 1991.

Zaffiri, S., *Hamburger Hill: May 11–20 1969*, California, 1988.

Index

Note. *In Vietnamese usage the family or surname is placed in front of the given name(s). In a few cases, however, a man is publicly known by his given name. Thus General Vo Nguyen Giap becomes General Giap, or even Giap; President Nguyen Van Thieu becomes President Thieu, or Thieu. Such departures have been cross-referenced.*